LOST WOLVERHAMPTON

ALEC BREW

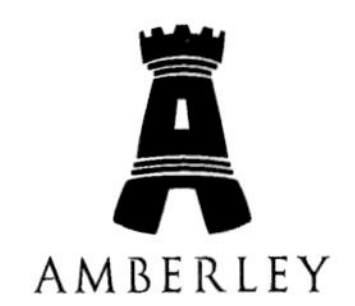

Acknowledgements

A large number of kind people have loaned me photographs of Wolverhampton over the las
forty years, especially the wonderful Dave Clare, Billy Howe, Ned Williams, Andy and Ra
Simpson, Simon Dewey, Francis Washer and recently Mervyn Srodzinsky, who not only ha
a motive in preserving for posterity, but also an artist's eye. Over those four decades man
other people have loaned me photographs, including Jim Boulton, Peter Brew, Harry Evan
Graham Hughes, Harry Jones, Ben Owen, Trevor and June Ridgway, and Doreen Seibot
I cannot always recall who supplied each, so if I have forgotten your name, forgive me
I'm old.

First published 2024

Amberley Publishing
The Hill, Stroud
Gloucestershire, GL5 4EP

www.amberley-books.com

British Library Cataloguing in Publication Data.

A catalogue record for this book is available from the British Library.

ISBN 978 1 3981 0530 0 (print)
ISBN 978 1 3981 0531 7 (ebook)

Origination by Amberley Publishing.
Printed in the UK.

Contents

1

Lost Landmarks

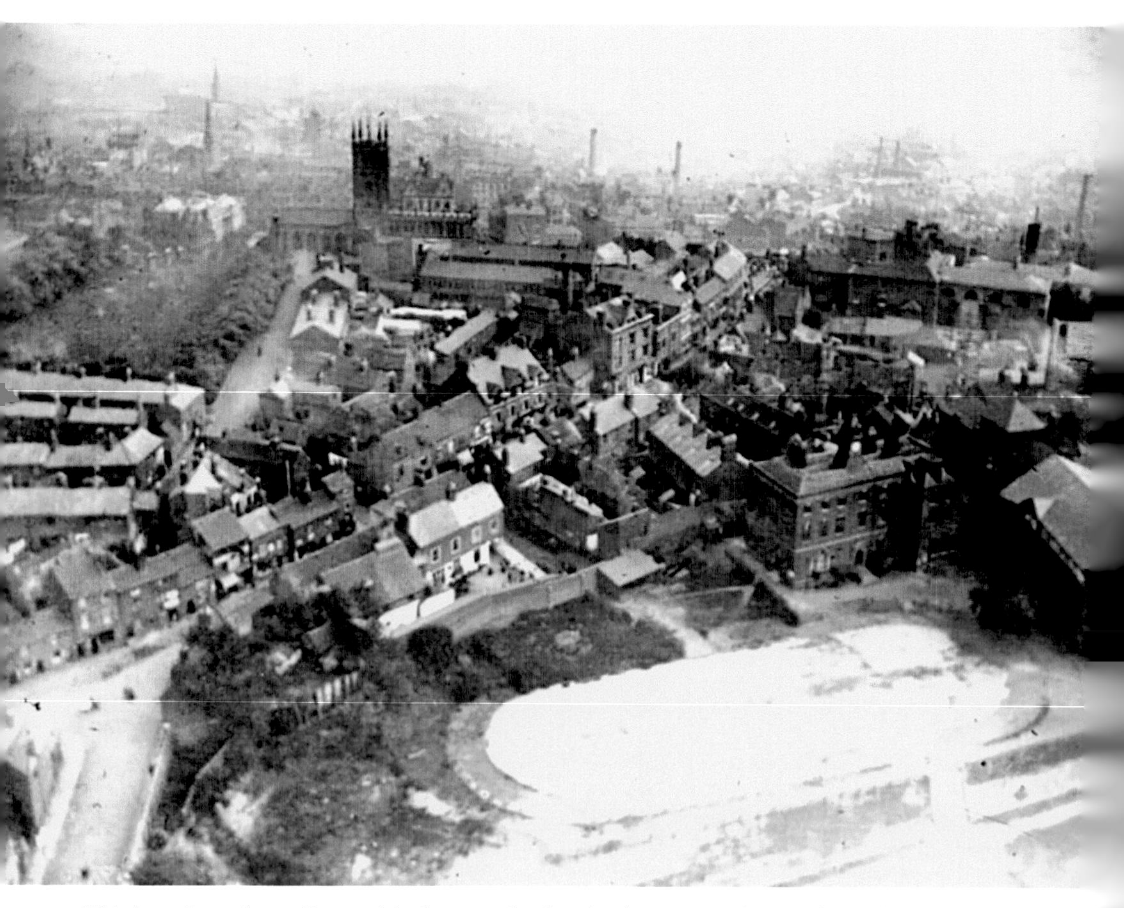

This is perhaps the earliest aerial photograph of Wolverhampton, taken in the mid-1870s, almost certa
from a gas balloon rising from Molineux Pleasure Gardens. Everything in the picture is now lost, apart f
Molineux House in the foreground and St Peter's Church in the centre, though the spire of St George's Ch
is just visible in the background. The white ellipse at the bottom is a skating ring, which for a short t
replaced the bowling greens at the rear of what was then the Molineux Hotel. North Street goes diagon
from the bottom left. Everything else in view has now gone, replaced by many of the buildings that featu
this book and are also now lost. It is important to remember that the things my generation think of as b
'lost' usually replaced something that an earlier generation remembered.

The Central Arcade is the landmark most missed by Wulfrunians of a certain age, including myself. Opened in 1902 and passing from Dudley Street to St John's Street, its cast-iron and glass roof covered an elegant shopping street. It was retained through public pressure when the Mander Shopping Centre was built in the 1960s, only to be destroyed by a disastrous fire in 1974 and replaced by the concrete tunnel that is there today.

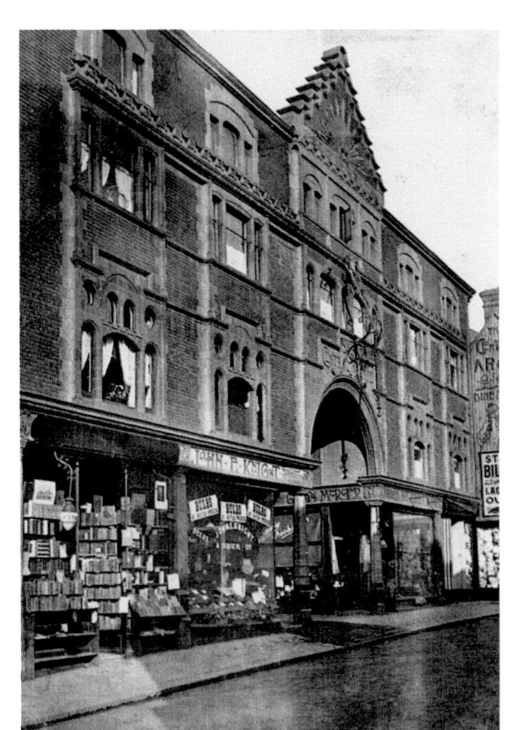

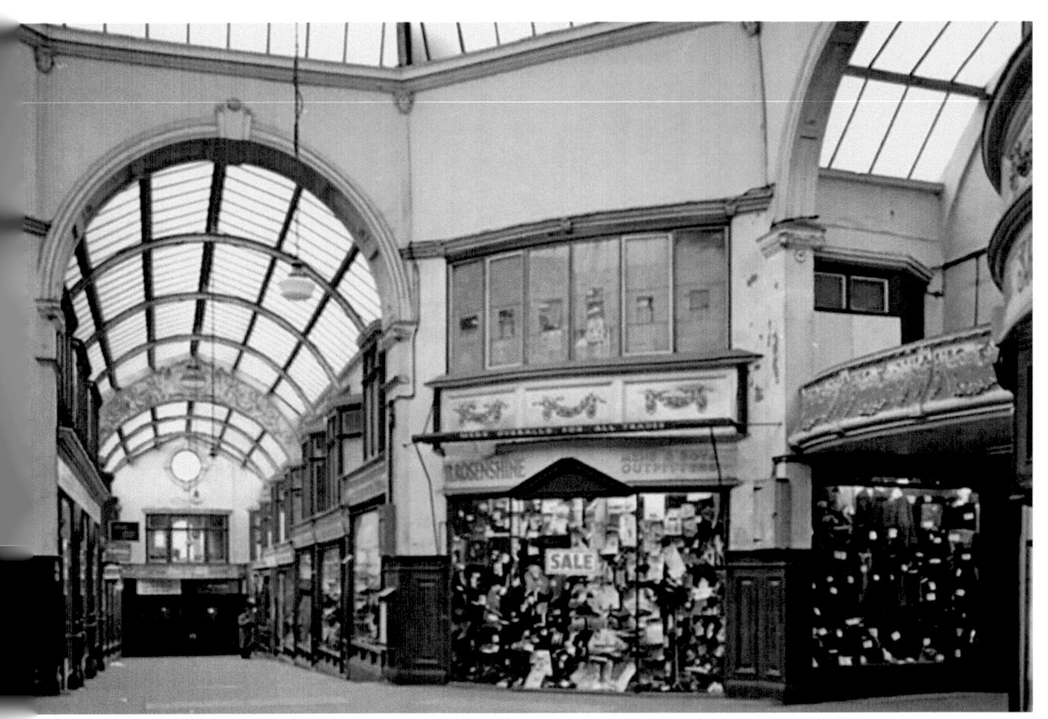

The Central Arcade's glass dome featured a bandstand at the first-floor level to the right, though few people can remember it being used as such. However, my favourite feature of the arcade, and that of many others, was the Sherwood Miller toy shop.

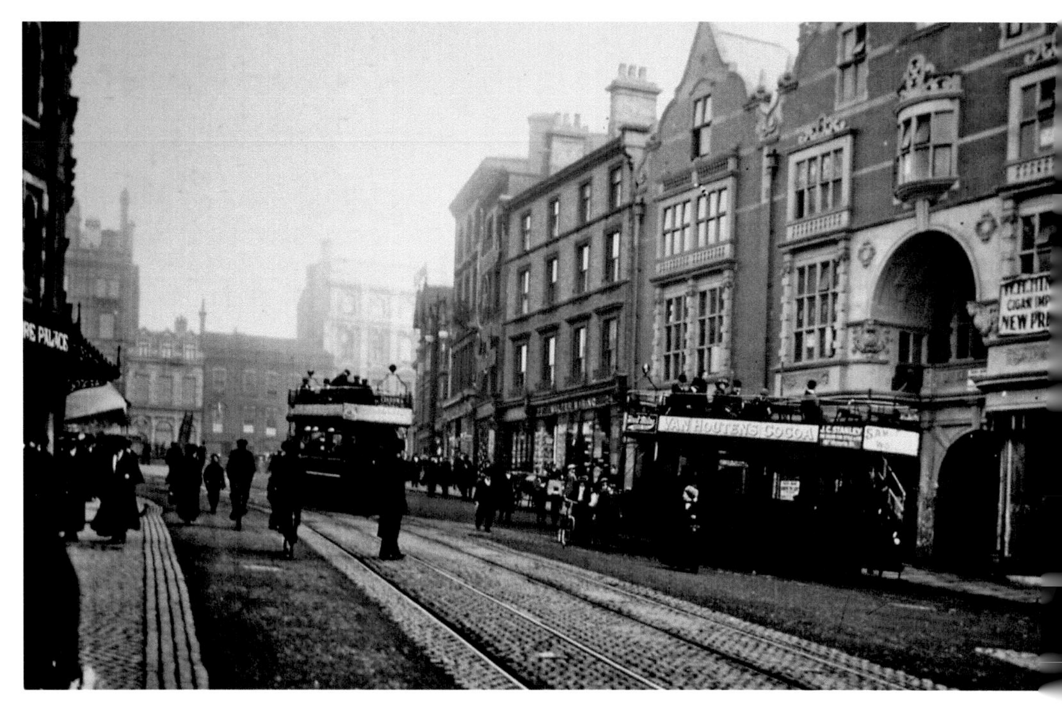

The Queen's Arcade entrance was off Queen Square, just behind the right-hand tram in this picture. It was built in 1902, like Central Arcade, but being a cul-de-sac was less well used. It was demolished in 1967 to make way for one of the entrances into the Mander Shopping Centre.

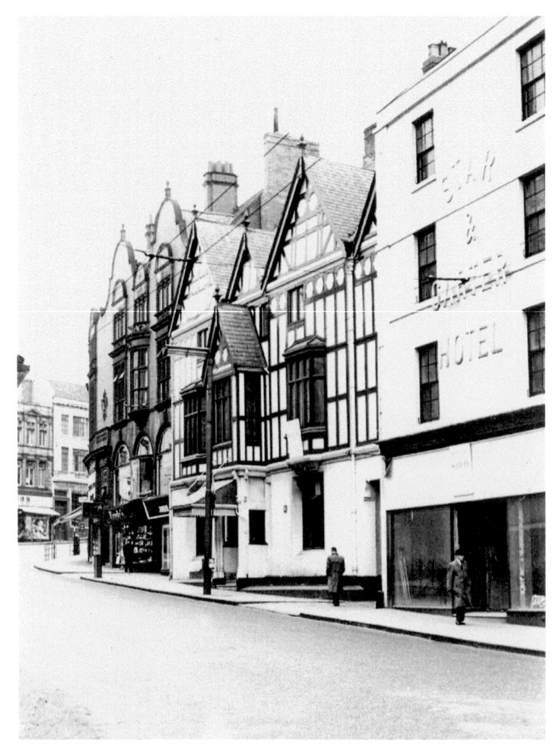

The Star & Garter on Victoria Street was perhaps Wolverhampton's premier coaching inn. It was built on the site of a half-timbered Tudor building, originally a private house where Charles II once stayed. It was demolished to make way for yet another entrance to the Mander Shopping Centre.

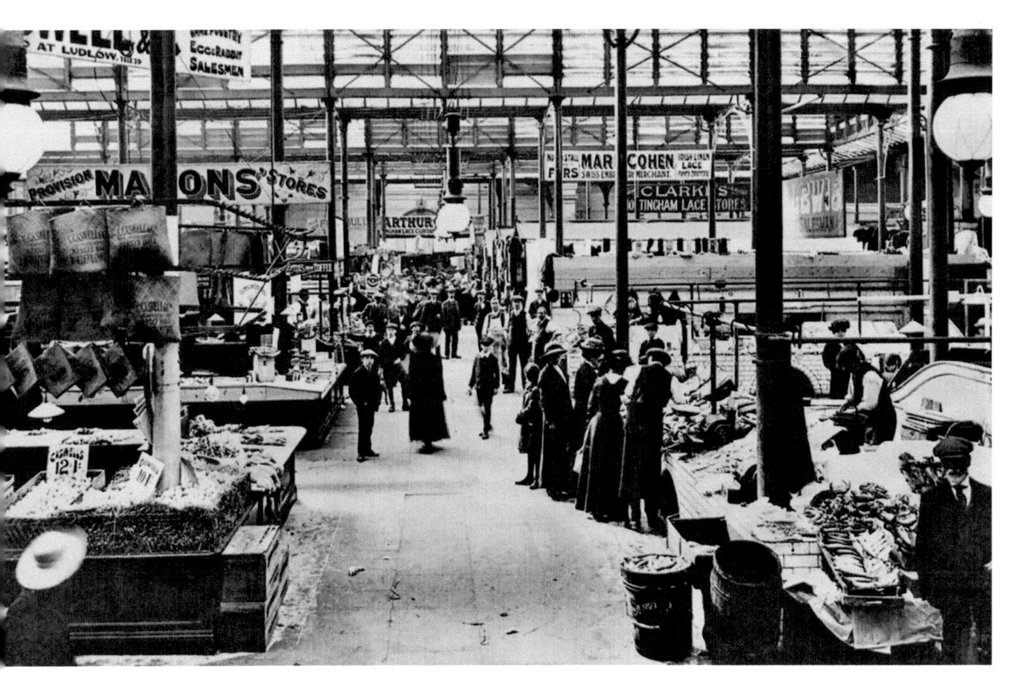

The old Market Hall opposite the Town Hall was built in 1853 of cast-iron pillars clad in stone, with a glass roof. Its loss is the second most lamented of Wolverhampton's buildings. Its demolition in 1960 was said to be because the pillars, which also drained water from the roof, had corroded too much.

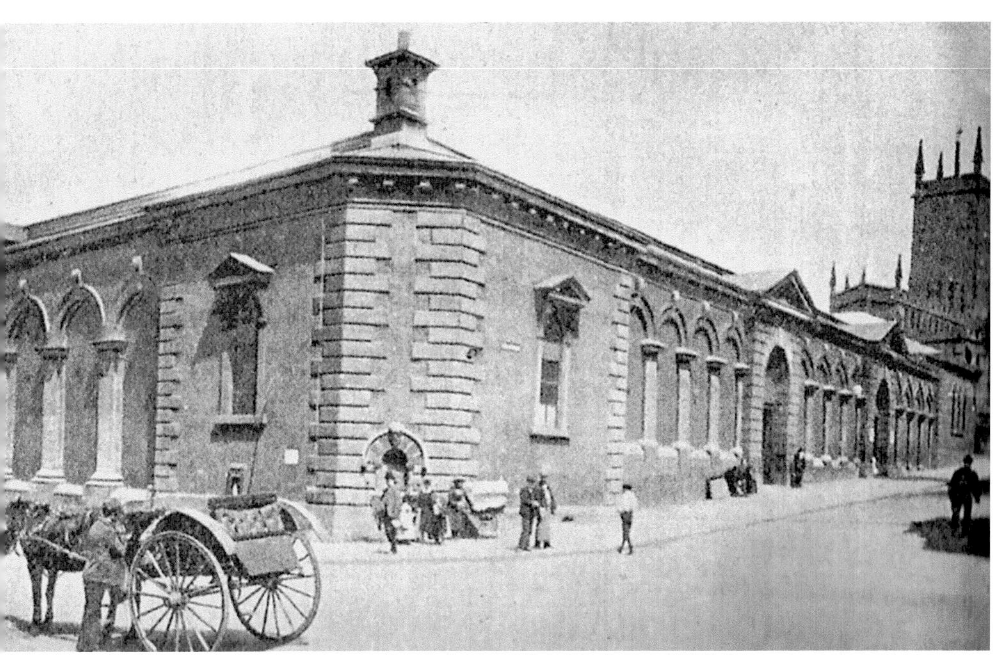

The Market Hall lay on the corner of Cheapside and North Street in the shadow of St Peter's, the heart of the town, where a market should be. It was replaced by a new market out by the Penn Road Island, now of course also gone. The recently named Old Market Square therefore causes some confusion with people of my age, who wonder to which 'old market' it refers.

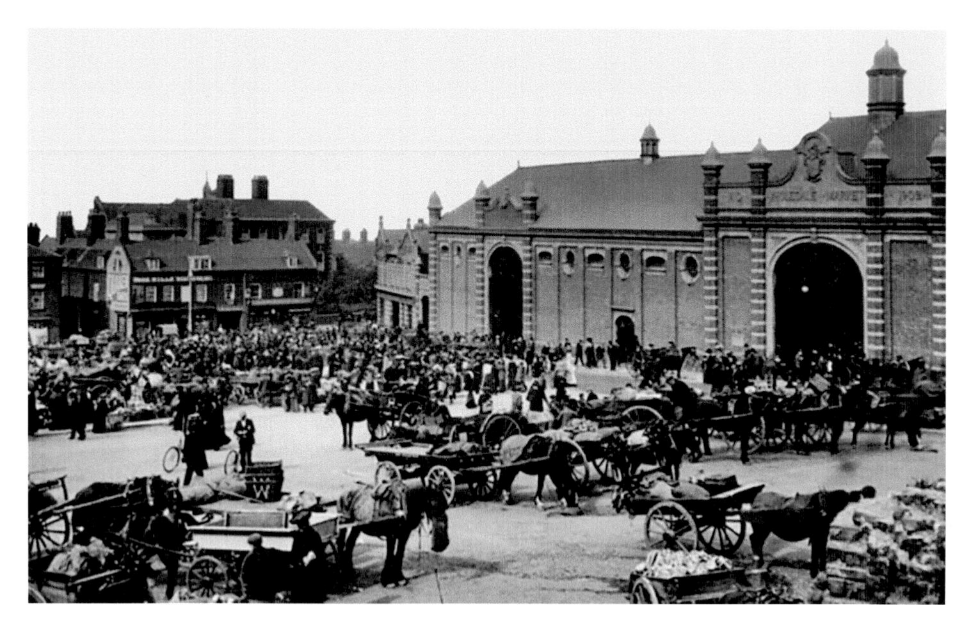

The brick and terracotta Wholesale Market building was opened in 1902, conveniently next to the outdoor Market Patch, which lay between it and the Market Hall. Its demolition in 1974 was much lamented, as the council eyed up the market's site for its new Civic Centre, and the beautiful Wholesale Market was replaced by a merely functional building in Monmore Green.

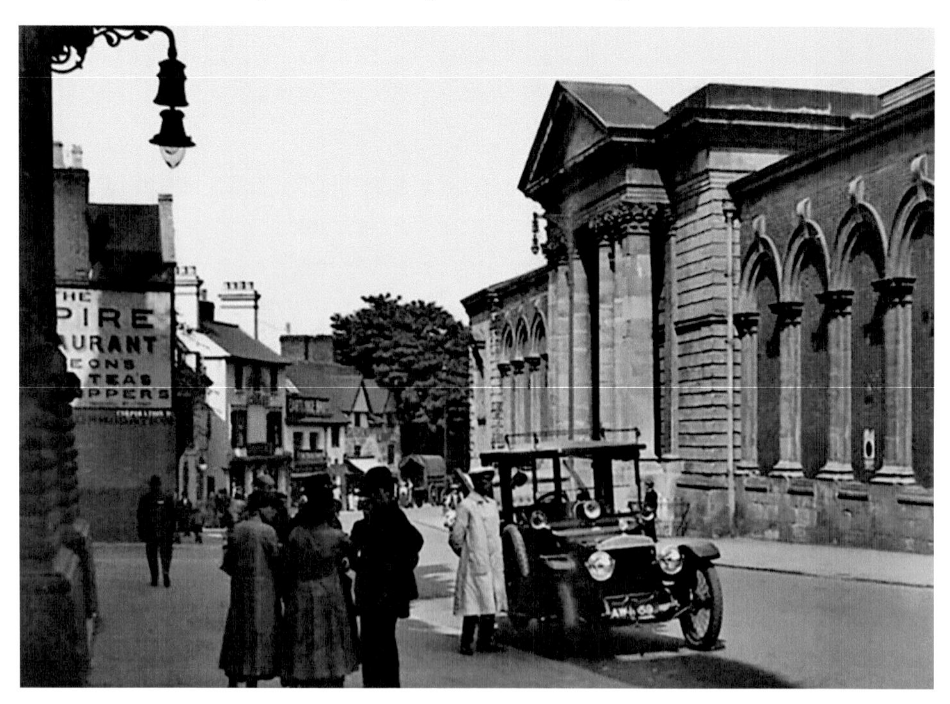

As the name suggests, North Street was the main route out of the town to the north, this section lying between the indoor Market Hall to the right and the Town Hall and Empire restaurant opposite. When the ring road cut North Street in two, this section became a one-way cul-de-sac, and is now pedestrianised as part of the Civic Hall redevelopment.

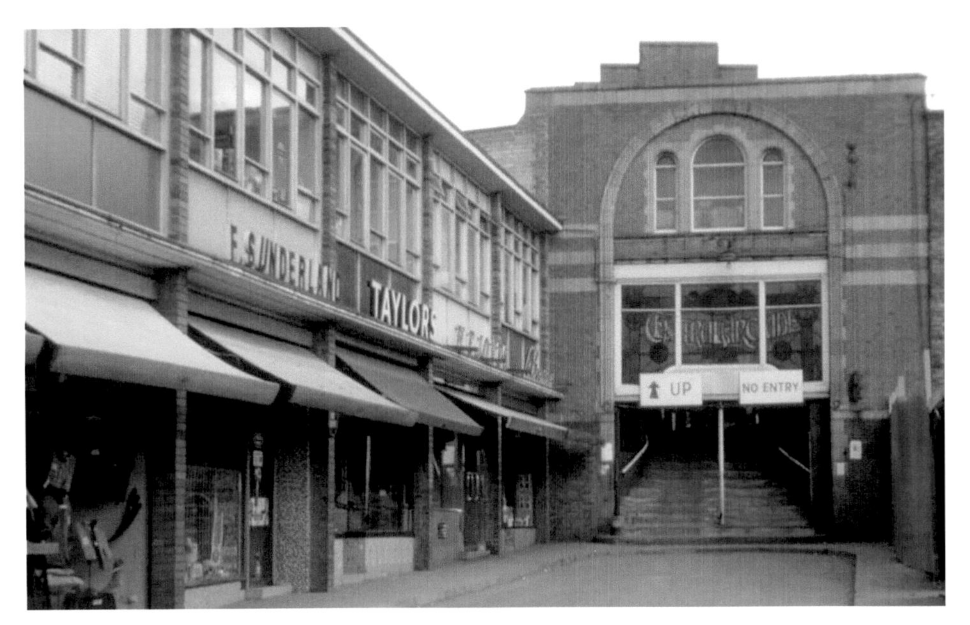

St John's Street used to pass from the bottom of Victoria Street to Dudley Street, passing by Mander Bros Paint & Varnish factory on the way. When the Mander Shopping Centre was built on the old factory site, this section of the street is all that remained, with new shops on the left leading to the rear entrance of the Central Arcade. The one-way signs on the steps up to the arcade have a Covid-like familiarity about them. When the arcade burnt down a new sloping entrance was built without steps.

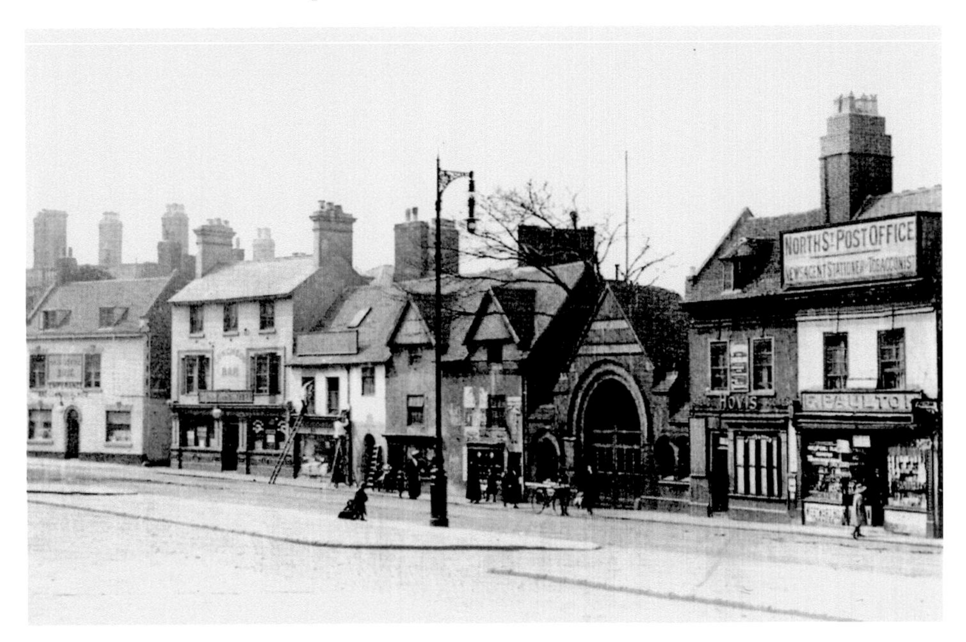

North Street used to be just a normal urban street with shops like the North Street Post Office, Newsagents and Tobacconists shown here and houses further away from town. There are no longer any such buildings along the whole of its length, which is now in two sections, cut by the ring road.

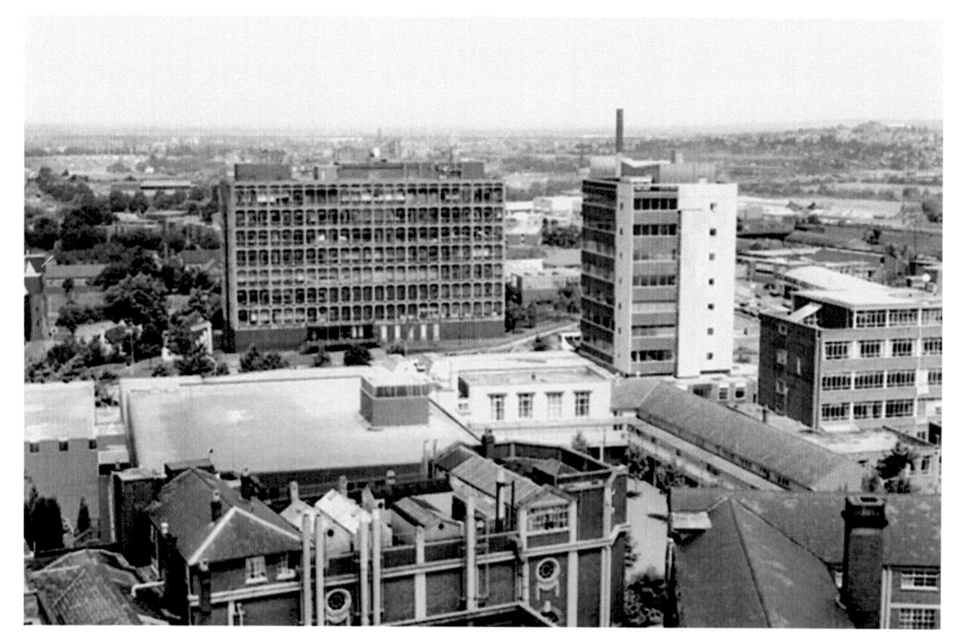

A view from the top of St Peter's Church reveals an apparently modern scene over the university, though when it was taken it was the Wolverhampton Polytechnic. The College of Art, now the Faculty of Art (ironically one of the ugliest buildings in the city), is still there in the centre, as are the buildings in the foreground, but the more modern-looking blocks to the right have been replaced.

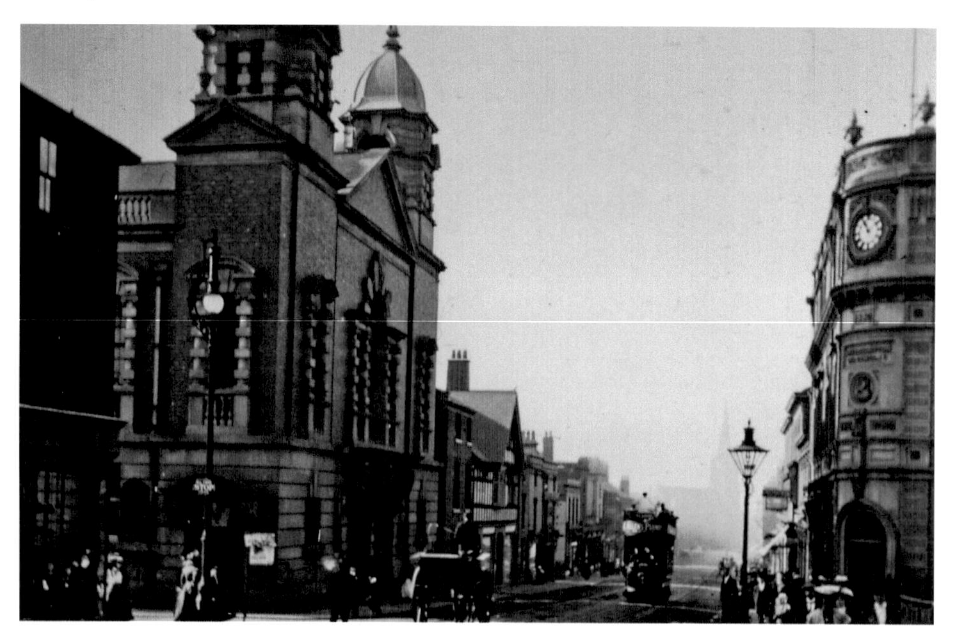

Apart from the Methodist Church on the left and St Mark's Church looming out of the mist, everything in this scene at the bottom of Darlington Street is now gone, cleared away for the ring road and new buildings on the right. The Lorain system (surface contact) tram is the only traffic apart from the horse and cart.

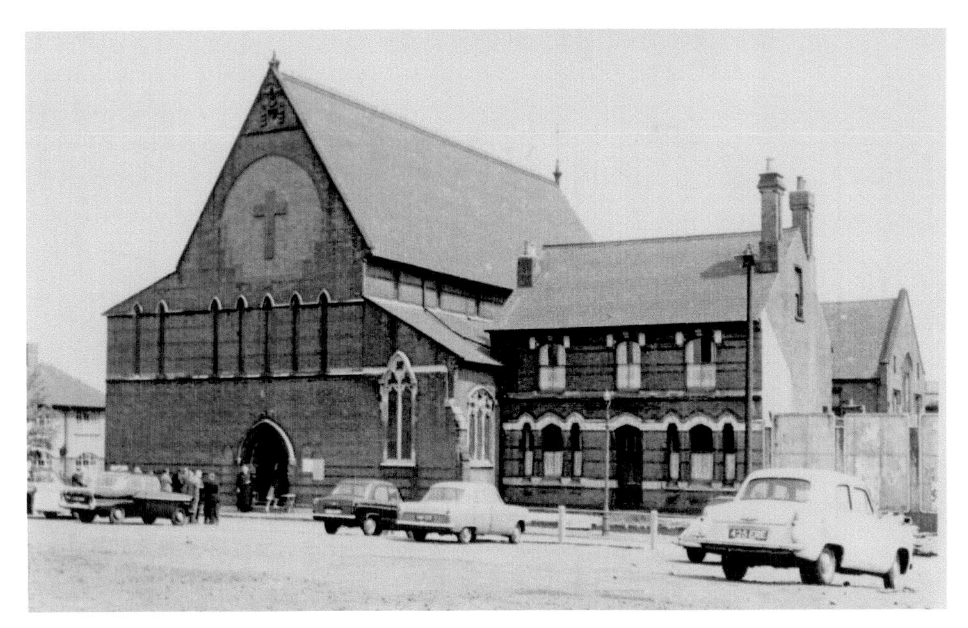

St Patrick's Catholic Church in Westbury Sreet was built in 1867 to cater for the large Irish community (around 2,000 strong) that lived in the area between Stafford Street and the canal. This area was generally known as 'Carribee Island', named after Carribee Street, Westbury Street's former name. Another casualty of the ring road, the church was demolished in 1972 and replaced by a new St Patrick's in Heath Town, the community of 'Carribee Island having already largely been cleared away.

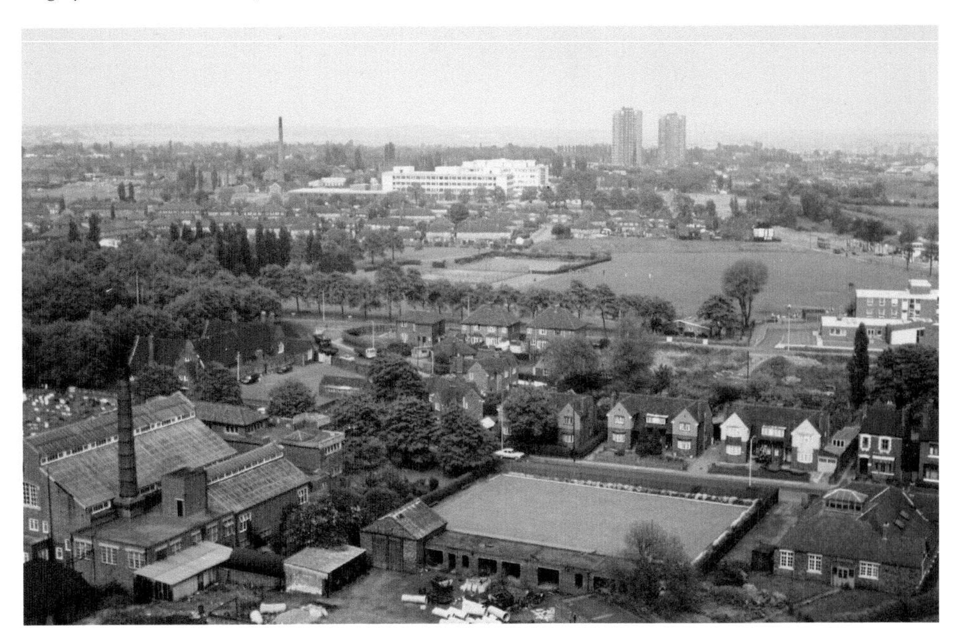

This view from the new Heath Town flats shows the much-lamented Heath Town Baths in the foreground, long closed and now having suffered one of those fires that always seem to proceed old buildings being cleared away. The bowling club next door has already been replaced by houses, but the new St Patrick's Church had not yet been built on the far side of Heath Town Park.

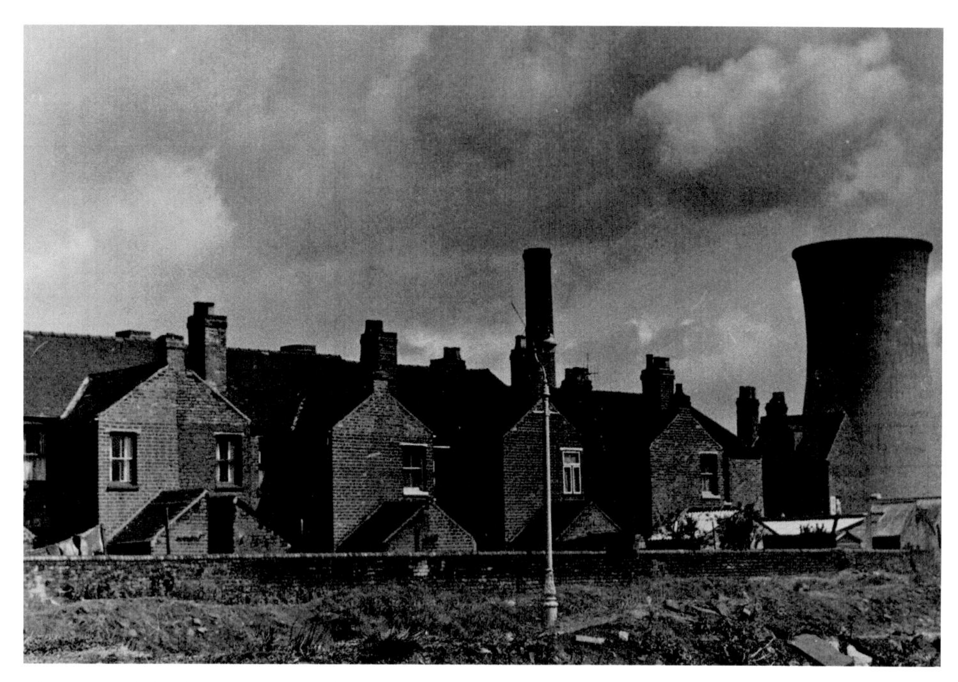

The rear of the houses in Gordon Street in 1970, a street that ran from Steelhouse Lane in All Saints. The cooling tower of Wolverhampton's Commercial Road Power Station looms in the background, as it does in so many of the photographs of this part of the town until decommissioned in 1976. The lower half of Gordon Street now has new housing.

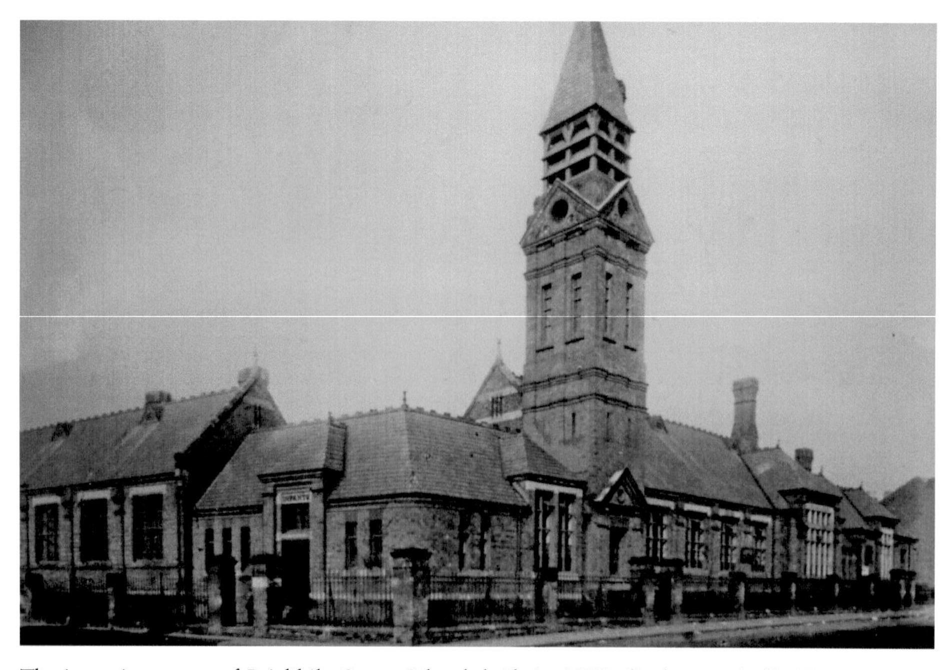

The imposing tower of Brickkiln Street School, built in 1878, displays typically Victorian civic pride. While the tower has since been demolished the school remains, now named Nishkam Primary School.

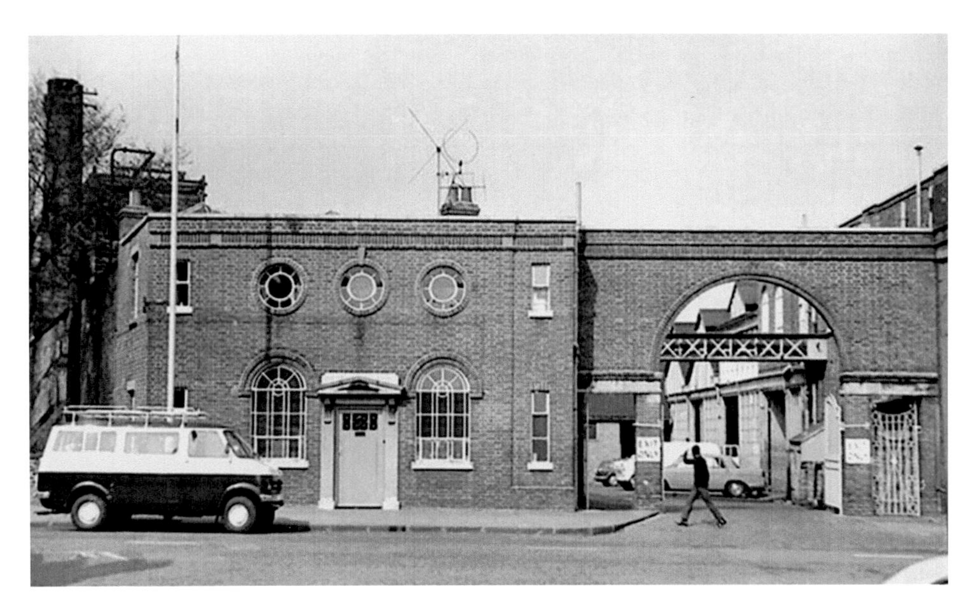

Wolverhampton was always a market town, with local produce brought in for sale from the countryside, including livestock originally sold at the top of High Green (Queen Square). A large municipal cattle market was opened on Cleveland Road in 1848, gathering together all livestock sales on one site. In 1929, a 1.5-acre abattoir was added, as were these offices on Cleveland Road, near St George's Church. The cattle market moved into private hands shortly afterwards. The last livestock auction took place in November 1970, after which the site was cleared to make way for the ring road.

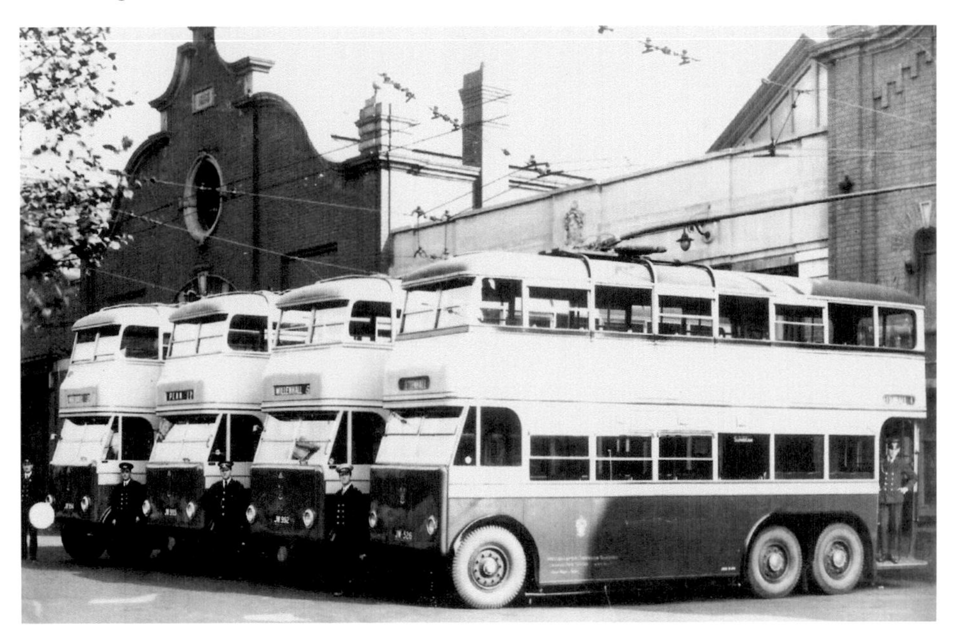

The first four Sunbeam MS.2 three-axle trolleybuses stand outside the Cleveland Road bus depot, which opened as the Municipal tram depot in 1902. For a while, Wolverhampton had the largest trolleybus network in the world and two major manufacturers, Sunbeam and Guy. The bus depot has since been demolished and replaced by housing.

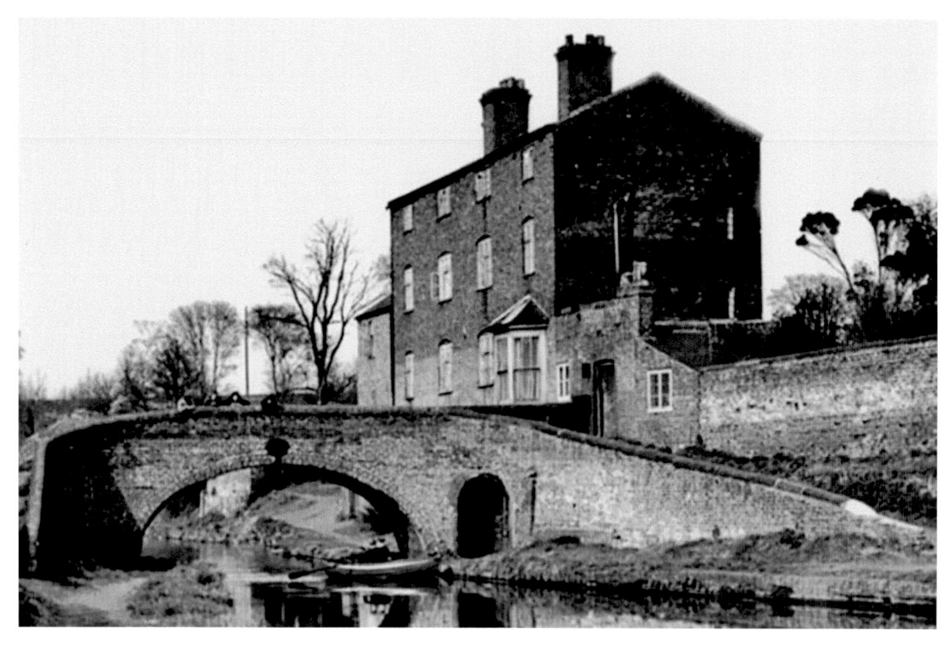

In 1792, the Birmingham Canal Navigations junction with the Staffs & Worcs Canal opened at Aldersley. This terrace of four cottages housed the canal workers, with the hexagonal tollhouse on the corner. There were stables in the cellars and an arch through the bridge to lead the horses through. The small village at Aldersley, only accessible by canal and footpath, has now been cleared away.

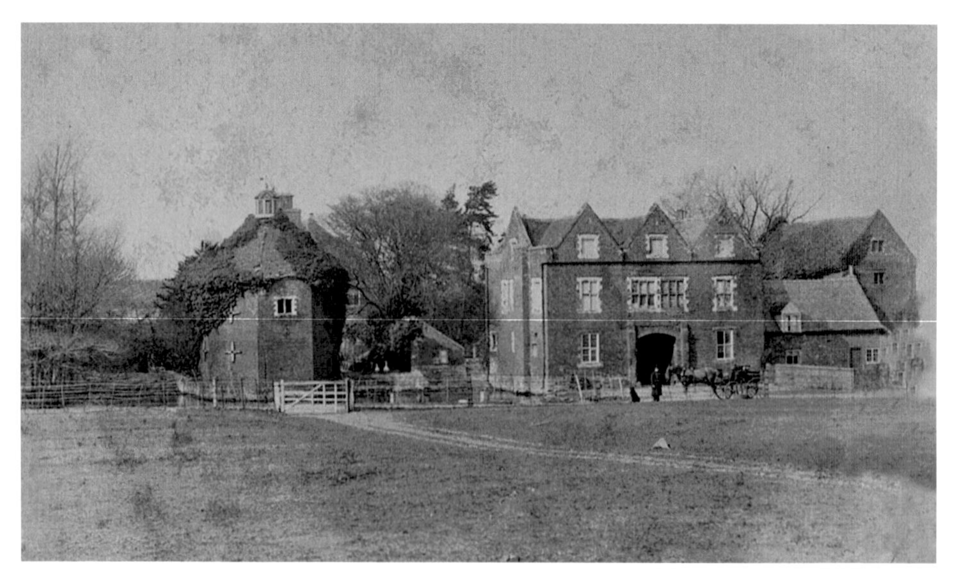

The medieval Barnhurst Farm at Pendeford was bought by the council in 1867 to build the sewage works, it being downhill from most of the urban area. The sewage works opened in 1870 and have been developed extensively ever since. In 1936, the Municipal Airport opened on another 178 acres of Barnhurst land. The moated manor house shown here was replaced in 1963, and the new house was demolished when a new housing estate was built on the site. Thankfully the seventeenth-century dovecote was listed and preserved, giving its name to the new estate.

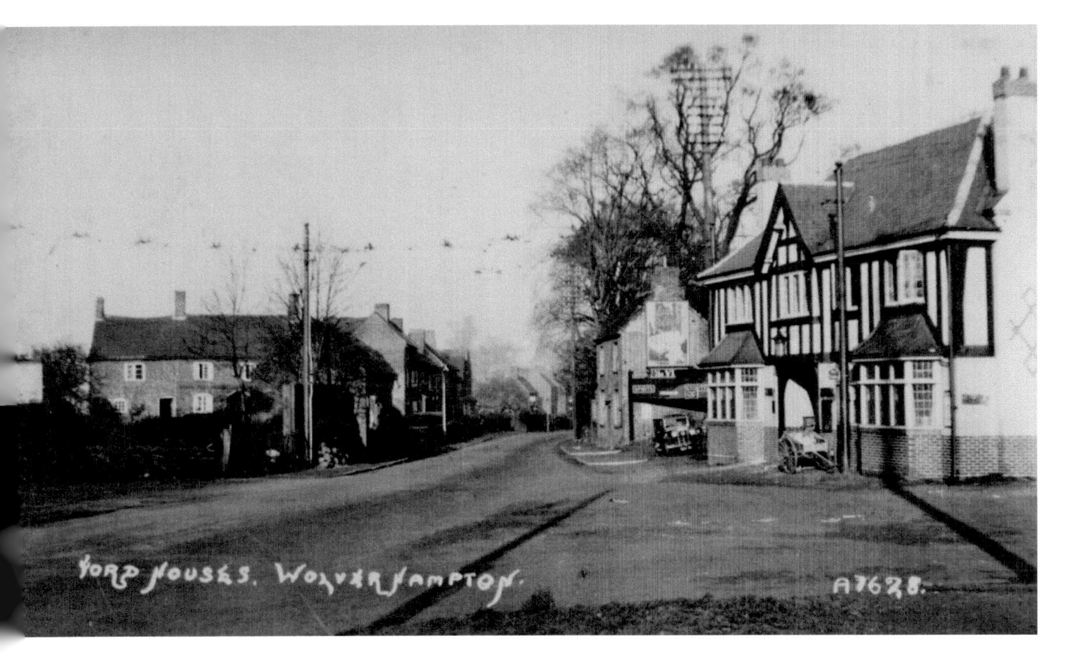

Before the Stafford Road was widened to a dual carriageway, there was a small community around the crossroads at Fordhouses and the Vine pub sat on the corner. Further along, on the other side, the Gate pub also served. Everything in this scene is gone today, with factories now on the far side of the road and housing where the Vine once stood. The name survives as the traffic island is known as the 'Vine Island'.

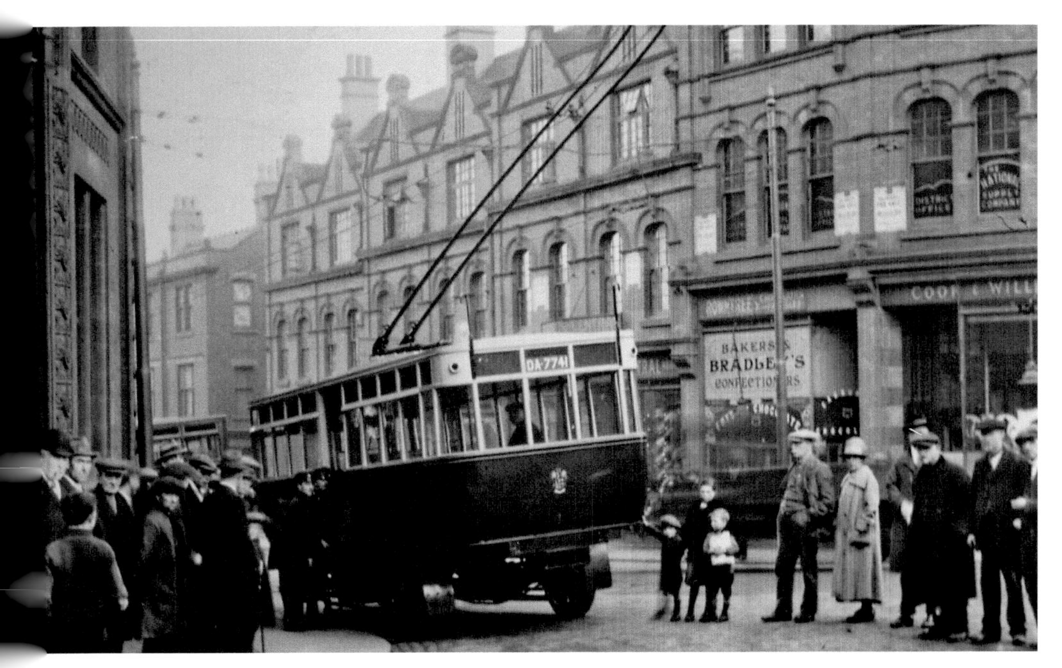

In 1923, a Tilling-Stevens single-decker trolleybus (fleet No. 1) stands ready at the top of Broad Street to make the journey to Wednesfield. A crowd has gathered to stare in wonderment at this new form of public transport. Trolleybuses are no more, but all of the buildings here survive.

2

Lost Companies

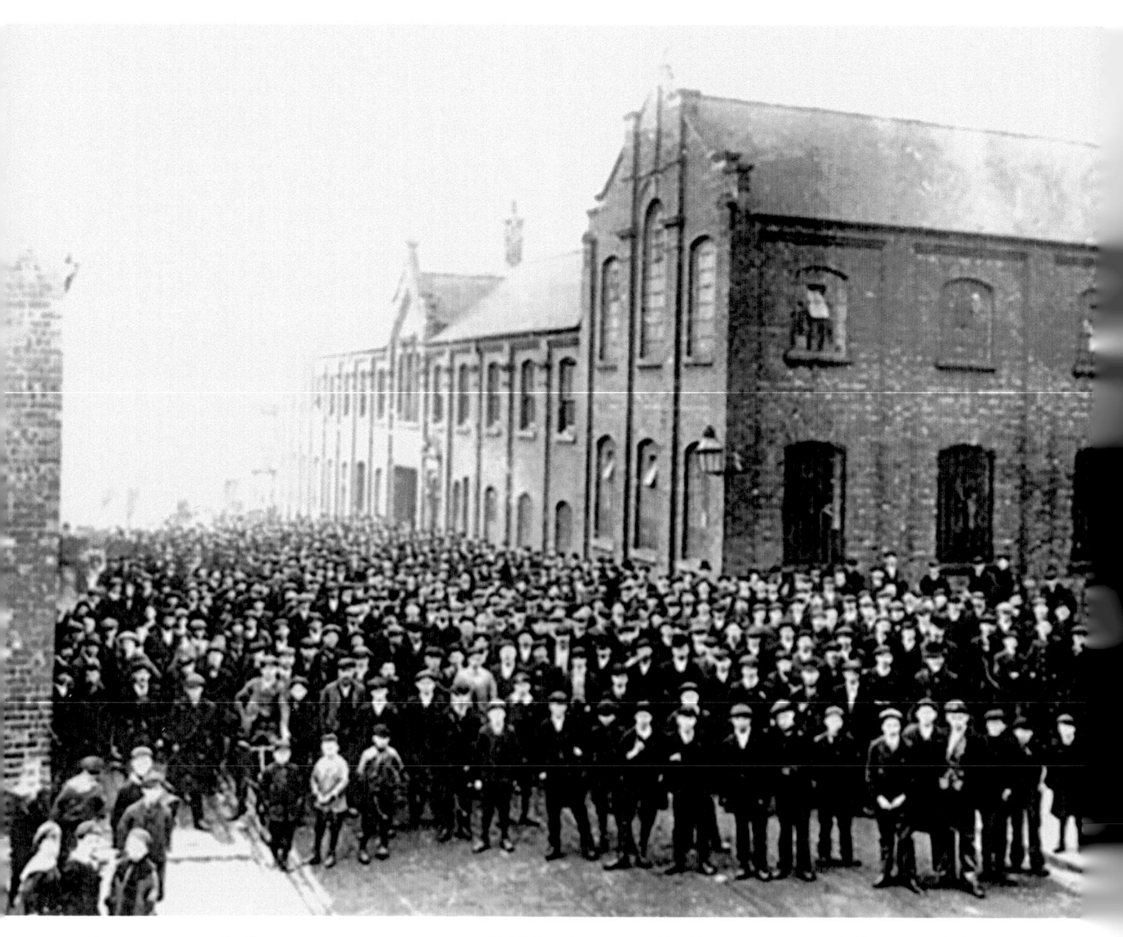

A scene typical of many companies around Wolverhampton in the early part of the twentieth century. The workforce of the Star Motor Car Co. are photographed outside the factory in Frederick Street, Blakenhall, all in flat caps. They will probably have all lived within walking distance, as each area of the town had its own large employers, so many of which have now gone. Edward Lisle began making bicycles as the Star Cycle Co., and built their first motor car in 1896. It soon expanded into Stewart Street and elsewhere, becoming the sixth-largest car maker in the country. This factory is still there but has been repurposed, now being in the leisure industry.

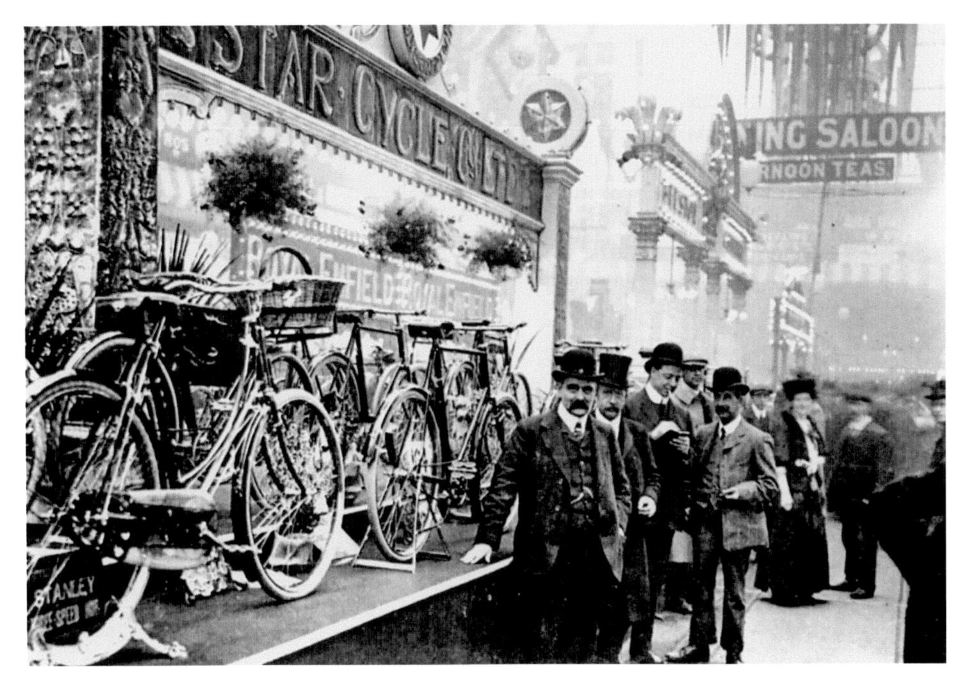

A Star Cycle Co. stand at an industrial exhibition with eager sales staff awaiting customers. Wolverhampton became one of the largest centres for cycle manufacture in the country because of local metalworking skillsets. As many as 198 manufacturers have been identified, but few of them were as large as Star.

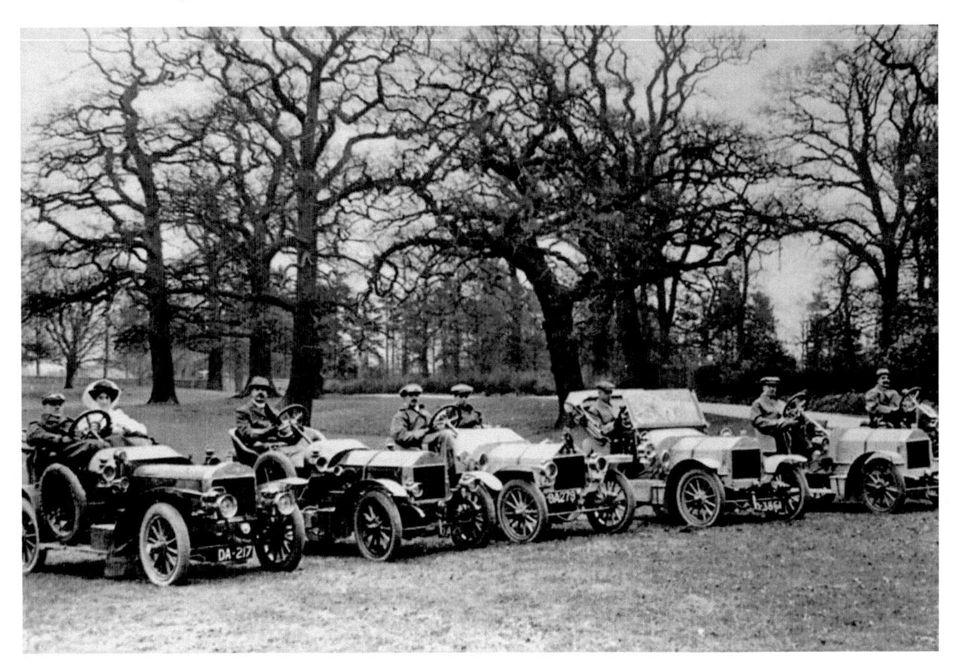

A line of six Star cars on an outing with the local gentry. Star Engineering made high-quality automobiles, but the Lisle family also branched out, building cheaper Starling and Briton cars in factories in Stewart Street and Walsall Street. They went into receivership in 1920.

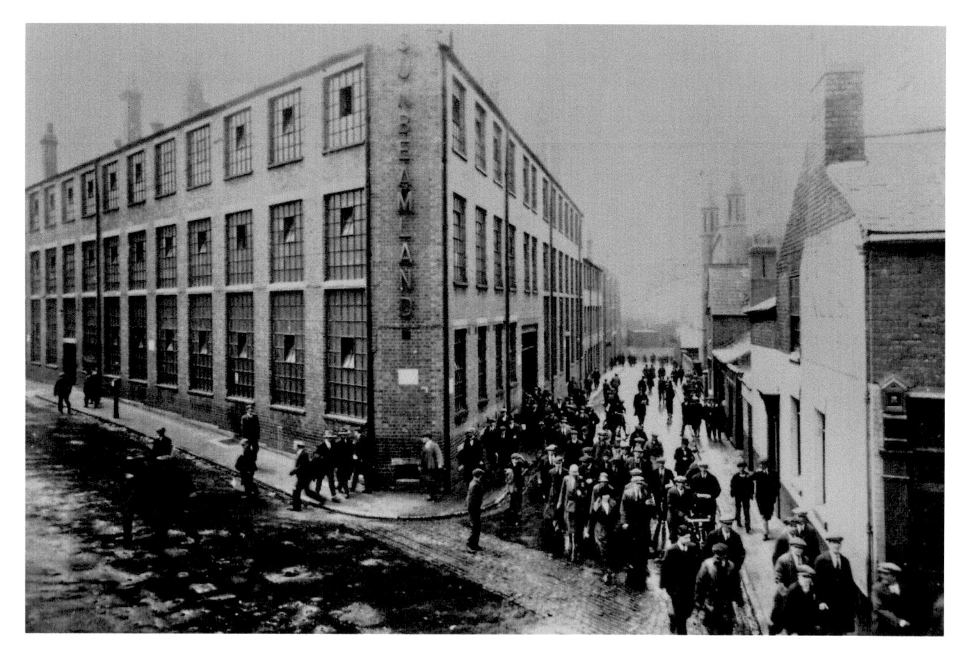

Just round the corner from Star workers pour out of Sunbeamland, where Sunbeam bicycles, and later motorbikes and car radiators, were made. John Marston Ltd was a 'japanware' maker who turned to bicycles in the 1880s, and built the highest quality cycles. They build their first car in 1899, but the Sunbeam Motor Car Co. was separated from the parent company in 1905, moving to a factory in Upper Villiers Street. Sunbeamland has been redeveloped into apartments.

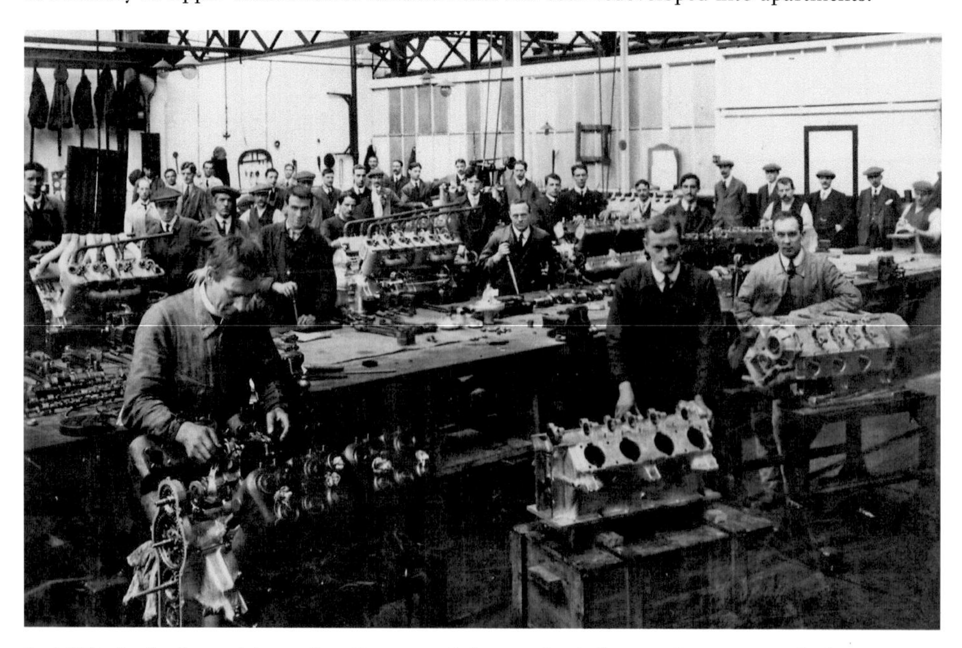

In 1912, the Sunbeam Motor Car Co. entered the sunrise industry of aviation with the country's first high-power aero engine, a side valve V8. At the start of the First World War, Sunbeams were the only high-power aero engines available. Here, side valve V8 Crusaders and V12 Mohawks are under construction for the Royal Naval Air Service.

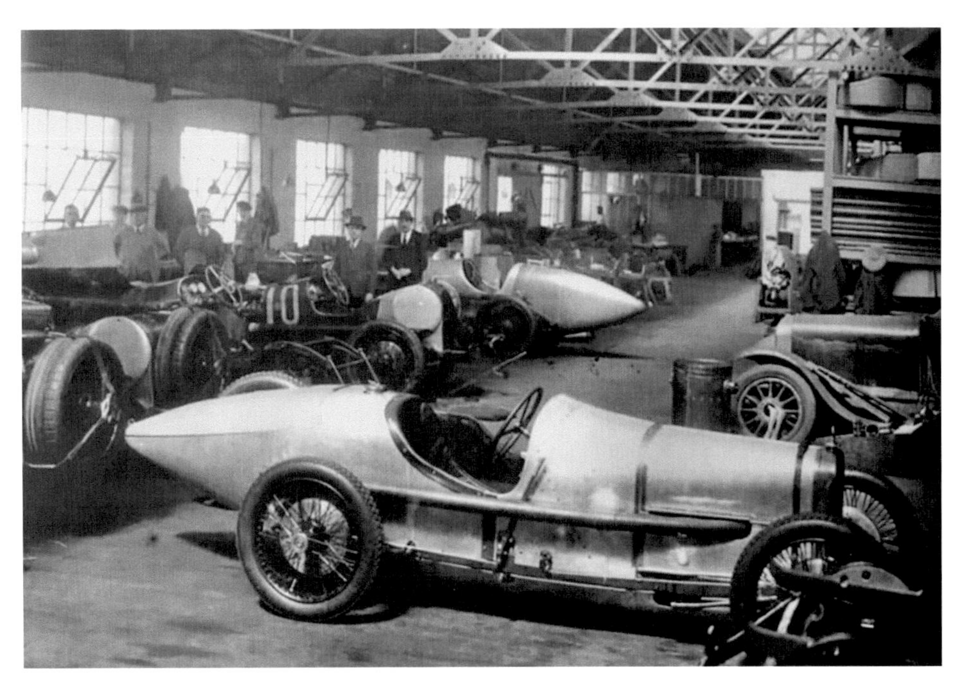

The French chief engineer of the Sunbeam Motor Car Co. believed in racing to improve and promote their cars. This is one floor of the Experimental Shop in the 1920s, with various racing cars being built and refurbished. This block still exists but has been converted into offices; however, the car lift, dating from before the First World War, is still in occasional use.

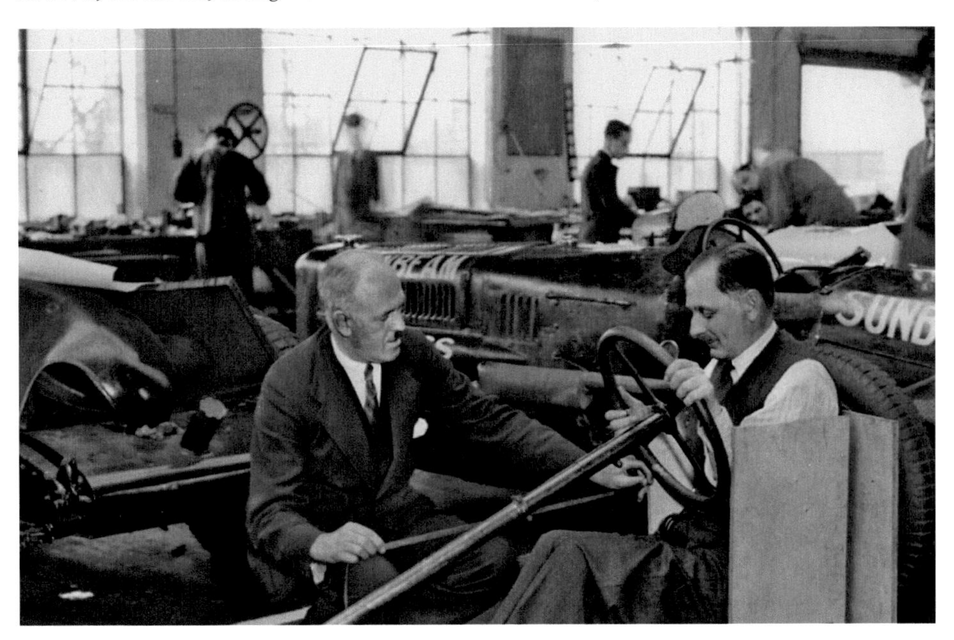

Sunbeam built the first car to take the World Land Speed Record beyond 150 mph. After this record was broken they set about building a car to take it beyond 200 mph. Here, in the Experimental Shop in 1928, the steering column is being installed in what became known as the '1,000 hp Sunbeam'.

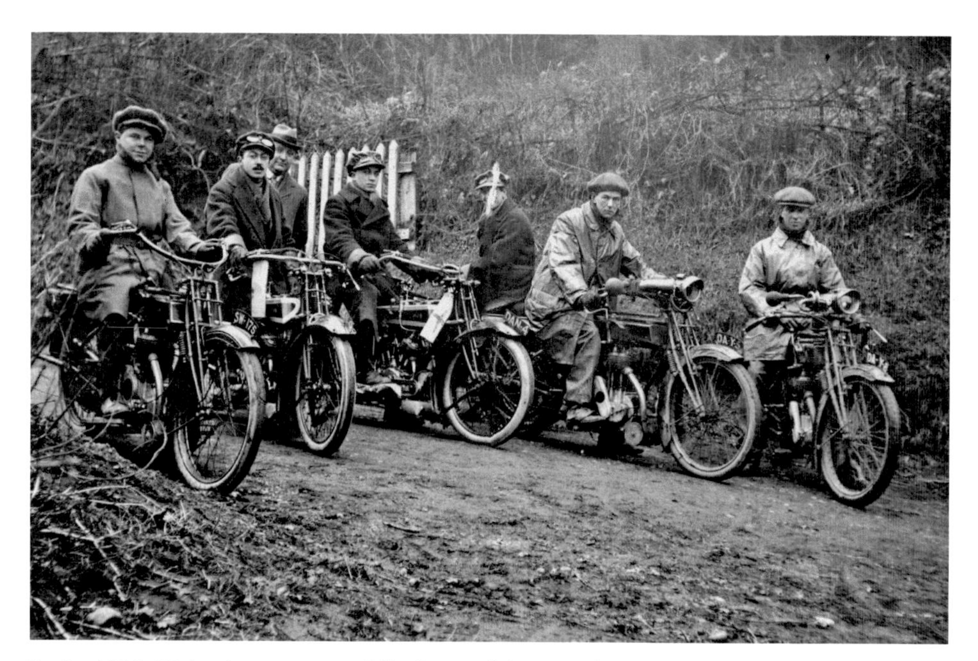

In the 1920s Wolverhampton was full of motorbike manufacturers, and their road testers were often to be seen roaring out of town, especially to Penn Common. Here Sunbeam and AJS testers meet up, despite the two companies being great rivals and often competing in the prestigious Isle of Man TT races.

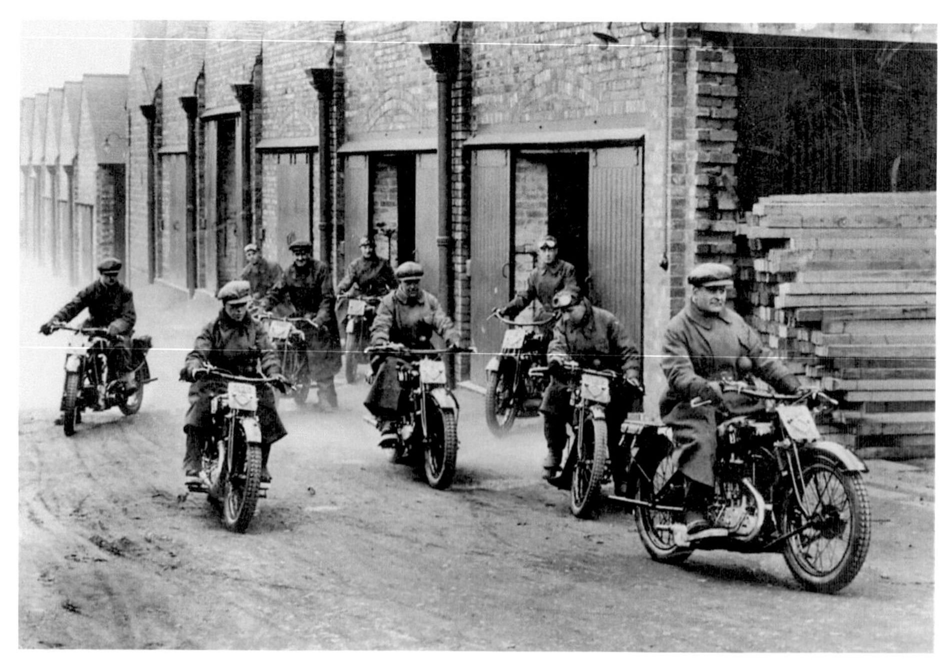

AJS was founded by the Stevens Brothers, who developed a huge reputation in motorbike racing. They eventually bought Graisley House, a mansion with large gardens next to the Penn Road, and built a large factory where Tesco is now situated. Here a group of the factory testers roar out of the rear of the factory before waking up the people in the fine houses down Penn Road.

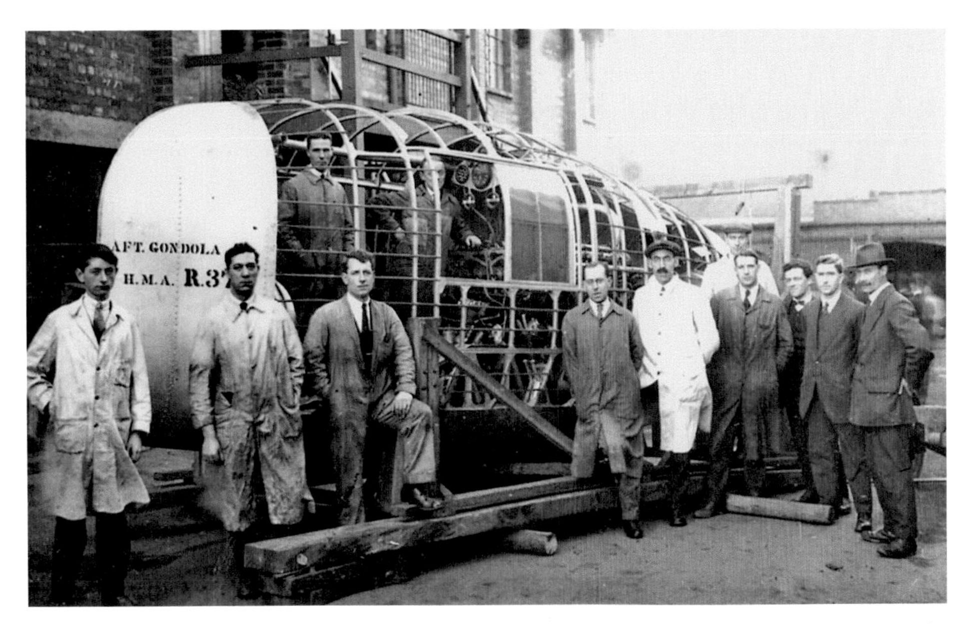

The aft gondola of the R.37 airship, ready for delivery from the Sunbeam works in 1919. The R.37 was to be powered by six Cossacks, but was cancelled when 95 per cent complete. Sunbeam built the engines and gondolas for many British airships, including the R.34, the first aircraft to fly over the Atlantic to America.

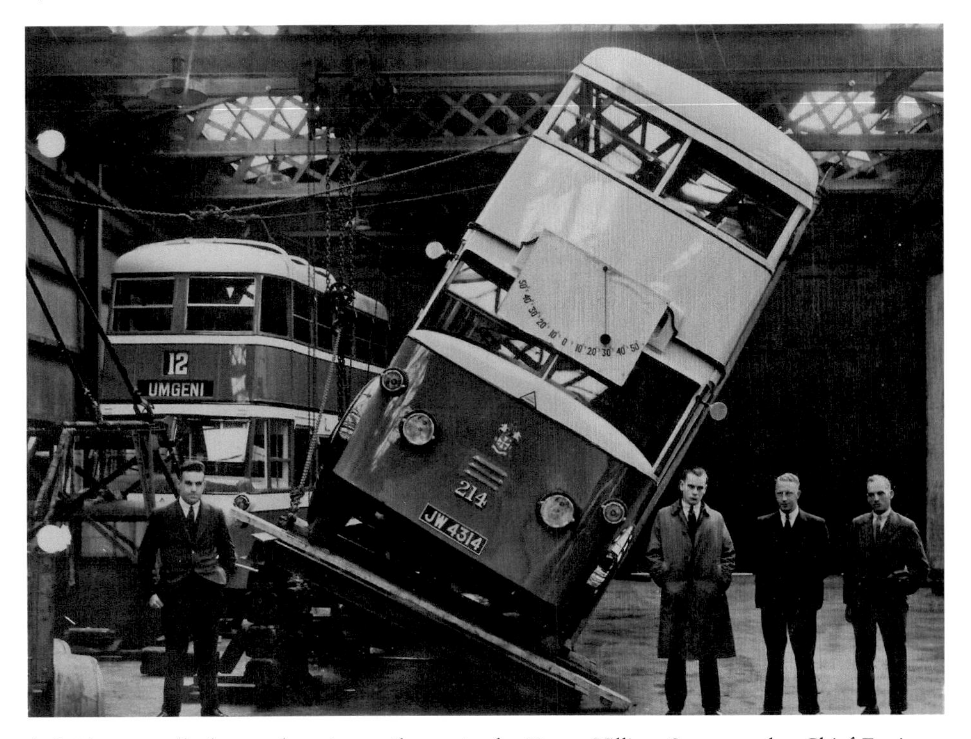

A Sunbeam trolleybus undergoing a tilt test in the Upper Villiers Street works. Chief Engineer Cyril Dabbs is on the left, and the bus behind is awaiting export to South Africa. The Sunbeam trolleybus business was later bought by Guy Motors and moved to its Park Lane factory.

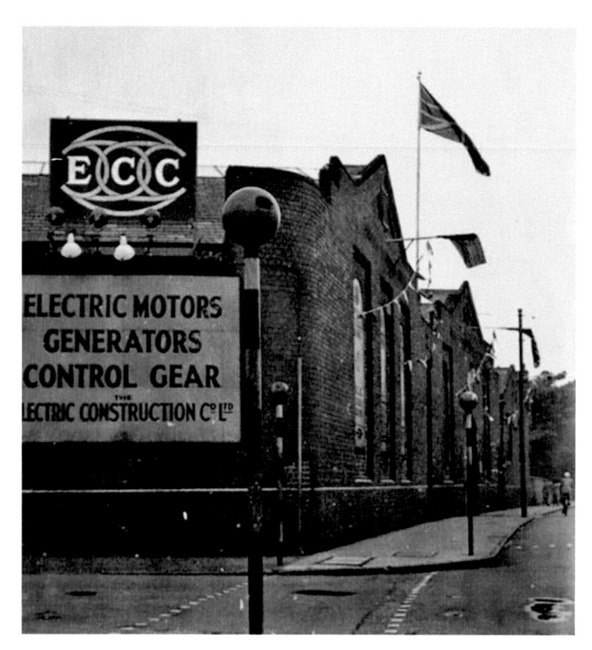

The Electric Construction Co. factory on Stafford Road, Bushbury. They were formed in 1889 by the amalgamation of three other companies, including Elwell-Parker of Commercial Road. They built the Bushbury factory and became leaders in the manufacture of power-generating equipment and electric vehicles.

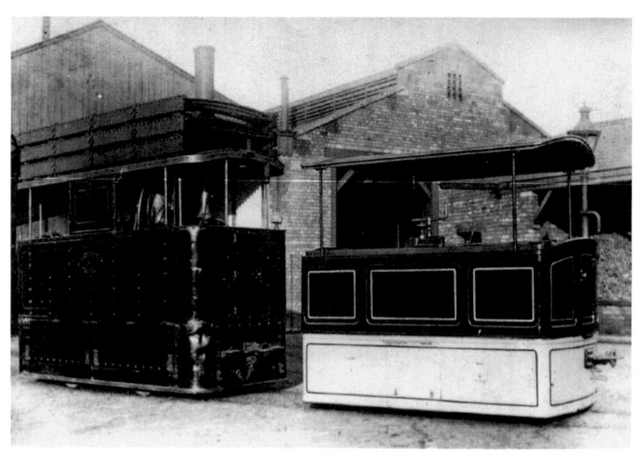

An Electric Construction Co. accumulator tram. They also built battery trams and overhead power trams, as well as the first powered public transport vehicles licensed in London in 1891 – two twenty-six-seat electric buses. By the start of the twentieth century they had largely given up vehicle manufacture and concentrated on generating equipment until closure in 1985.

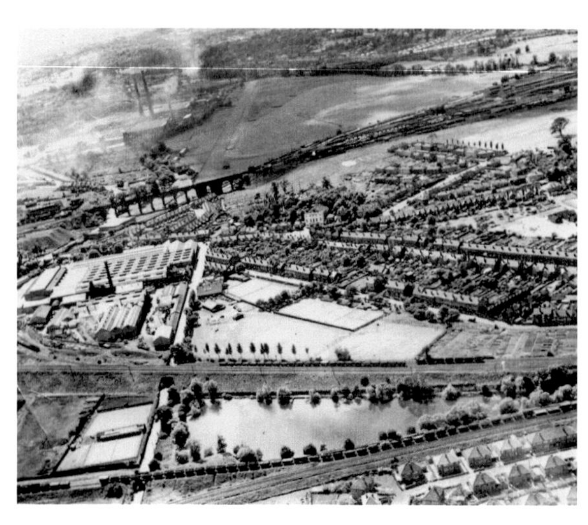

An aerial view of the Electric Construction Co. works to the left, just below Stafford Road, with Bushbury Pool in the foreground. In the background, beyond Dunstall Viaduct, is the triangle of Wolverhampton Racecourse with the Courtaulds factory to the left. Almost everything in this photograph has now gone.

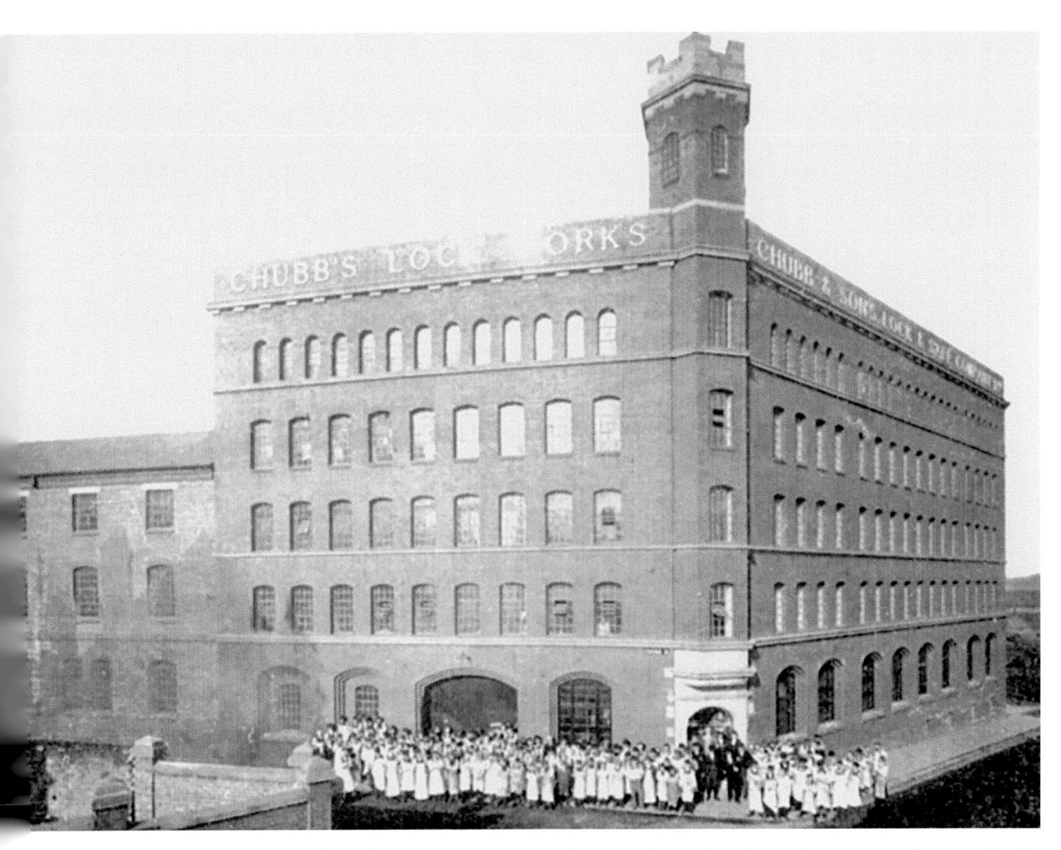

Many of the workforce gathered in their aprons outside the Chubb Lock works in Fryer Street. Chubb had come to Wolverhampton in 1820, initially occupying premises in Temple Street and elsewhere in the town until the Fryer Street factory was opened in 1889.

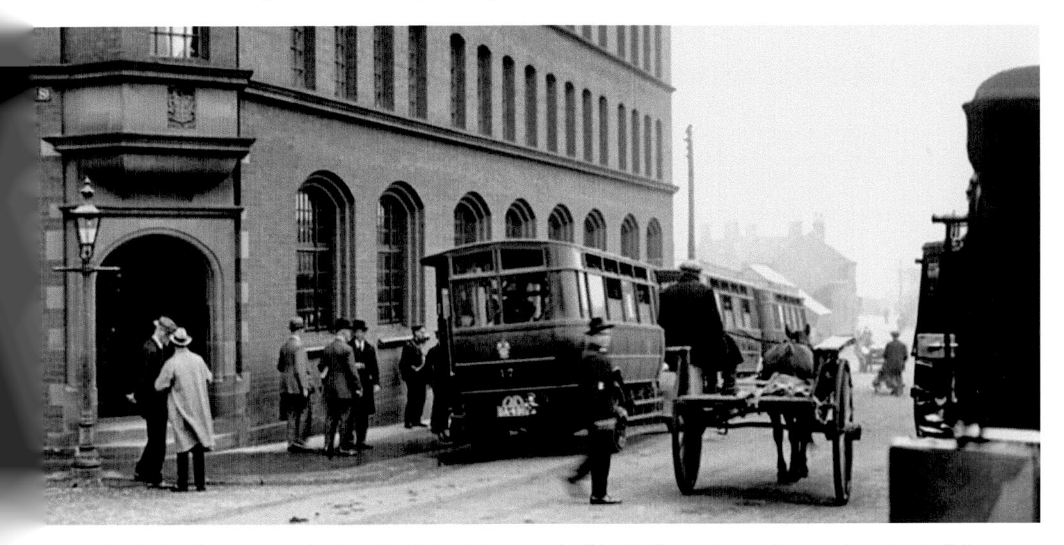

Single-decker buses outside the Chubb building, parked in Railway Street. Even when the building was taken over by Baelz Equipment it was still known as the Chubb building. It now houses offices and the Light House Media Centre.

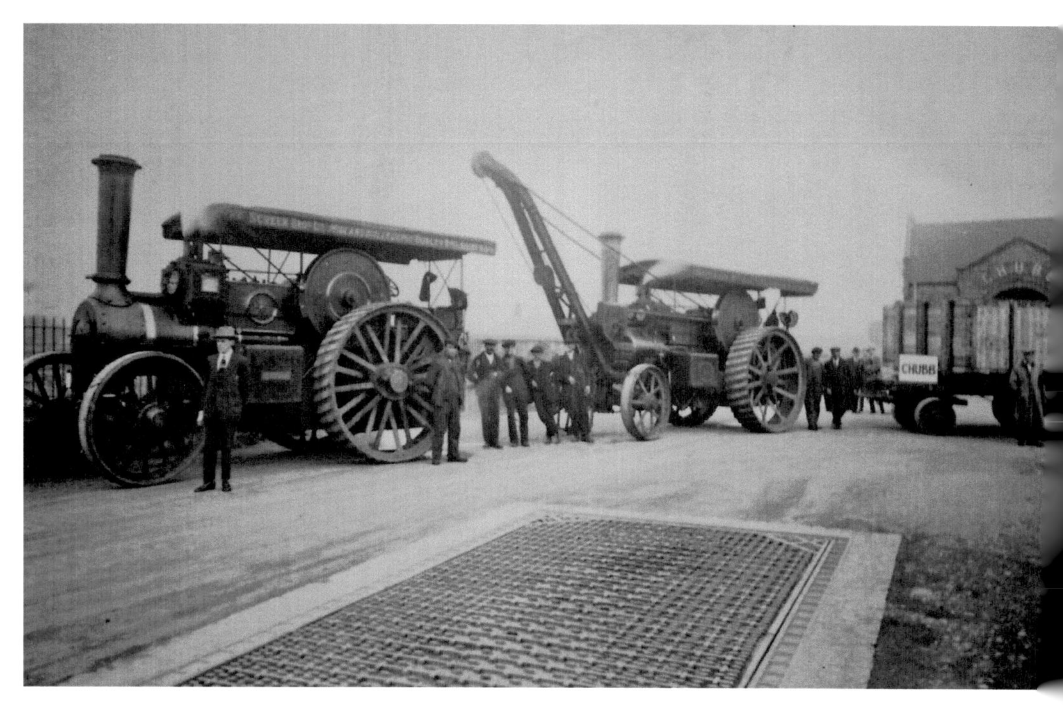

Chubb settled on Heath Town. Here two traction engines, one with a crane, haul a load of crated safes.

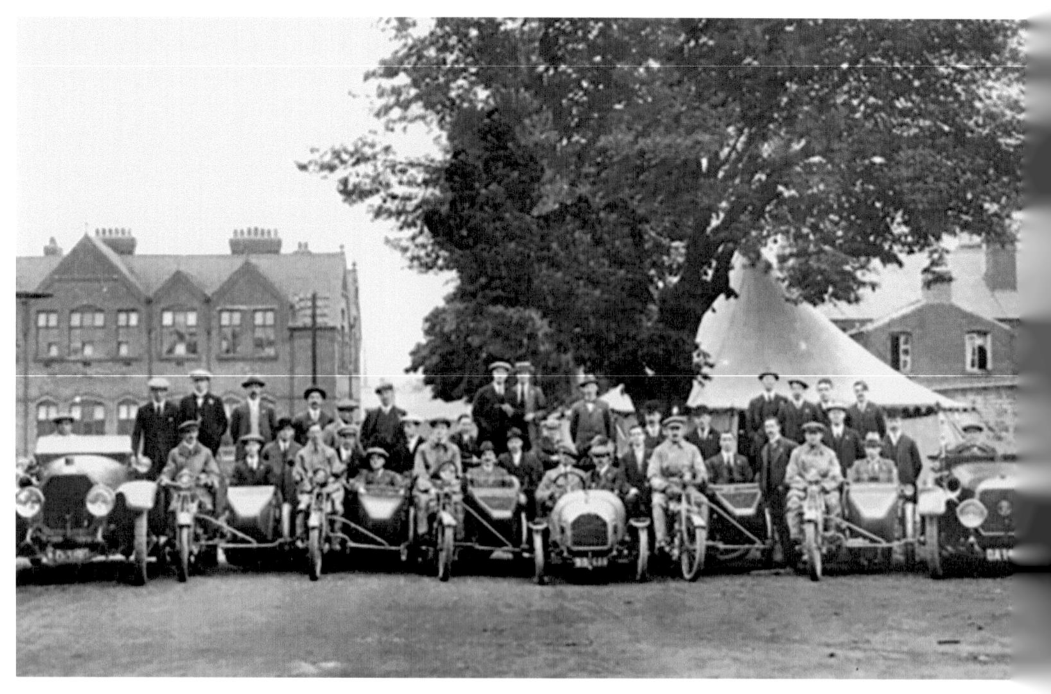

Clyno cars and motorbikes lined up for a works outing across the corner of Humber Road and Great Brickkiln Street, facing towards the Pelham Street factory. Clyno moved from Northampton to Retreat Street before the First World War. They later moved into larger premises in Pelham Street where they began making cars. The building behind is the United Services Club, now the Tayyaba Mosque.

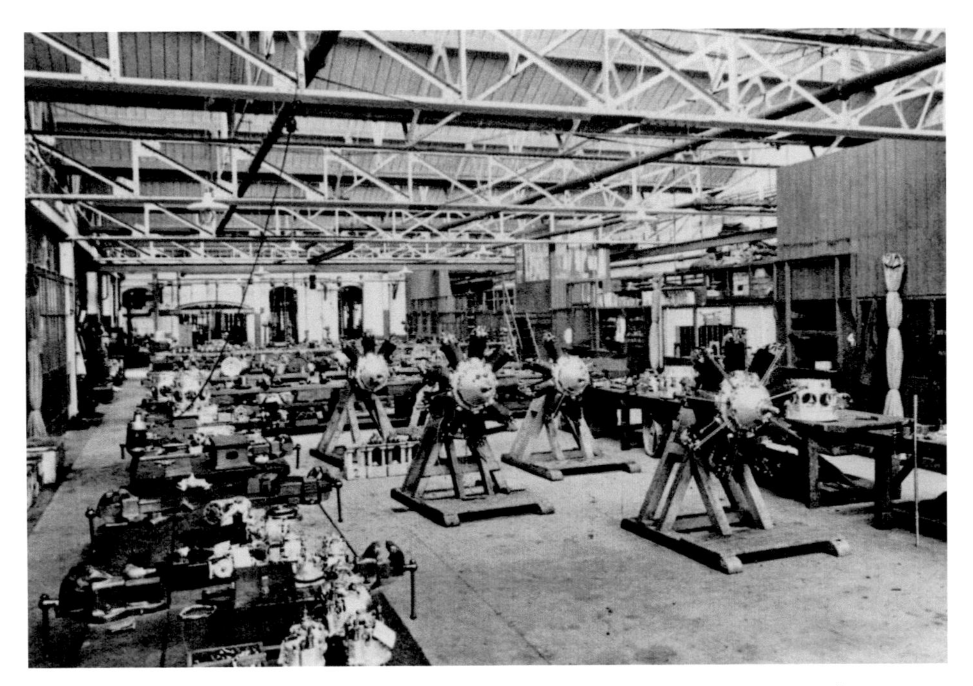

At the end of the war, Clyno built forty 350 hp ABC Dragonfly aero engines in Pelham Street, four of which are shown here. They then expanded car production to the point where they were the third-largest manufacturer in the country, after Morris and Austin.

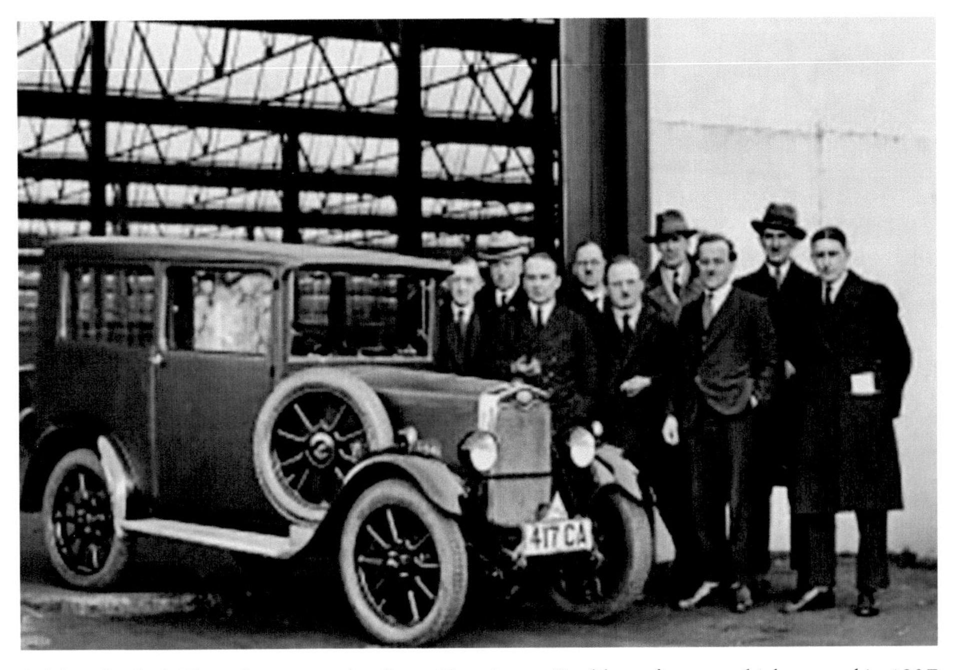

A fabric-bodied Clyno 9 car emerging from Clyno's new Bushbury factory, which opened in 1927 after the Pelham Street works became overcrowded. Clyno entered into a price war with Morris and offered a version of the 9 called the Century for only £113. It was a failure and Clyno could not compete with Morris, and went into liquidation.

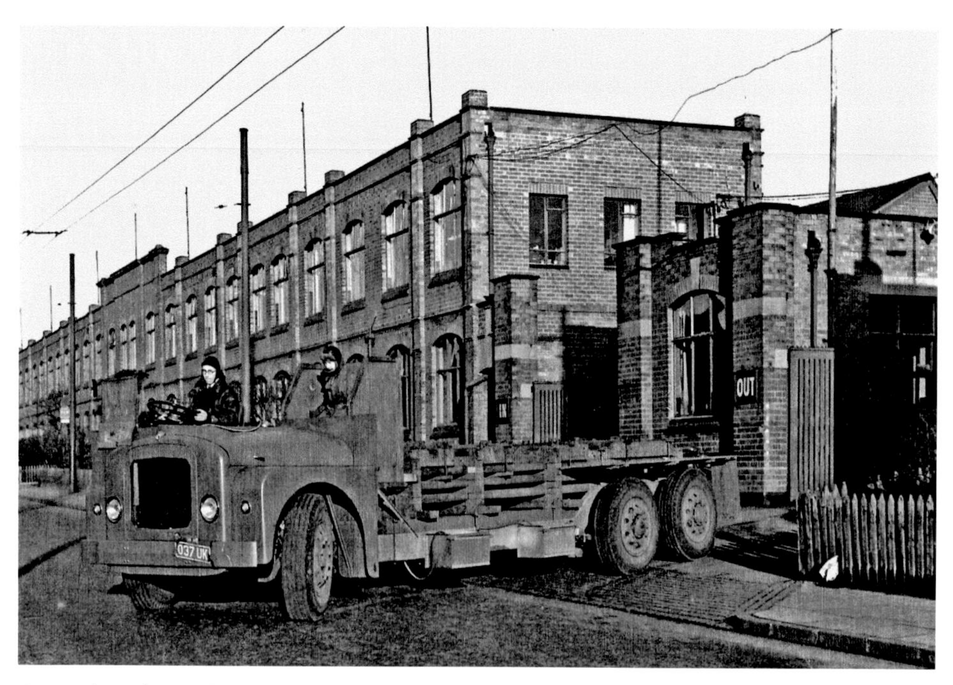

A Guy bus chassis being driven from the Guy Motors Park Lane factory. The drawing office building is in the background. This was normal sight in the town as the chassis would be driven to a bodywork manufacturer for completion. The poor drivers had to wrap up warm during the winter.

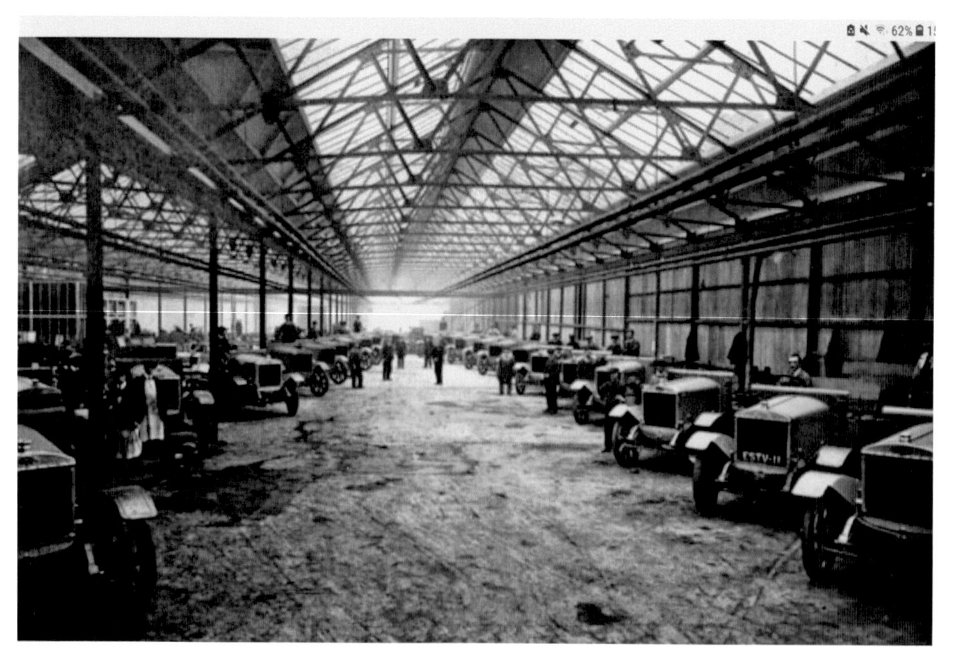

Sydney Guy resigned as Sunbeam Works Manager in 1913 and started his own company, building a factory in Park Lane primarily to make commercial vehicles. Here, light trucks are being built in the 1920s.

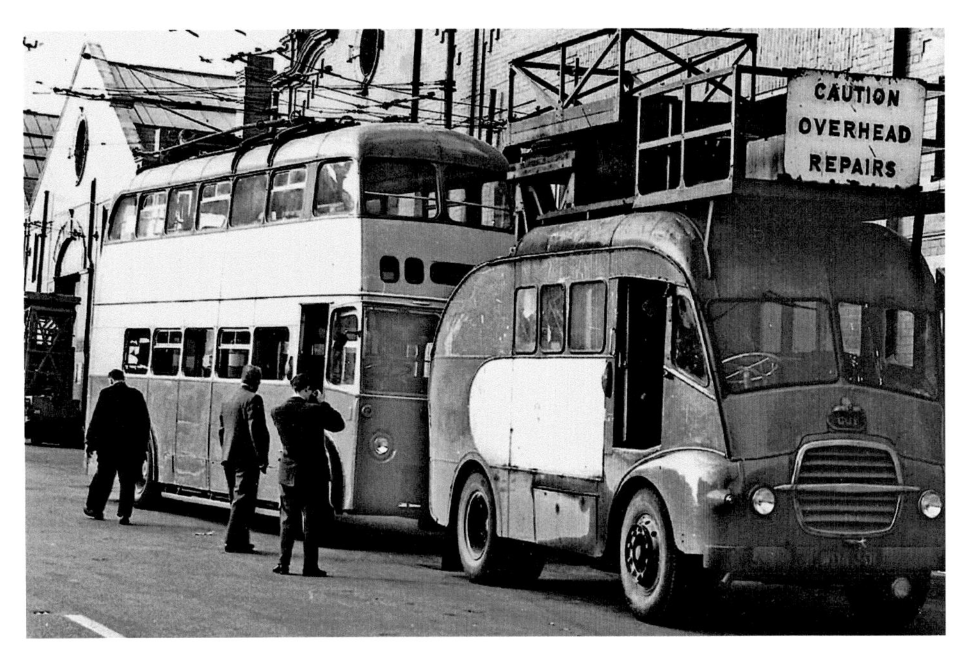

Guy Motors not only produced their own motor buses and trolleybuses, but they took over the Sunbeam trolleybus business. Wolverhampton Corporation Transport Department were a faithful customer, and here, outside the Cleveland Road bus depot, a Guy Warrior overhead maintenance vehicle is pressed into use to tow a Sunbeam trolleybus that was being retired.

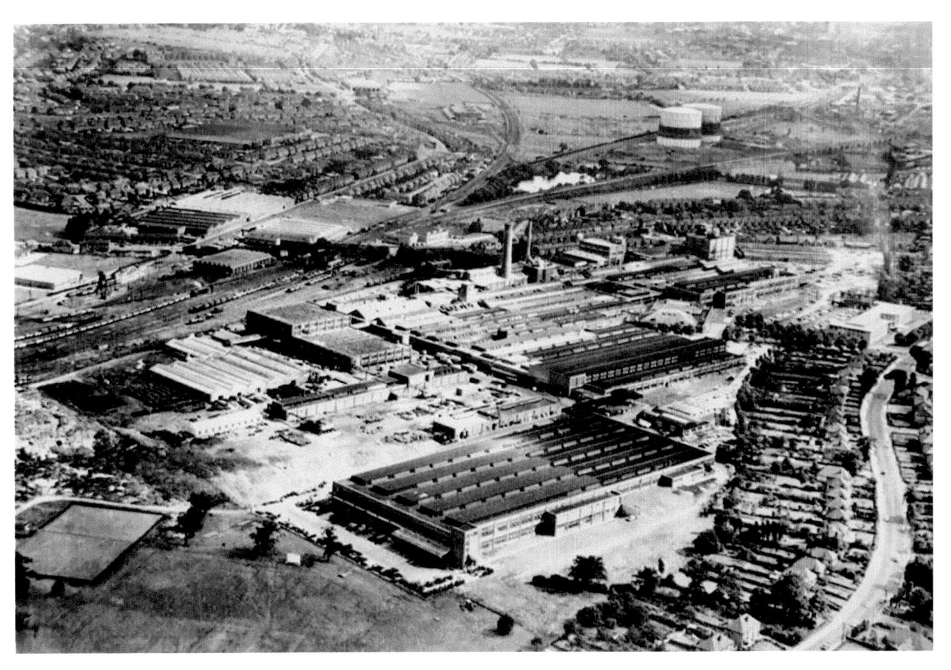

An aerial view of the huge Goodyear factory, with the single-carriageway Stafford Road running through the centre. In the distance there are two gasometers on Wolverhampton Gas Works site, and beyond that is the ubiquitous Commercial Road Power Station. After over ninety years of Goodyear being one of the biggest employers in the town, this whole site is now housing.

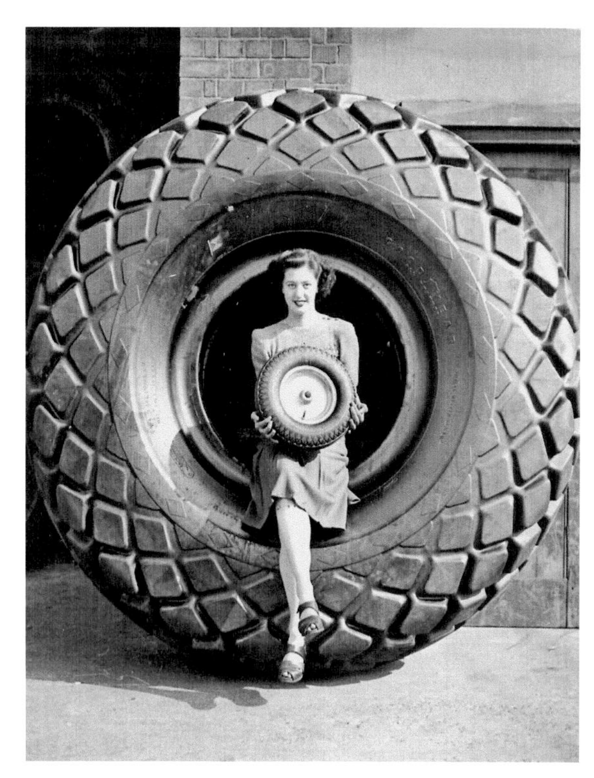

Little and large, Goodyear made them all. A member of the office staff shows off the extremes of tyre production.

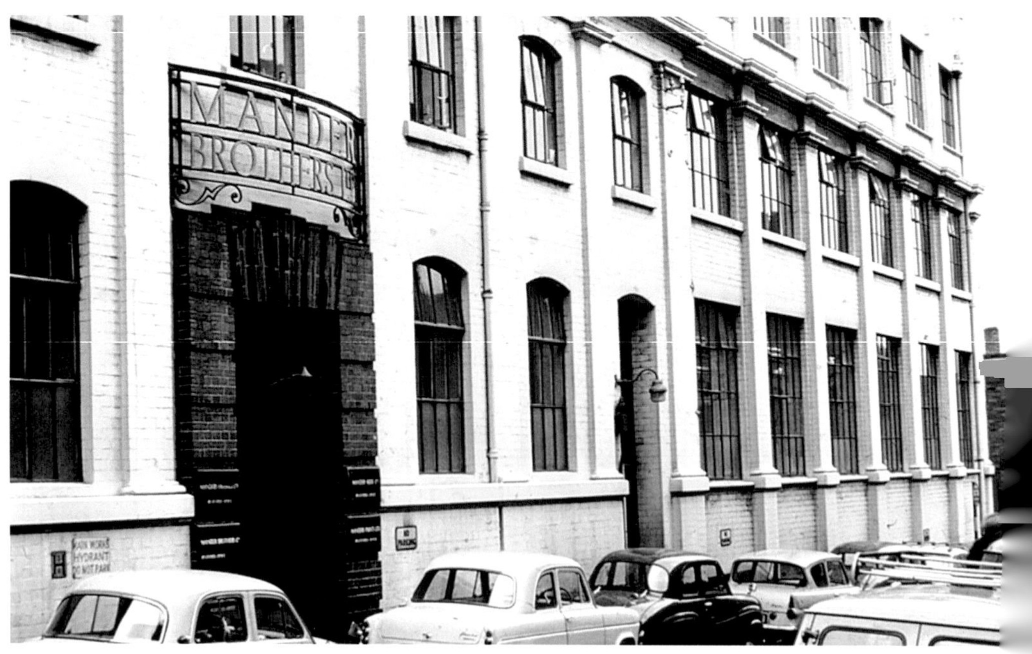

Mander Bros paint and varnish works in St John's Street, right in the heart of the town. The Mander family moved here in 1790 and later opened new factories in Wednesfield (1908) and Heath Town (1926). The original site closed in the 1960s and the company developed the Mander Shopping Centre in the released space.

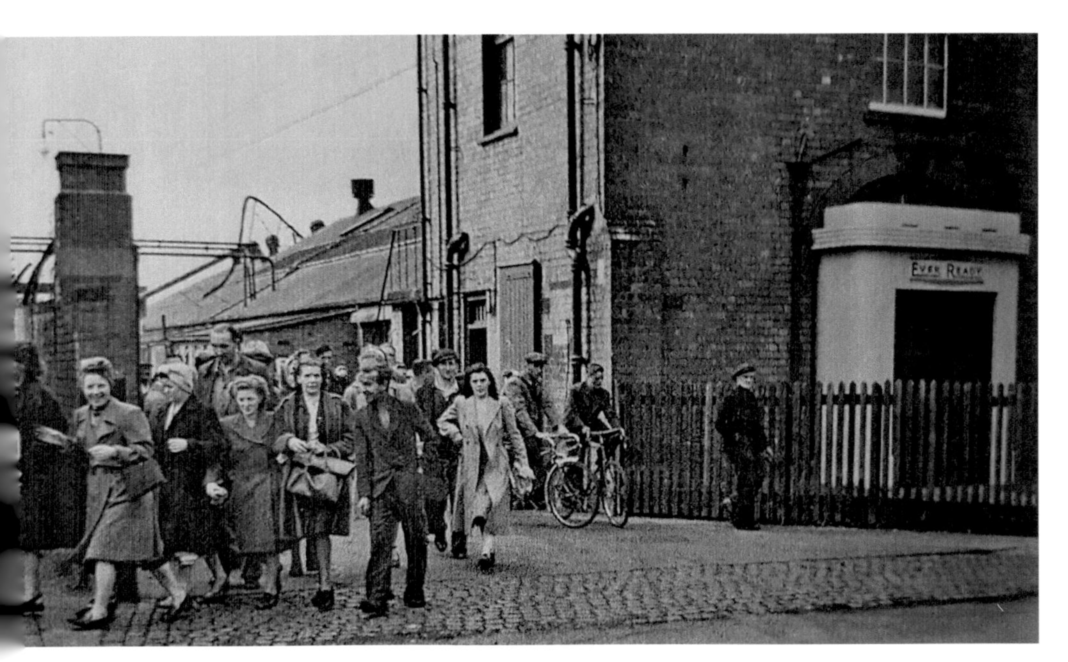

Workers pour out of the Ever Ready factory on Park Lane. The factory was opened in 1911 by a company called Efandam ('F and M', after the directors) who made electrical appliances and torches. Ever Ready (a subsidiary of the American company Eveready) bought Efandam in the 1920s. The Park Lane factory expanded to over 3,000 employees, with a second factory opening in the old AJS factory in Walsall Street. The factories closed in 1980.

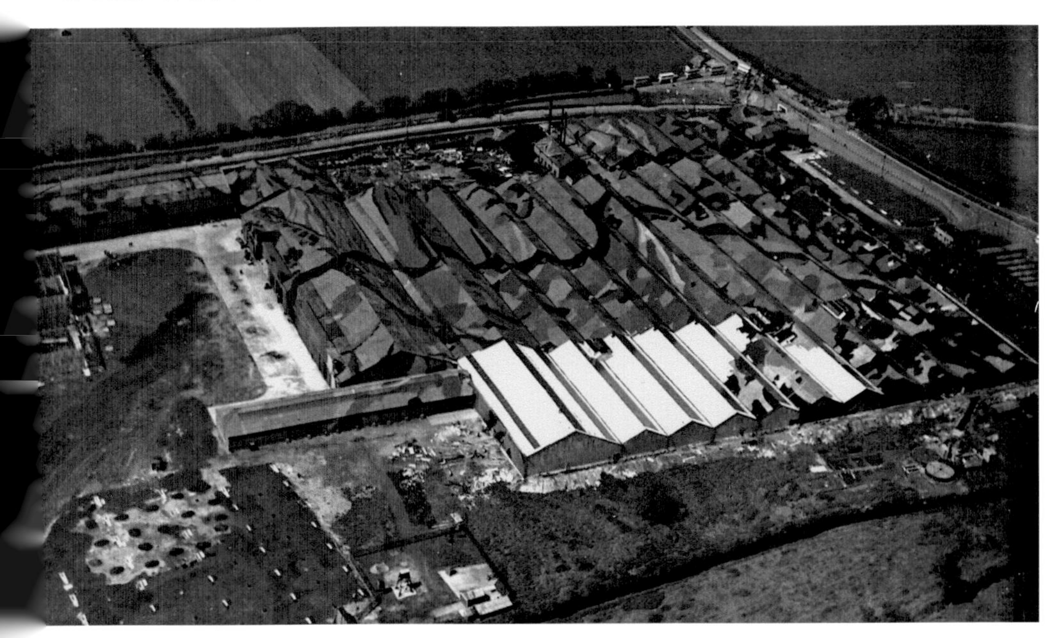

The Boulton Paul Aircraft factory in Pendeford during the war. The aircraft division of Norwich company Boulton & Paul Ltd moved here in 1936. The factory is camouflaged, and the roof of the new gun turret extension is also just being painted. A defiant fighter stands outside the first of the new Bellman hangars being built to the left.

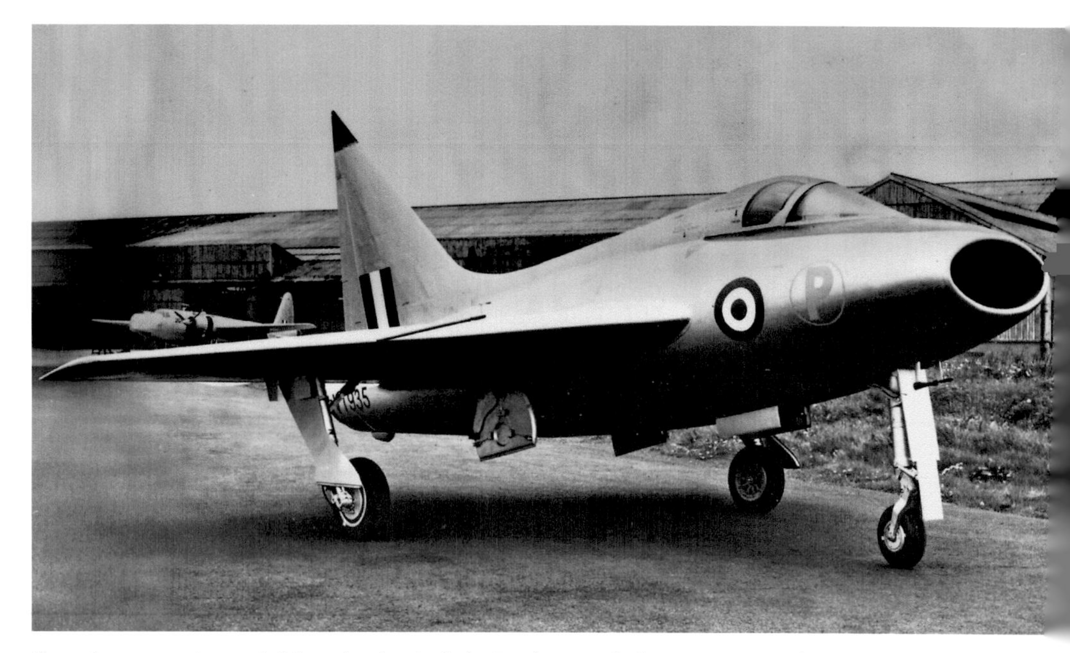

One of two experimental delta wing jets built by Boulton Paul, the P.111, sits in the taxiway, which ran round Pendeford Hill to Wolverhampton Airport. In the background is one of the Wellington bombers being refurbished and converted to navigation trainers. Aircraft production ceased in 1956, and the company concentrated on power controls.

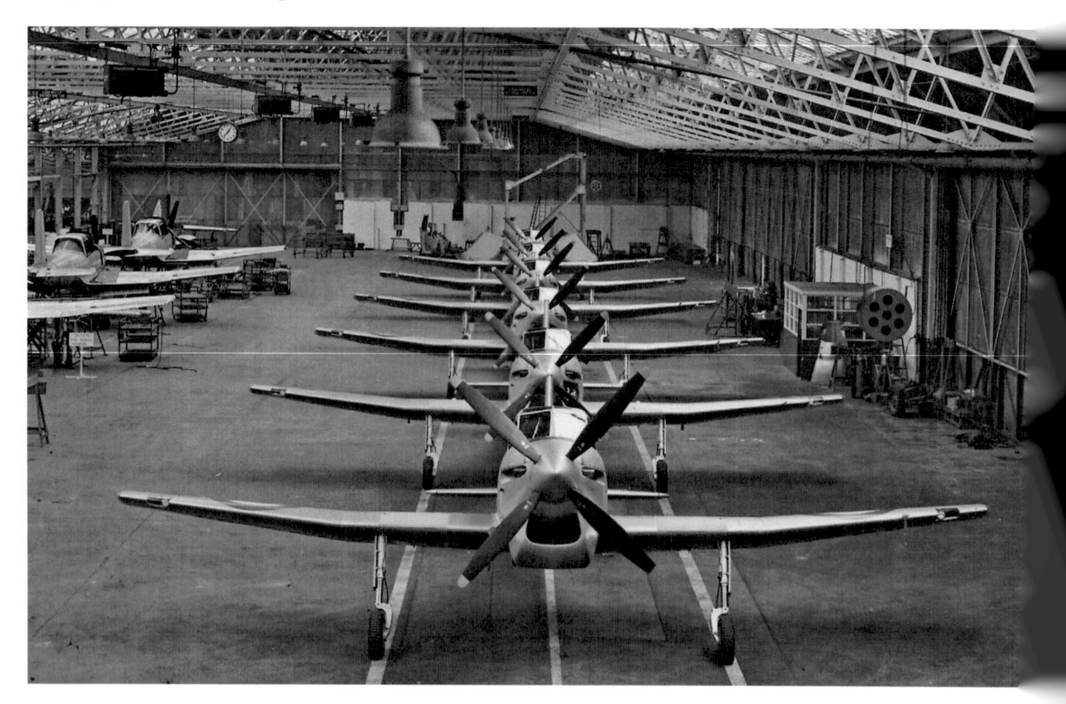

A line of Balliol advanced trainers in the flight shed await their first flight and delivery to the RAF. The last aircraft powered by the famous Rolls-Royce Merlin engine, the Balliol, was the last piston engine advanced trainer and the last aircraft type made in Wolverhampton.

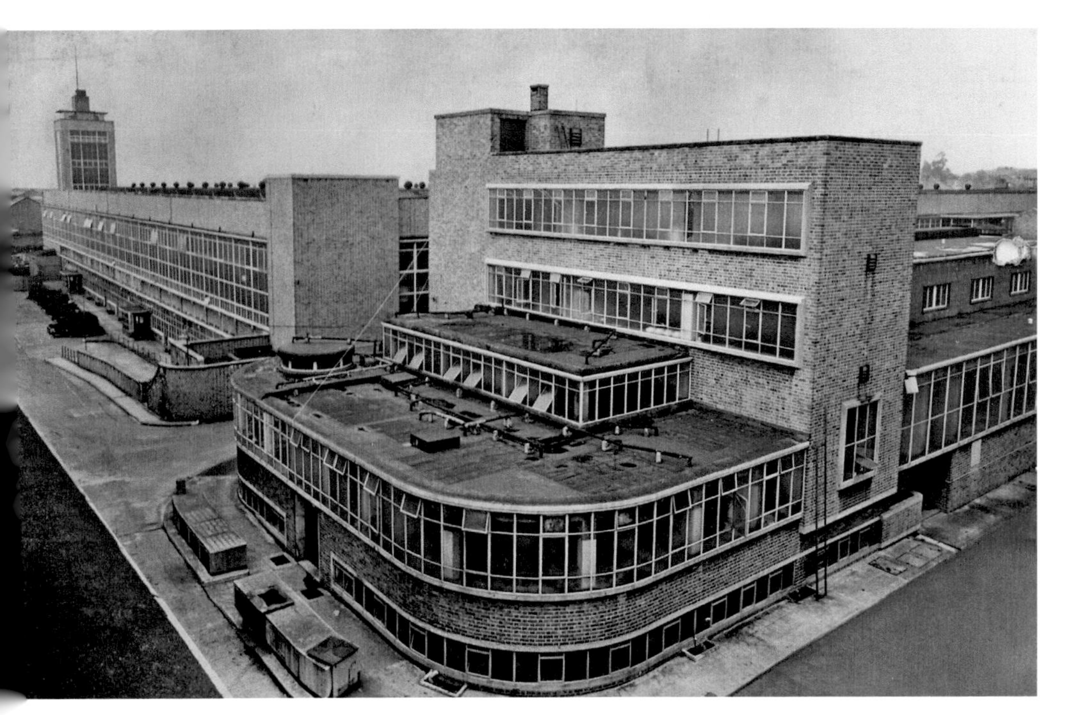

The 14-acre Henry Meadows factory on Cannock Road. Formed in 1919 by a local consortium to make commercial vehicle gearboxes, the company soon began making petrol and then diesel engines for a plethora of applications.

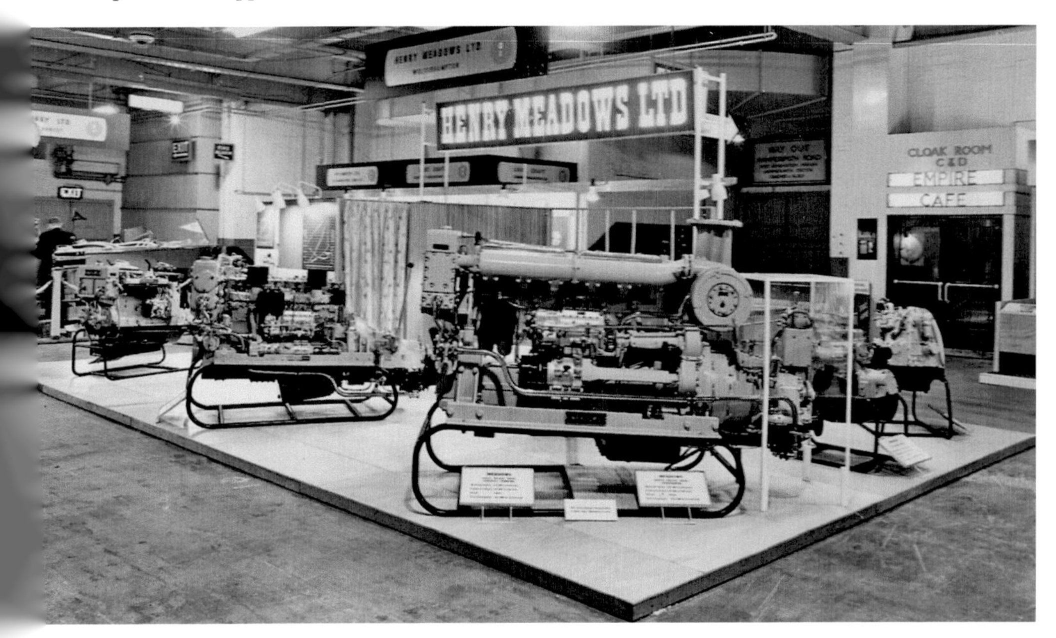

A Henry Meadows trade stand displaying five of the diesel engines their 1,200-strong workforce made for trucks, buses, locomotives, power boats, generating sets, and many other things. Bought by Jaguar in 1965 with the intention of integrating with Guy Motors next door, Meadows was soon part of the British Leyland Group and closed in 1968.

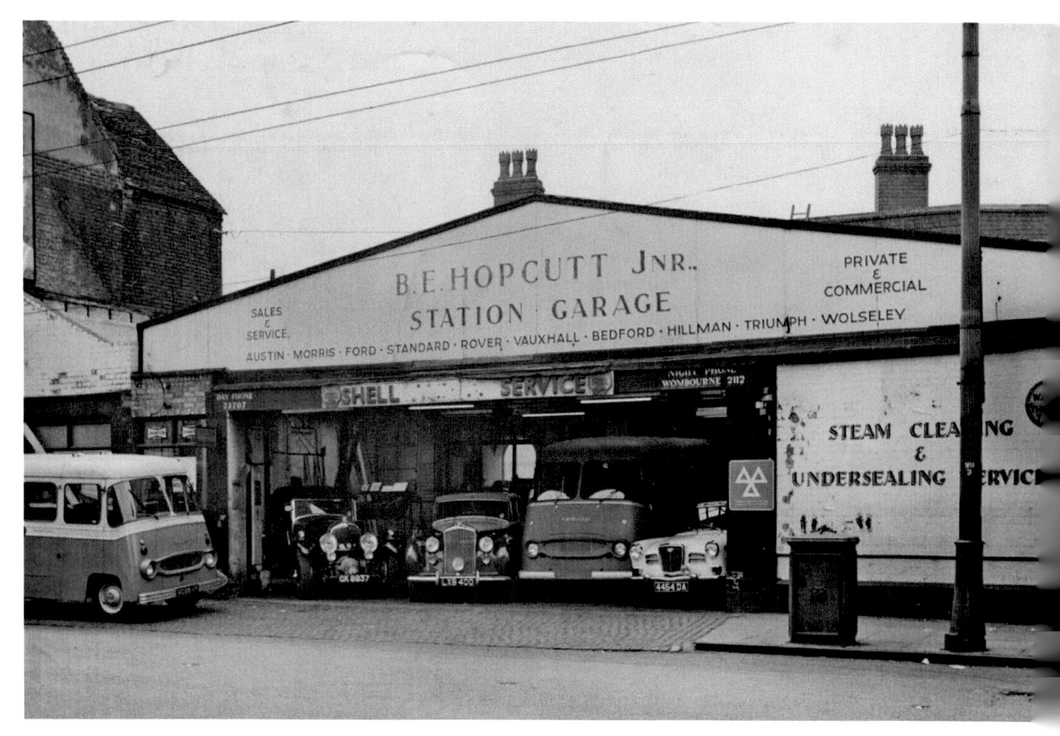

B. E. Hopcutt's Station Garage in Horseley Fields in the early 1960s, a typical urban garage at the time, advertising undersealing, a popular fashion in those days.

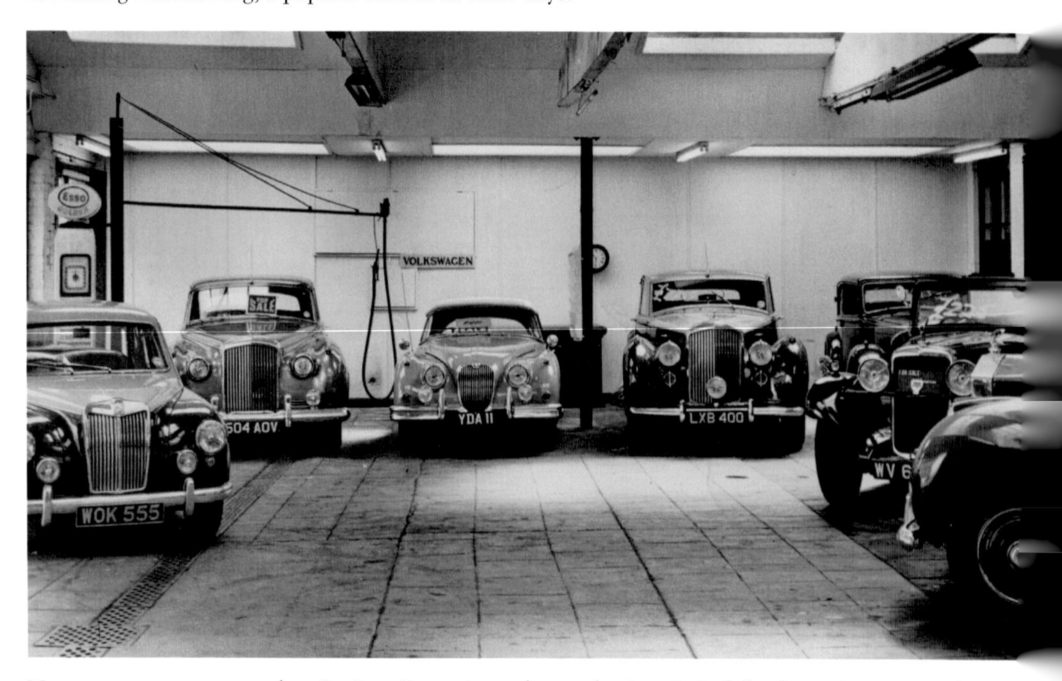

Not a transport museum but Station Garage's used-car selection. It is full of prestige cars, such as Bentleys, Rolls-Royce, Jaguar XK150 and MG Magnette. Station Garage was cleared away with the rest of the Horseley Fields community.

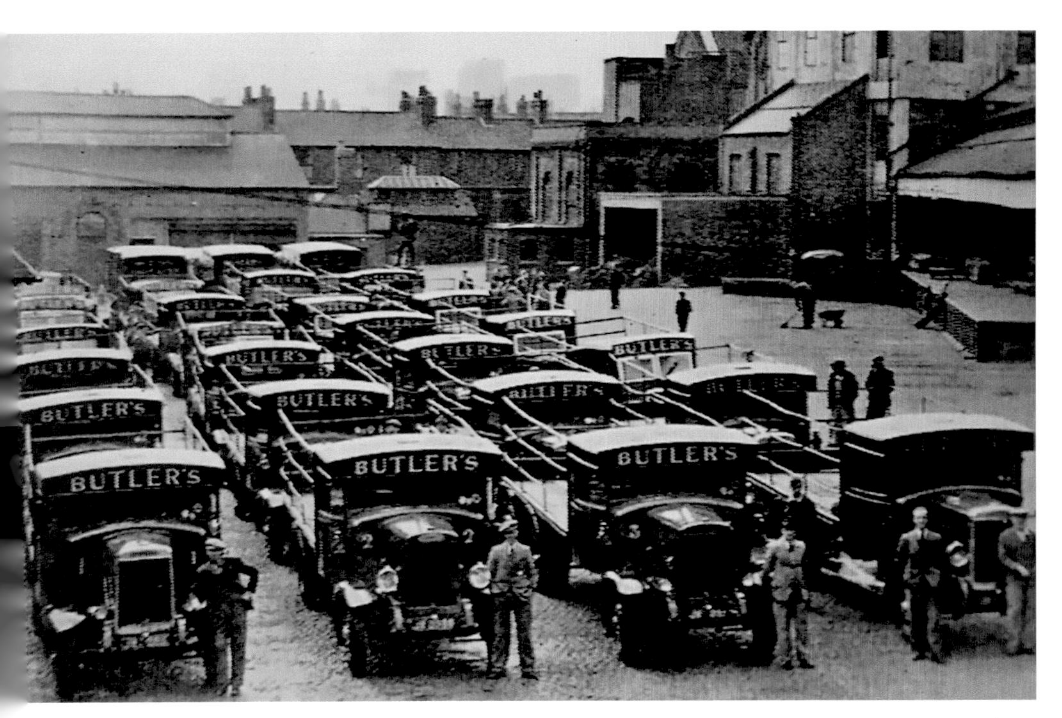

Over two dozen Butler's drays outside the Springfield Brewery in 1938. William Butler moved his brewery from Priestfield to Springfield in 1874 because of the local water supply, the source of Smestow Brook, and the adjacent railway for transportation.

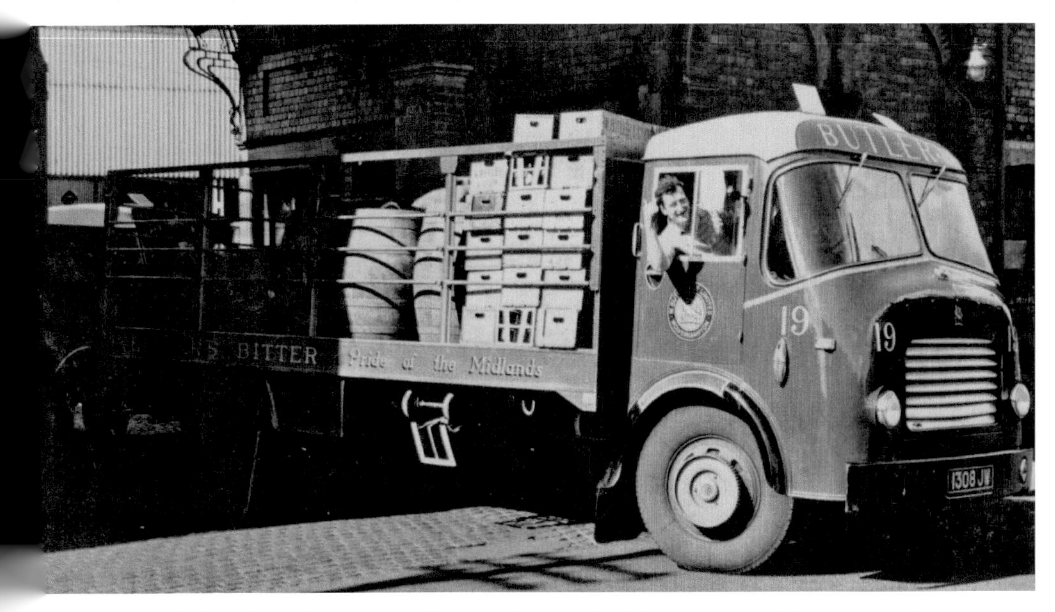

A lorry loaded with Butler's Ales pulls out of Springfield Brewery. In 1960, it was taken over by Mitchells & Butlers, and the following year there was a merger with Bass. After that there was a gradual run down, with departments closed as Bass, Mitchells & Butlers Ltd streamlined their operation until Springfield Brewery finally closed in 1991. After years of dereliction and then a fire, the premises were taken over by the university for redevelopment.

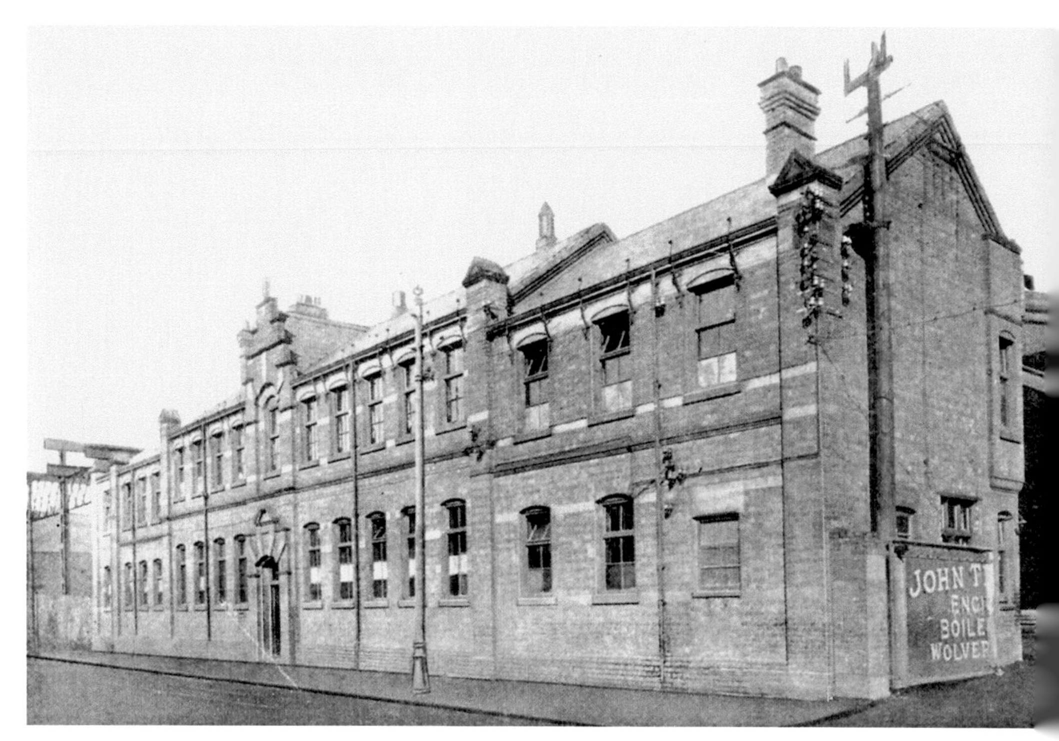

The offices of John Thompson on Millfields Road, Ettingshall, *c*. 1900. The Thompson family began in Bilston making narrowboat bodies and steam boilers, and moved to Ettingshall in 1870. Only the central portion of the office building now survives.

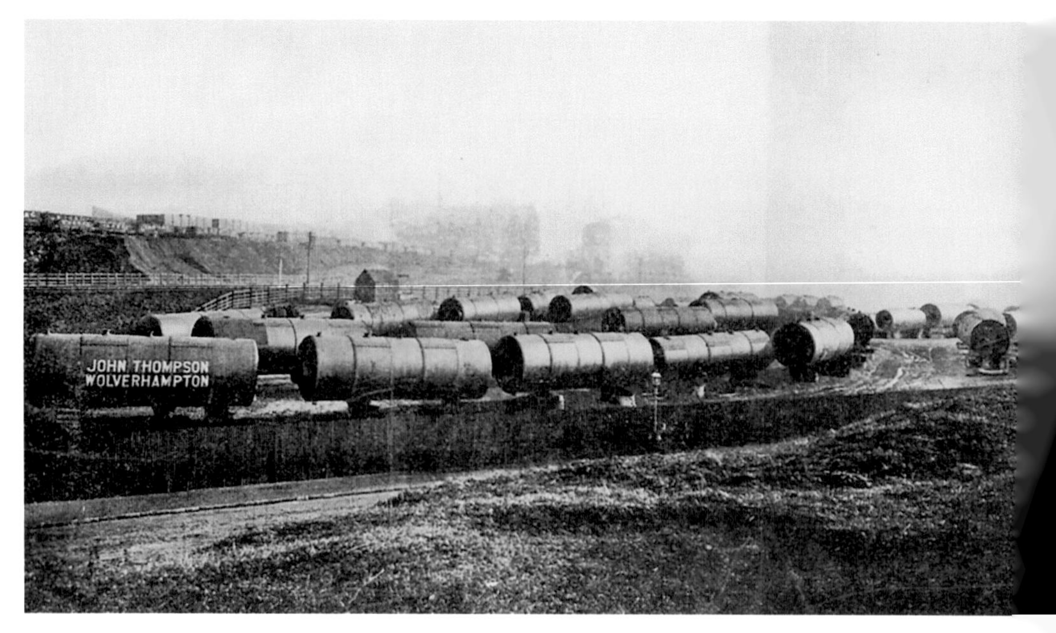

John Thompson's boiler stockyard. The company dominated the area with a site that covered 80 acres and encompassed many other products. Lots of the buildings survive, but have since been put to other uses.

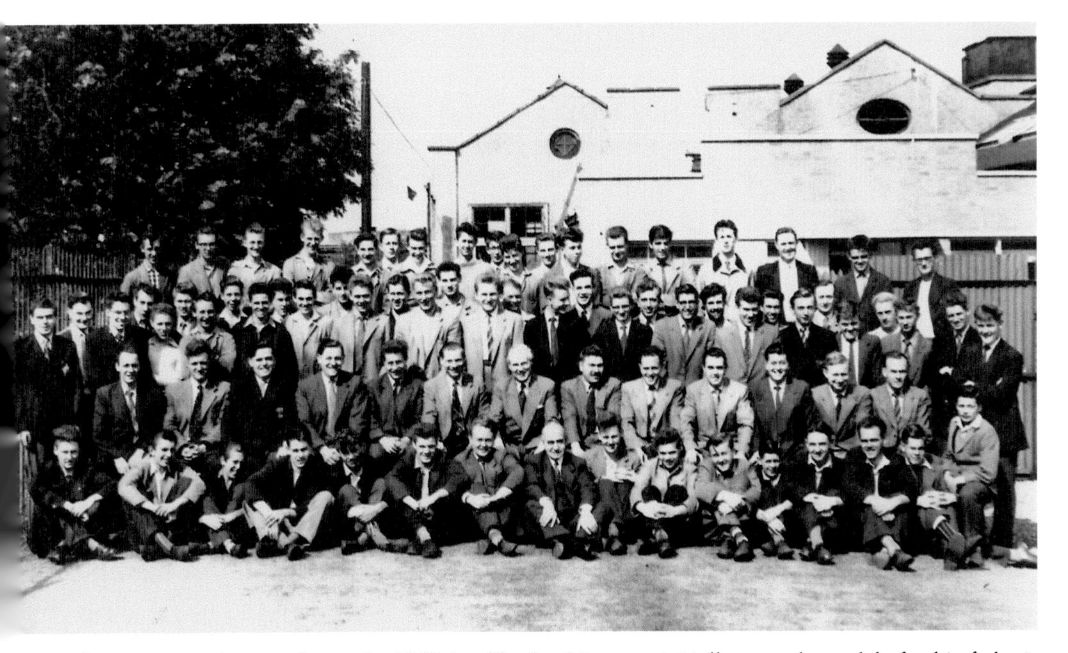

Villiers Engineering was begun in 1890 by Charles Marston, initially to make pedals for his father's Sunbeam bicycles, taking a licence for an American Pratt & Whitney design. Later they became famous for the millions of two- and four-stroke engines they made. Here a photograph of their apprentices is a reminder that many of the city's companies used to employ a huge number of engineering apprentices.

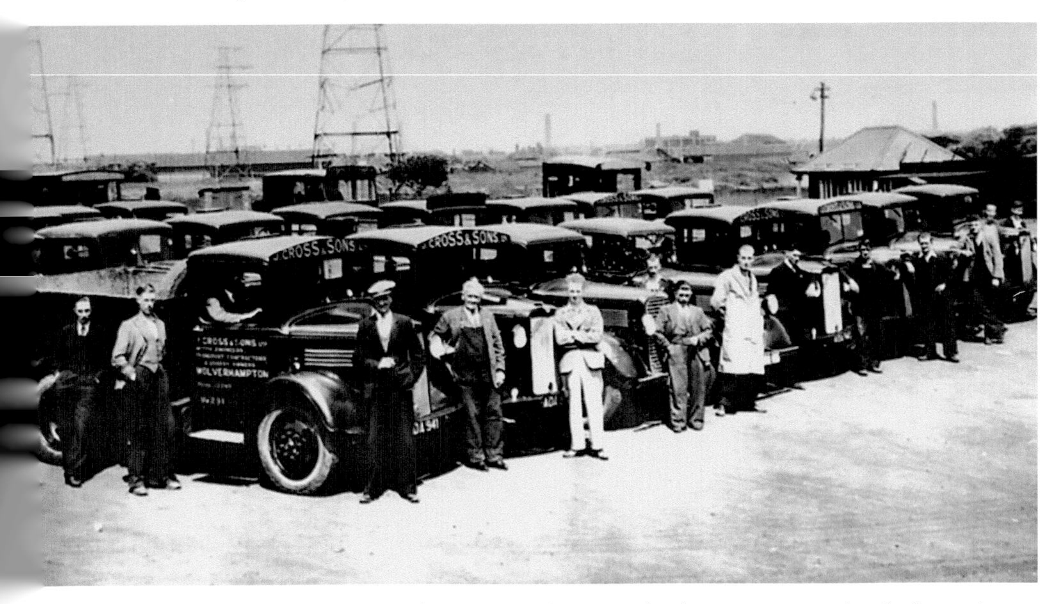

The assembled trucks and drivers of J. Cross and Sons, a haulage contractor that had premises at No. 55 Willenhall Road, Horseley Fields.

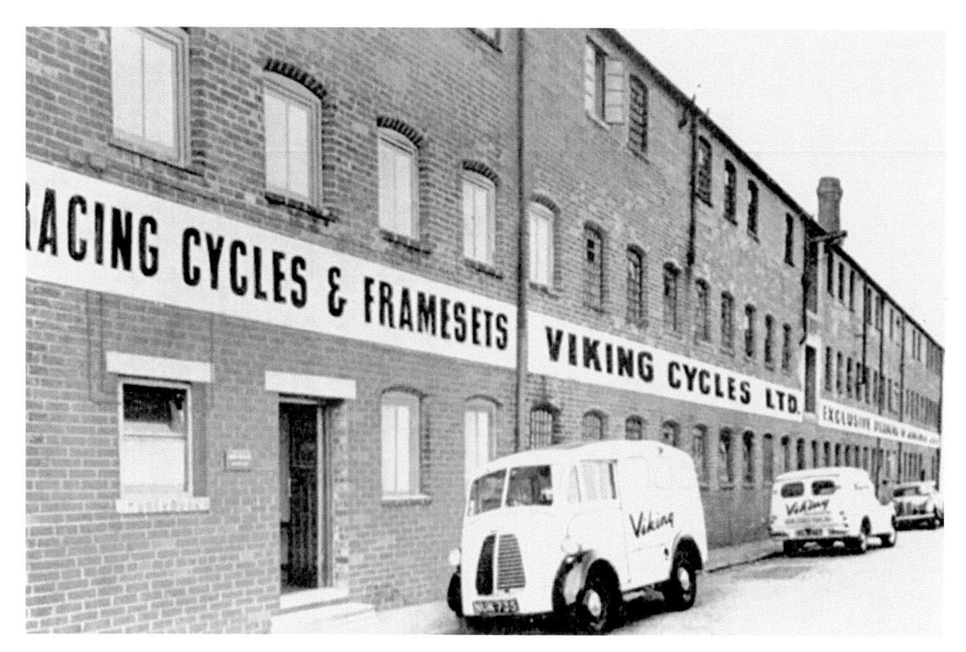

The Viking factory in Russell Street. The longest lasting of all the many Wolverhampton cycle manufacturers, Viking was started by Alfred Davies in Heath Town in 1908. They later moved to Princess Alley and then here to the Merridale Works, where they made up to 20,000 cycles a year until closure in 1967.

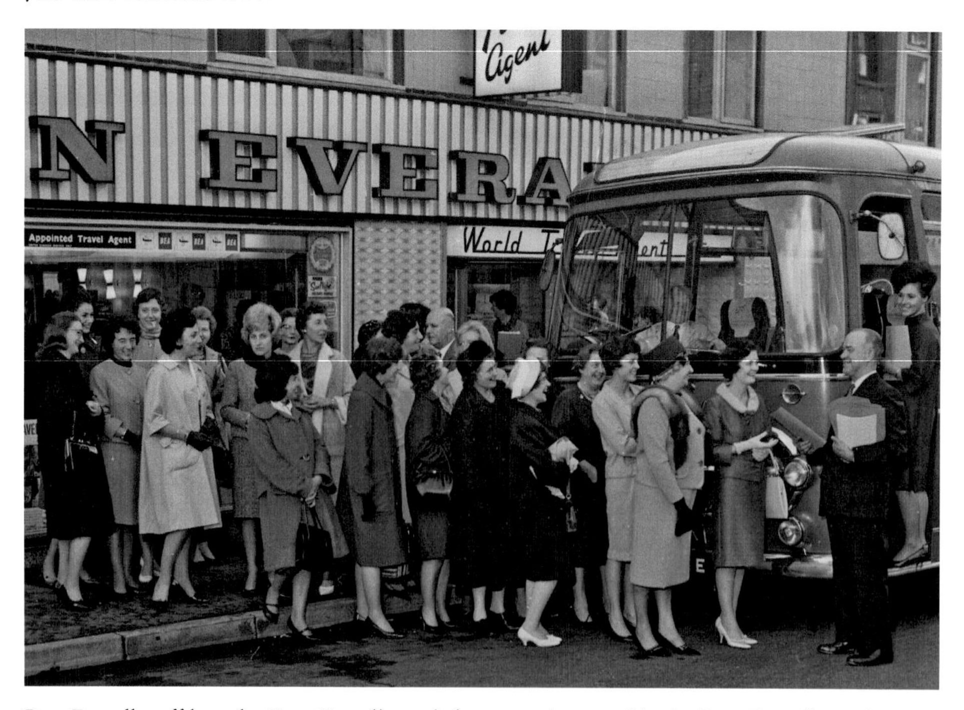

Don Everall staff board a Don Everall coach for an outing, outside the Don Everall travel agents in Bell Street. Don Everall started his coach company in the 1920s and eventually spread into many sectors of the industry, including running holiday camps.

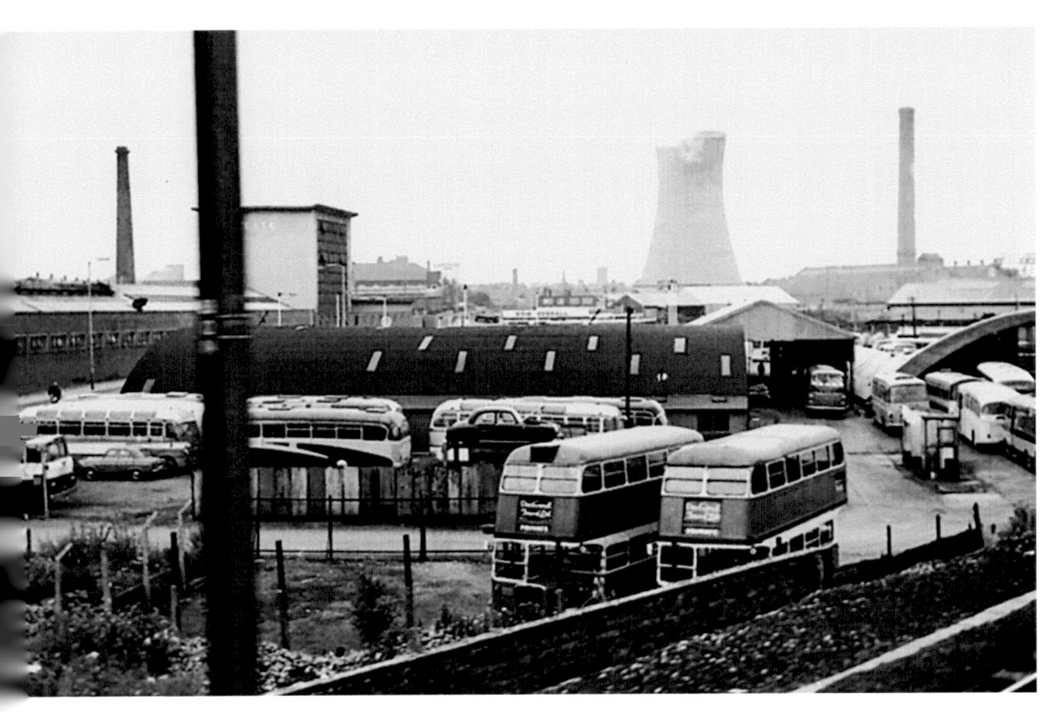

The main Don Everall coach and bus yard, which was behind the Don Everall Ford dealership on Bilston Road, Monmore Green.

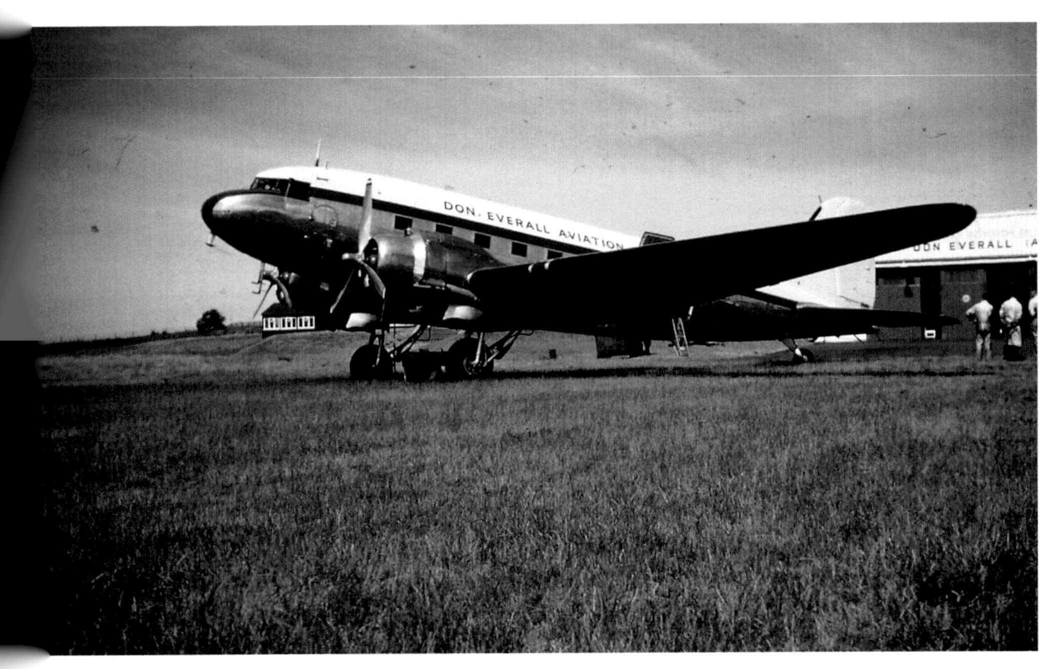

For a time, Don Everall ran an airline, operating inclusive tours from Elmdon (Birmingham Airport), though their DC-3 aircraft were serviced at Wolverhampton Airport, which the company also ran on behalf of the council. Here, a DC-3 stands in front of the maintenance hangar. For eighteen months in the mid-1950s they also offered scheduled flights from Pendeford.

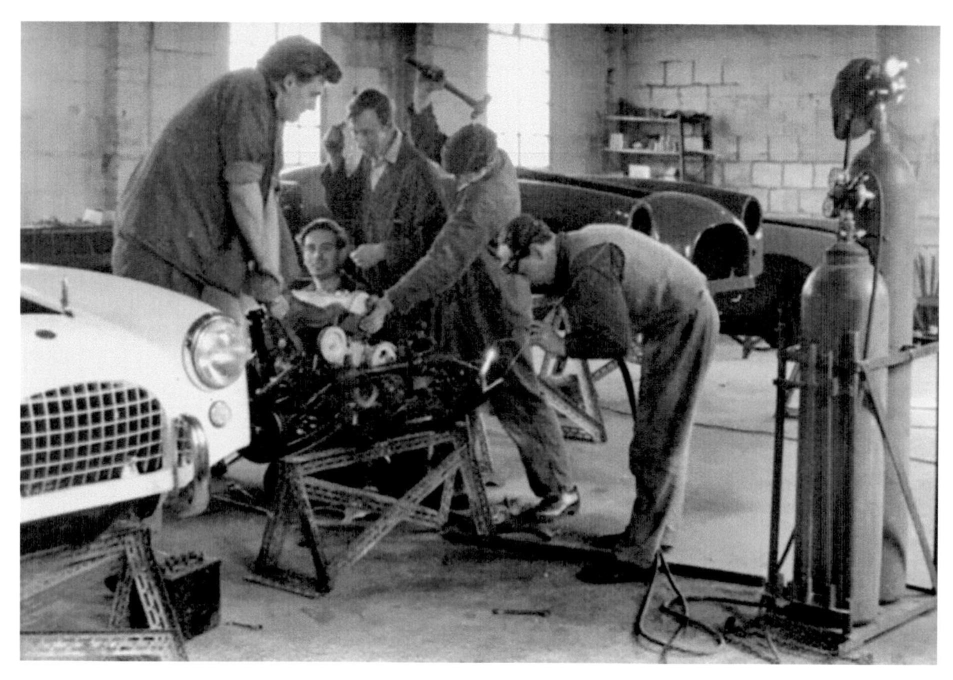

One of the wartime huts at Pendeford Airport was occupied by the last of the town's vehicle manufacturers, sports car maker Jack Turner. Jack began his company in Seisdon in 1949 before moving to the airport. He made over 600 of his two-seaters up to 1966 when he retired through ill health.

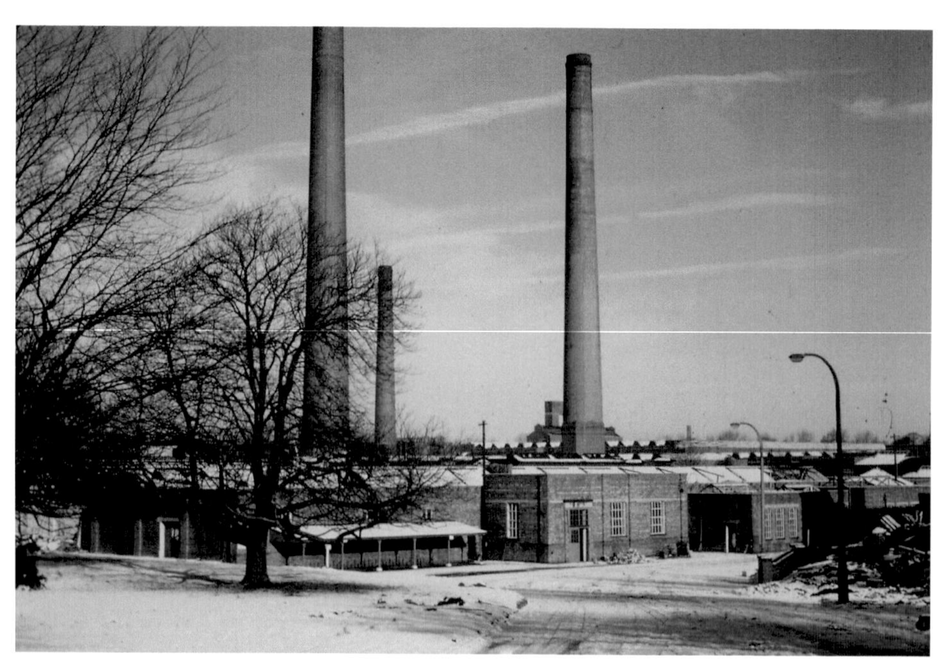

The rayon-manufacturing factory of the giant Courtaulds conglomerate was built in 1926. Its chimneys, known as the 'Three Sisters', dominated the area until closure in 1970 when as many as 1,350 people worked there, on what is now the Farndale Estate.

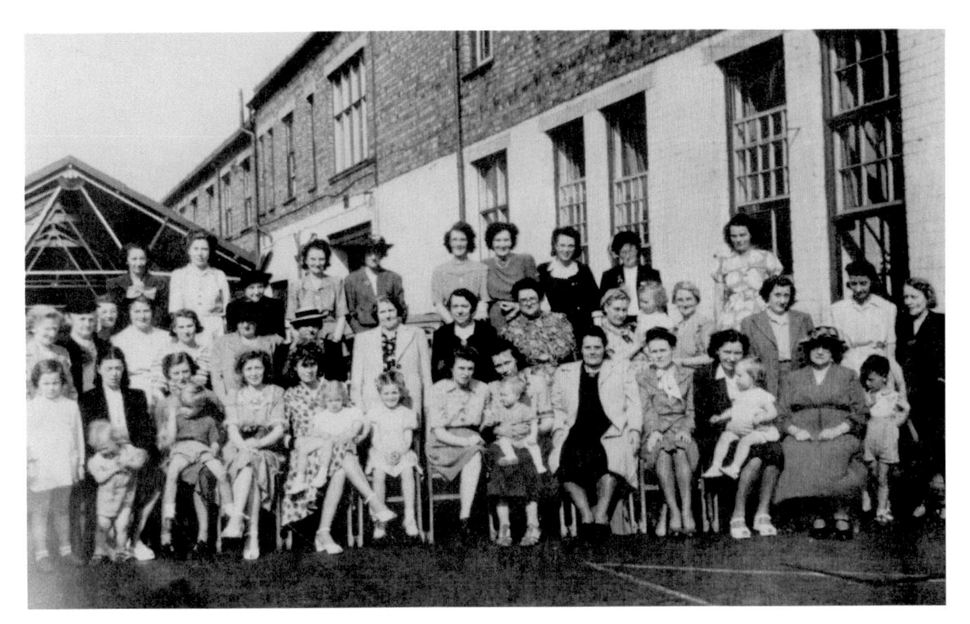

The German company Fischer Bearings came to Upper Villiers Street in 1936. After the war they were to have several name changes, to Fafnir Bearings and then Timken of America, before final closure in 2015. There were always a great number of female staff, many of whom are seen here at some kind of social event.

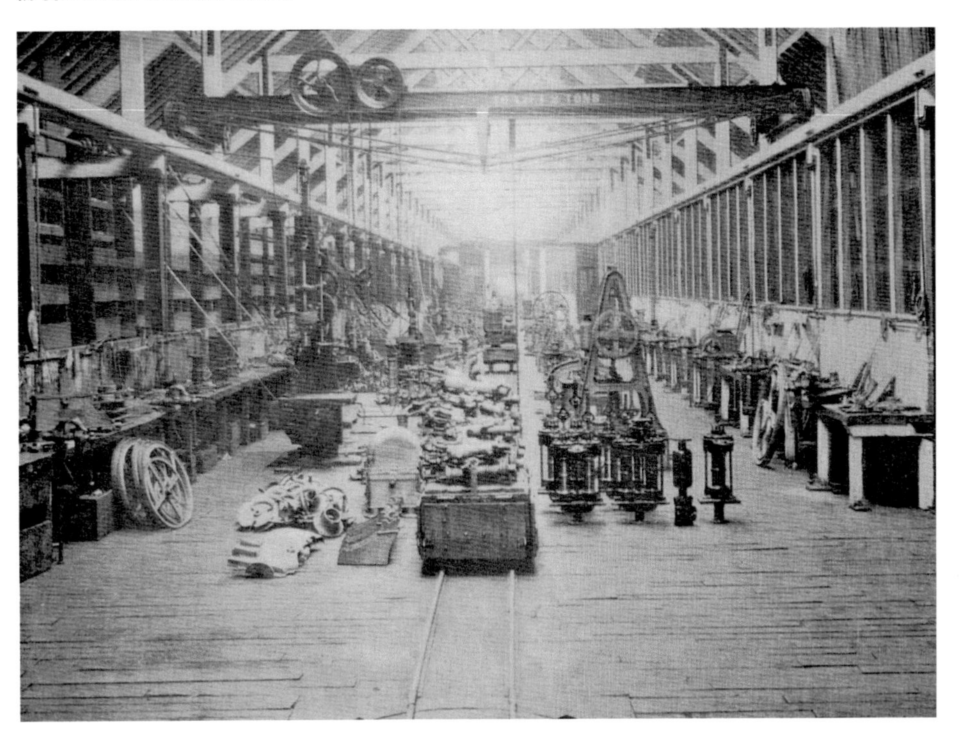

Joseph Evans pumps in Heath Town had origins in the early part of the eighteenth century making all kinds of pumps under their Lion brand logo. They eventually settled on the huge Culwell Works in Woden Road, one of the manufacturing bays before the First World War.

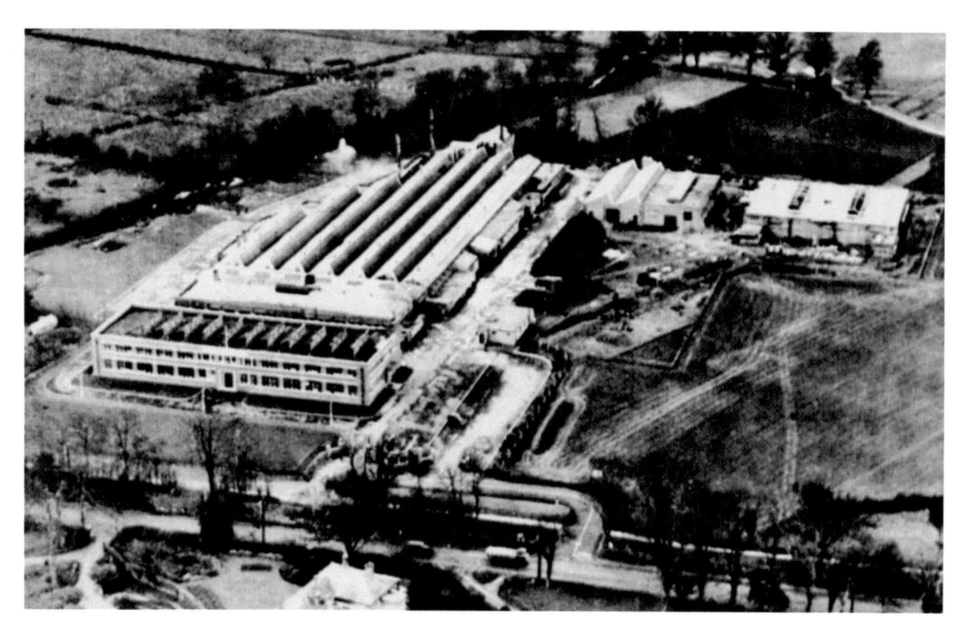

H. M. Hobsons were a London company who took a licence to build the French Claudel carburettor and were encouraged to come to Wolverhampton in 1913 by the Sunbeam Motor Car Co. They settled in the Accuracy Works in Blakenhall and became a major supplier of car and aero engine carburettors. In the Second World War this new shadow factory was built on Stafford Road, which later expanded considerably, becoming Lucas Aerospace, and is now part of Collins Aerospace.

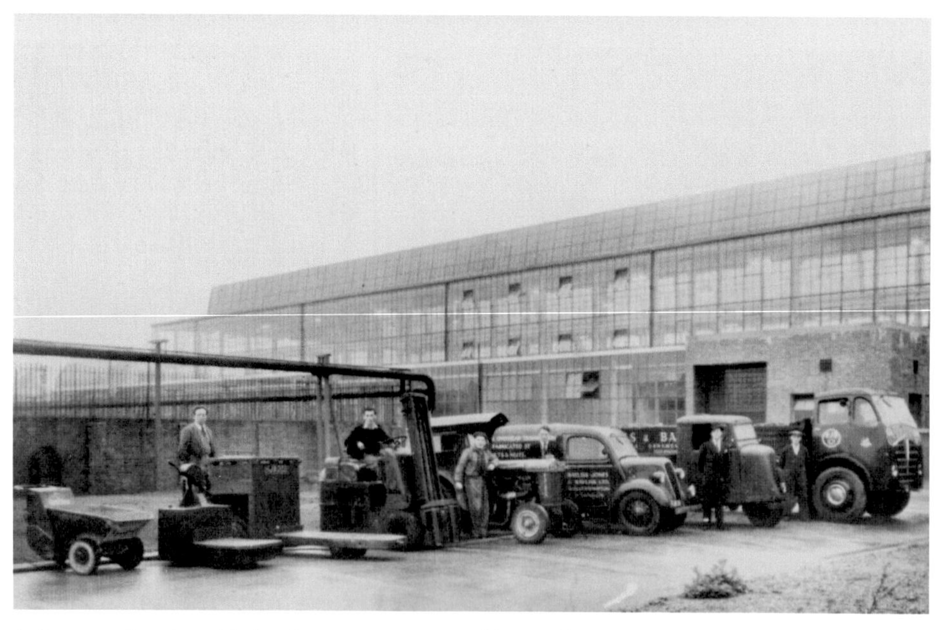

A line up of various kinds of transport operated by Bayliss Jones and Bayliss in Cable Street, Monmore Green. This Victorian firm expanded across a huge site, making largely wrought-iron products, but then also steel rolling and metal working machinery. It became part of GKN and was closed in the 1980s.

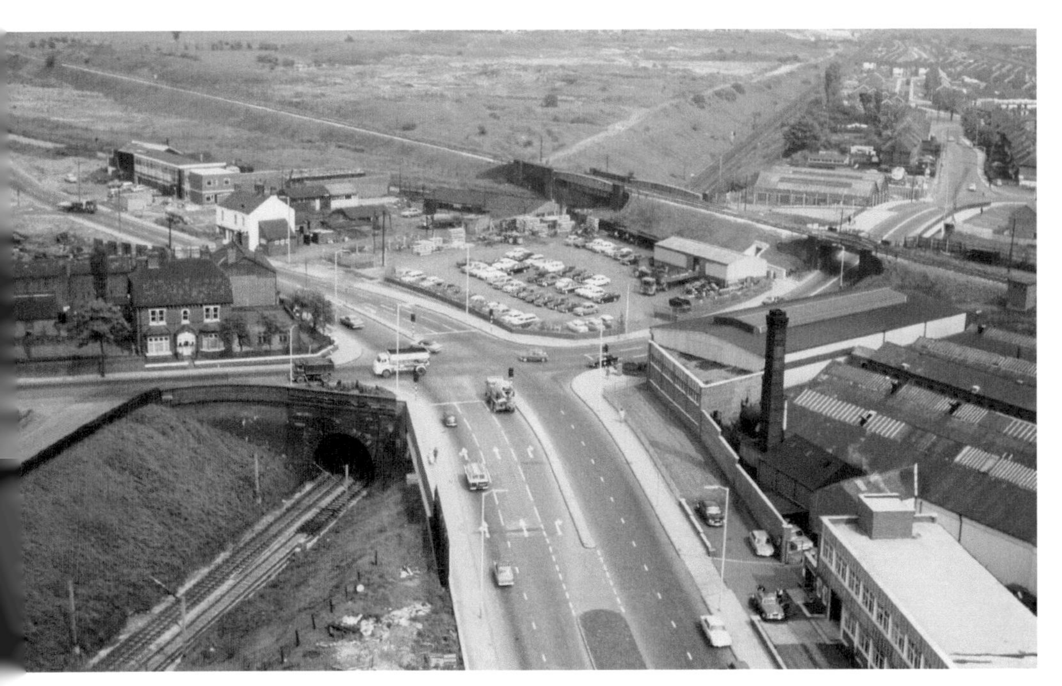

The Wednesfield Road and Deans Road junction, seen from the top of the Heath Town flats. The factory to the right was bought in the war by Redwing Aircraft of Croydon, who made Boulton Paul Defiant fuselage sections and other parts. After the factory was cleared away an early resident of the new shopping centre built there was Kwiksave.

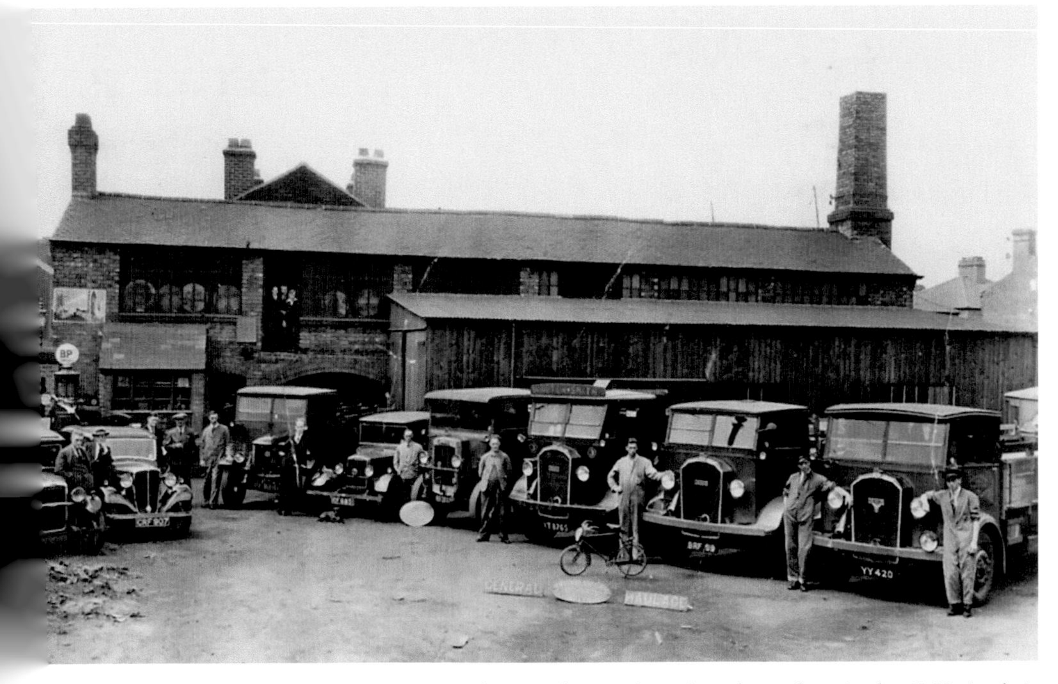

Another long-lost transport company is Walter Smith's Haulage Co., shown here in the 1930s in their yard on Parkfield Road, Ettingshall, with their full fleet of five lorries, three cars and a bicycle.

3
Lost Neighbourhoods

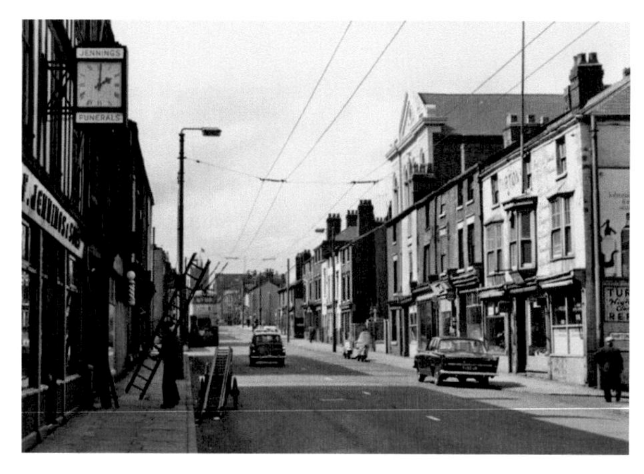

Around the town centre there used to exist a series of neighbourhoods that were practically self-contained, having houses, workplaces, shops and leisure facilities. This is the main Willenhall Road through Horseley Fields with the Jennings (undertakers) clock on the left. Jennings still exists, though in a new building, but everything else here was swept away.

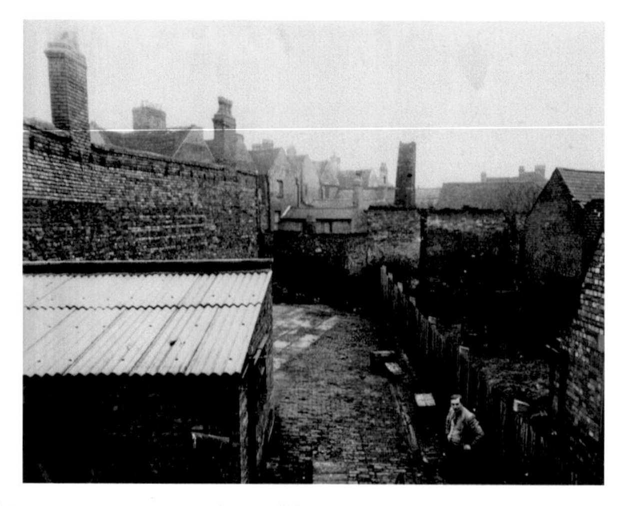

Mr Hopcutt of Station Garage, Horseley Fields, stands in the foreground on the space in which he hoped to build an extension in 1963, showing the jumbled nature at the rear of the businesses.

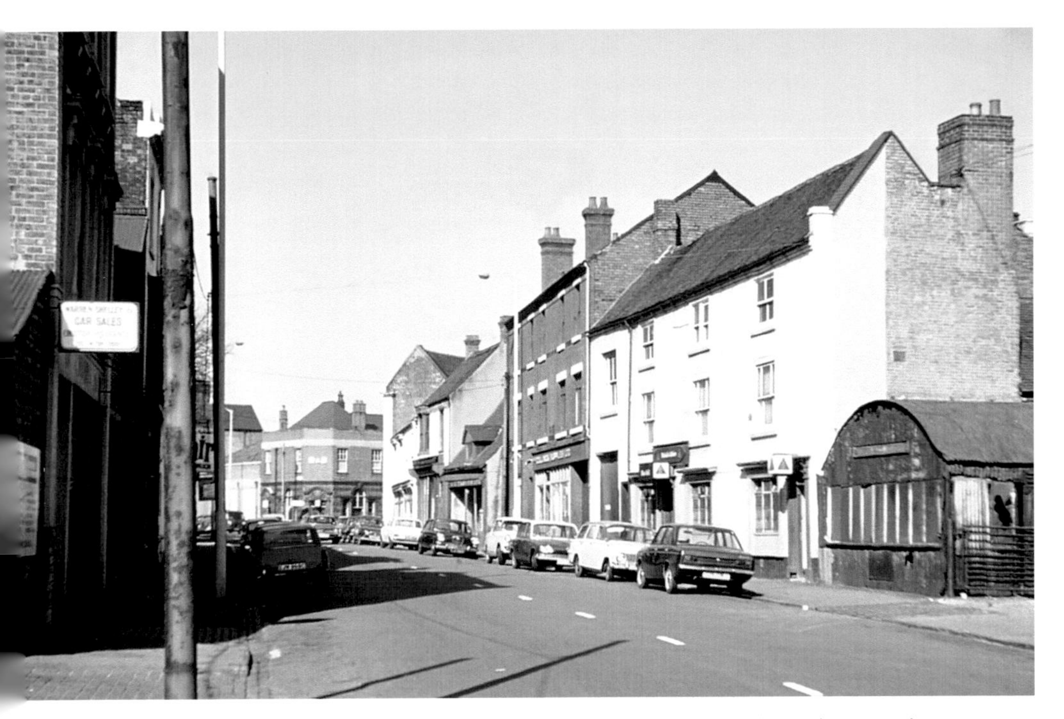

Bilston Street was another road leading out of the town centre that housed a varied community. The Blue Bell pub to the right was just one of many catering for the local thirst. The Blue Ball, straight ahead, was on Piper's Row.

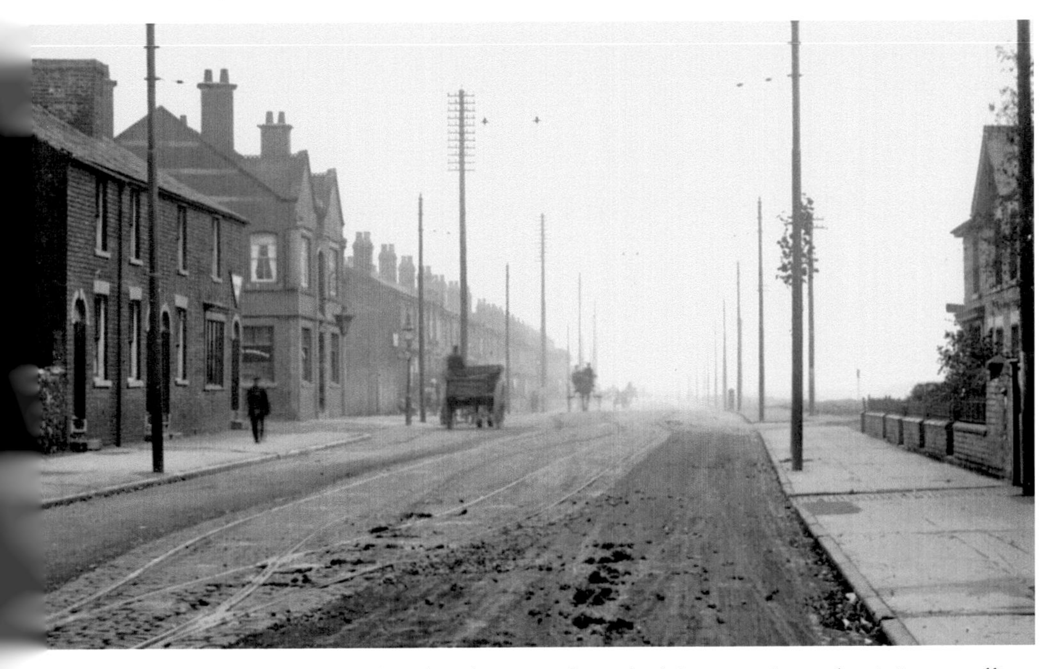

Seen to the centre left, the British Oak pub was at the end of Coventry Street, but it is now offices. The terrace of houses beyond still remains, but those this side of the pub have gone, as have the horse droppings in the road.

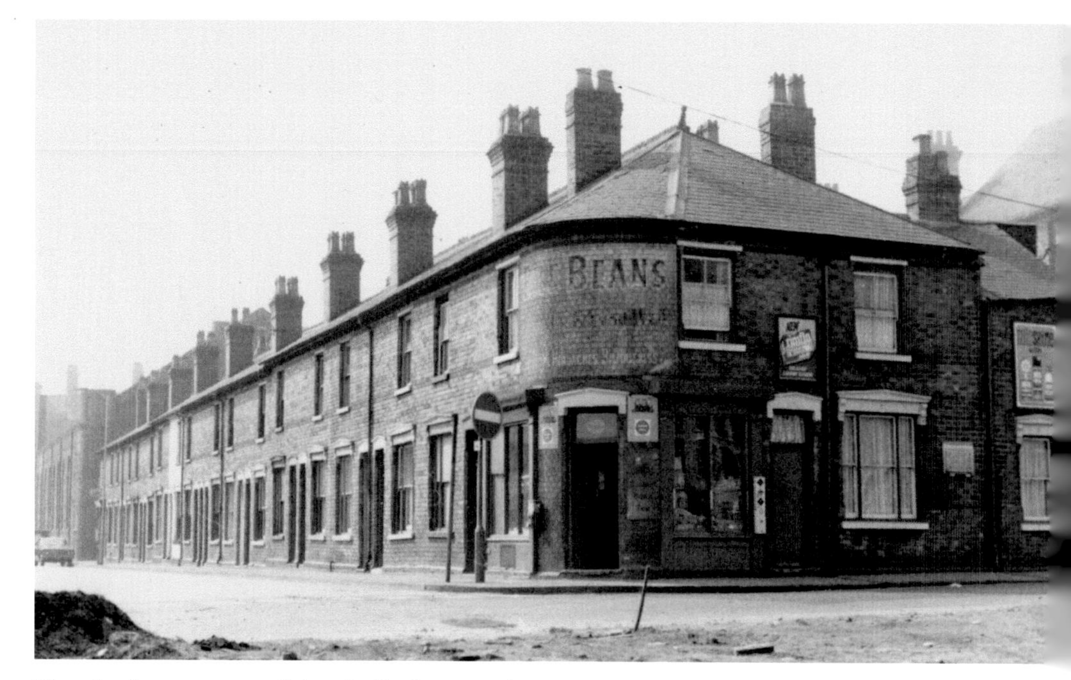

Thornley Street runs parallel to Stafford Street. This terrace starts at the corner with Littles Lane and still exists, but the terrace on the other side of the road is gone, together with the whole community of 'Carribee Island' behind it, replaced by a car park and the ring road. Littles Lane is now cut into two short cul-de-sacs.

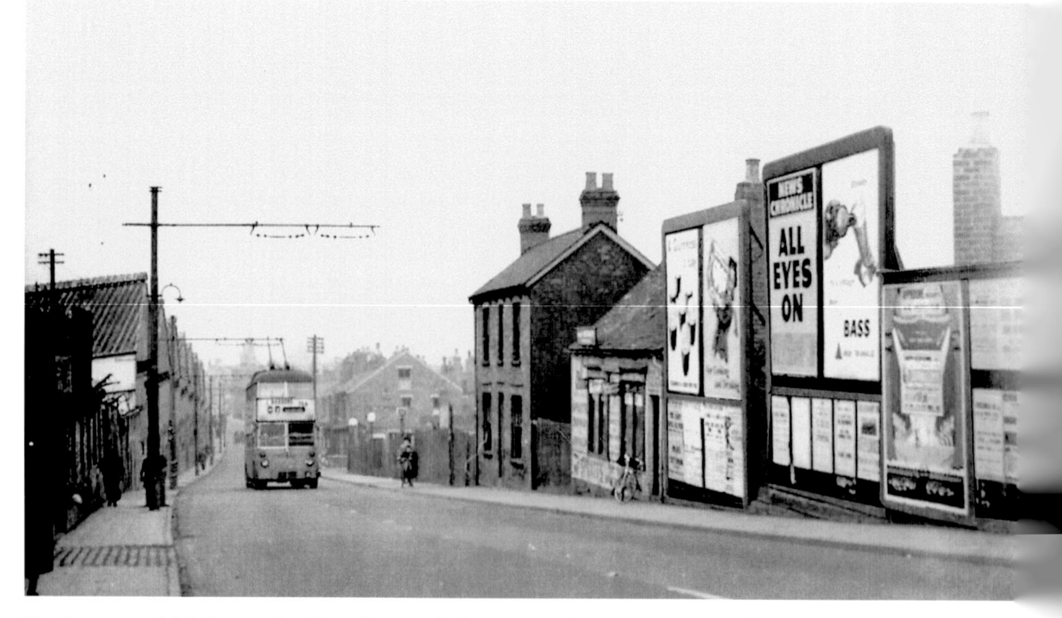

To the east of Molineux Stadium lay a whole community set in a triangle of roads: North Street, Waterloo Road and, on this side, Molineux Street, which a trolleybus is seen gliding up. The Wolves bought the houses on the other side of the street, which was then closed to construct the John Ireland Stand.

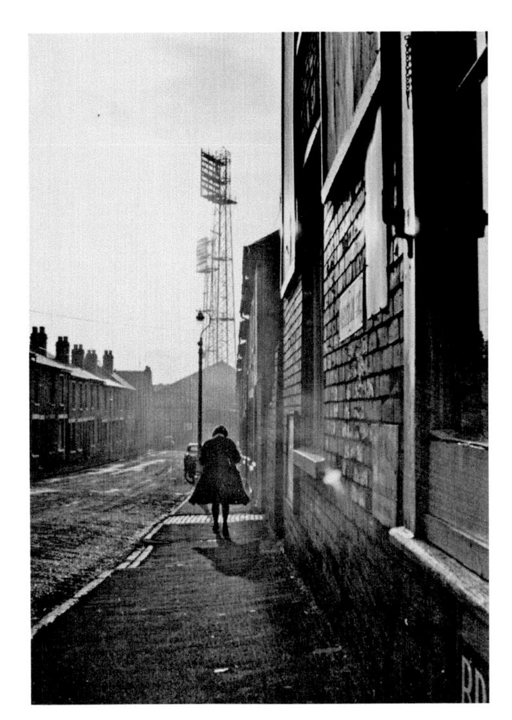

One of the streets of terraced houses in the area was Dawson Street, running down to Molineux's North Bank. The famous floodlight pylons lit the whole area on evening matches, when Dawson Street would be full of parked cars.

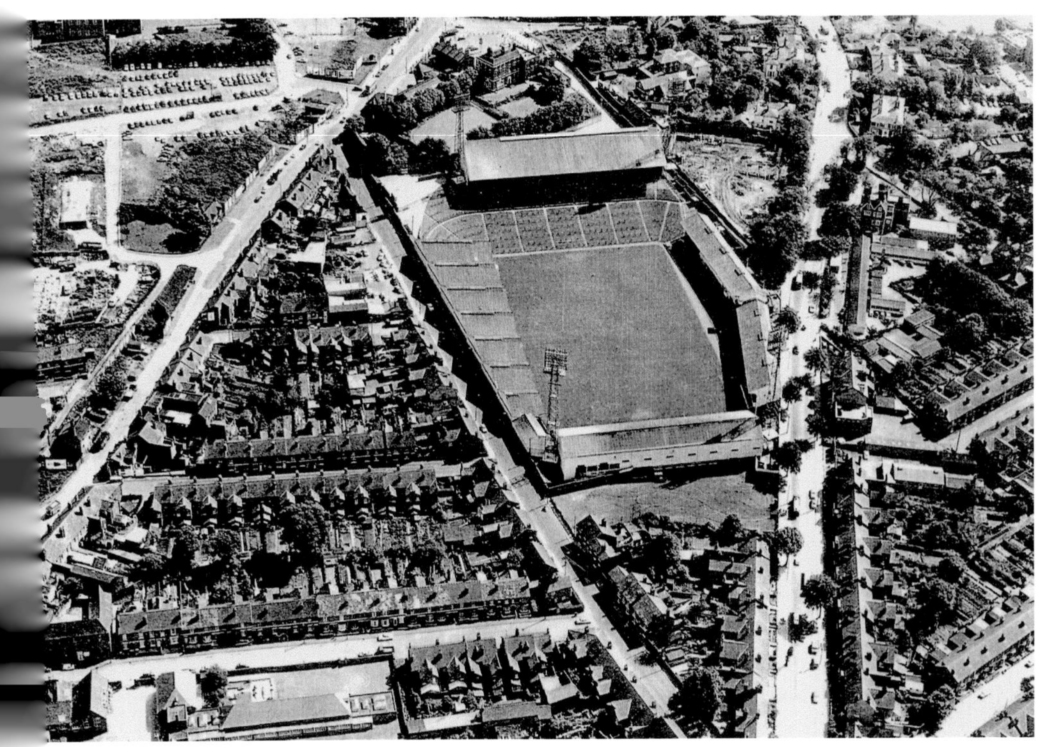

The old Molineux Stadium with the iconic multi-gabled Molineux Street stands to the left with the triangle of housing behind, now all replaced by car parks and an Asda. The second triangle of housing behind the North Bank has also gone.

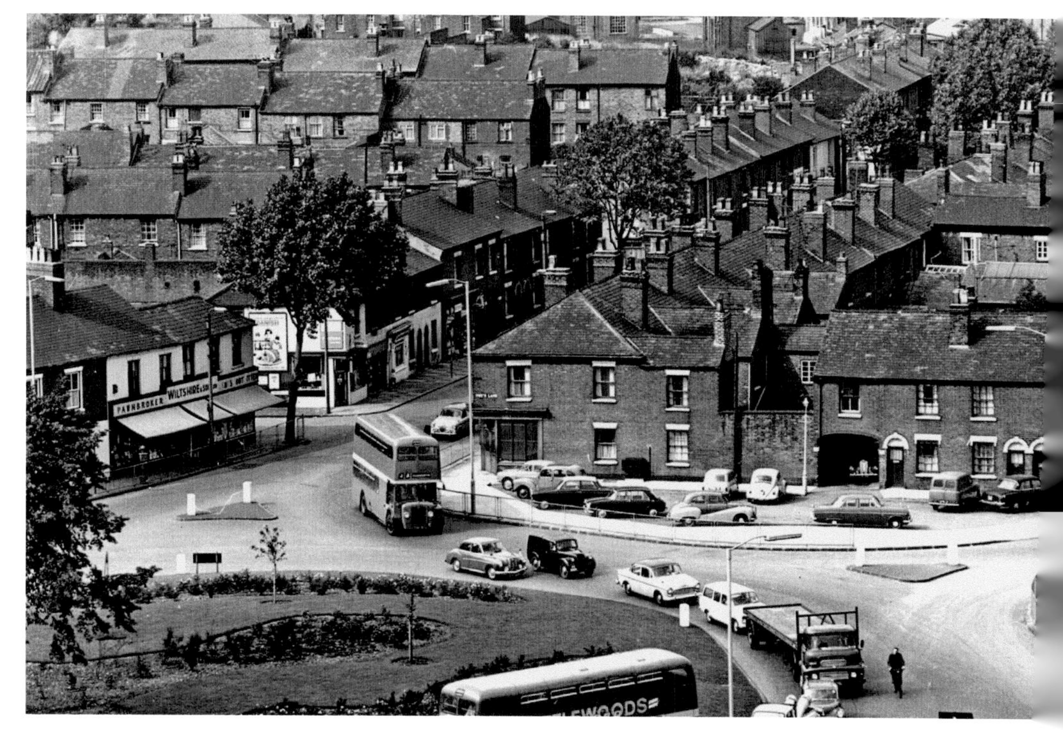

A view of Five Ways island with North Street heading to the Dunstall Road railway workshops complex in the background. The island is still there, but nothing else in this picture still exists. The scene today would be dominated by Wickes with the car showrooms behind.

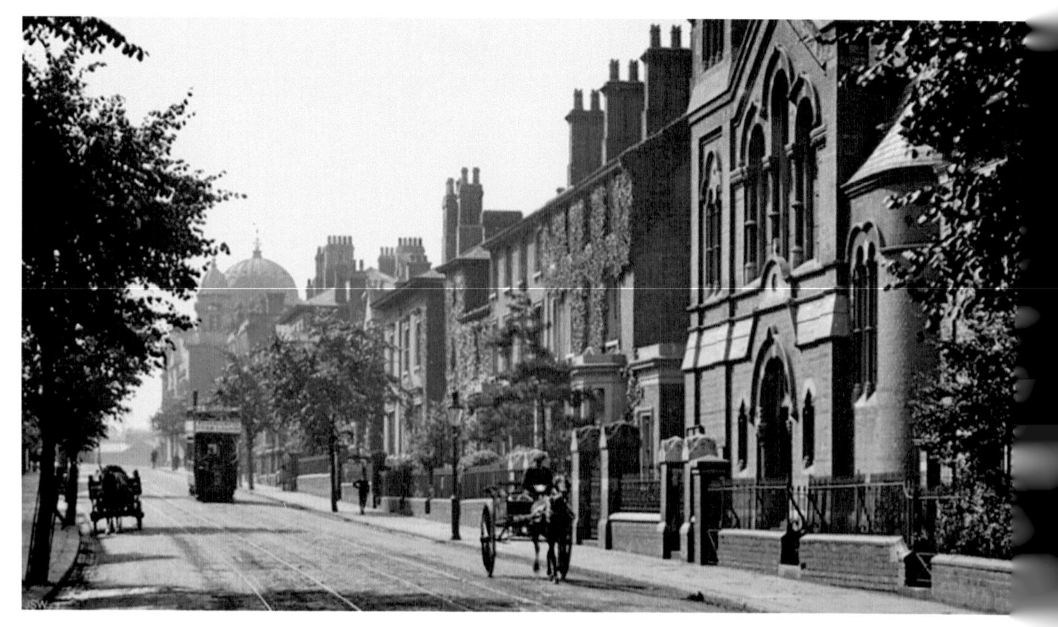

A genteel Waterloo Road with the Methodist Church in the background, and the only traffic being a tram heading to Whitmore Reans and a couple of carts. The old Baptist Chapel on the right is now gone but many of the houses are still there, though all now offices.

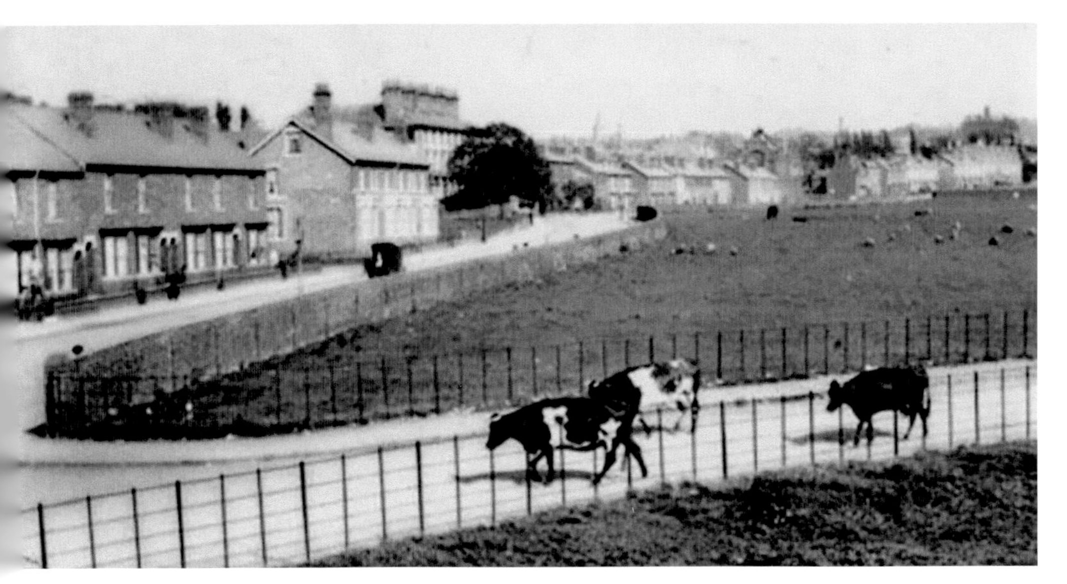

A slightly blurred but almost unbelievable scene as cows wander along Devon Road towards Newhampton Road to the left. There are sheep in the field in which West Park Primary School is currently located. There is no sign of the tram tracks down Newhampton Road, which dates the image to before 1902.

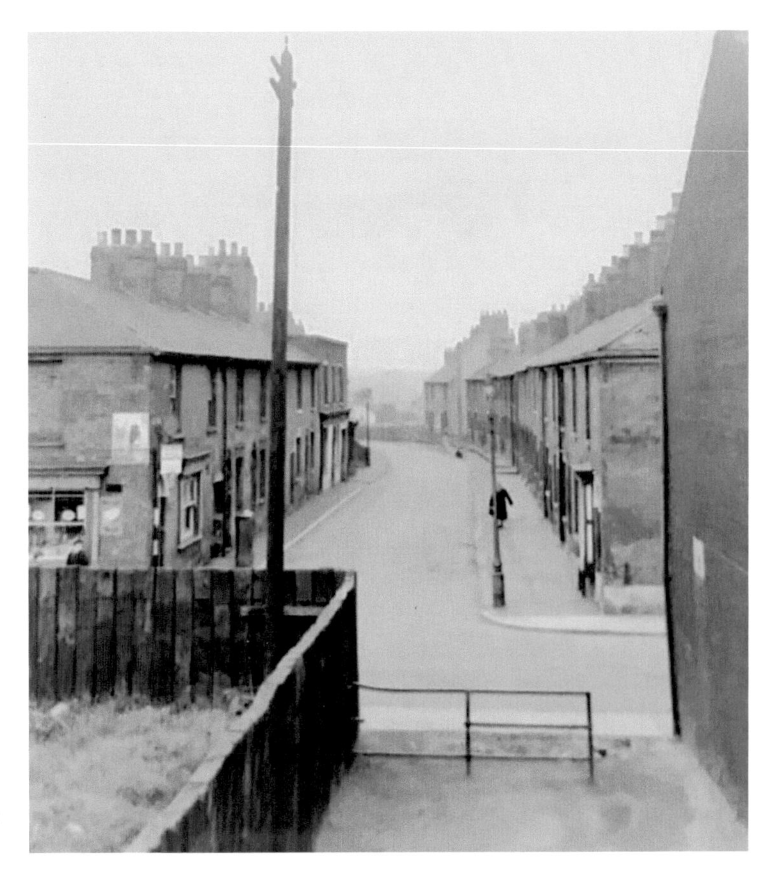

The Springfield area of town looking from the top of the 'Nineteen Steps' (there were only ever eighteen) along Culwell Street. There are no houses here anymore, apart from the student flats alongside the steps, just industrial buildings.

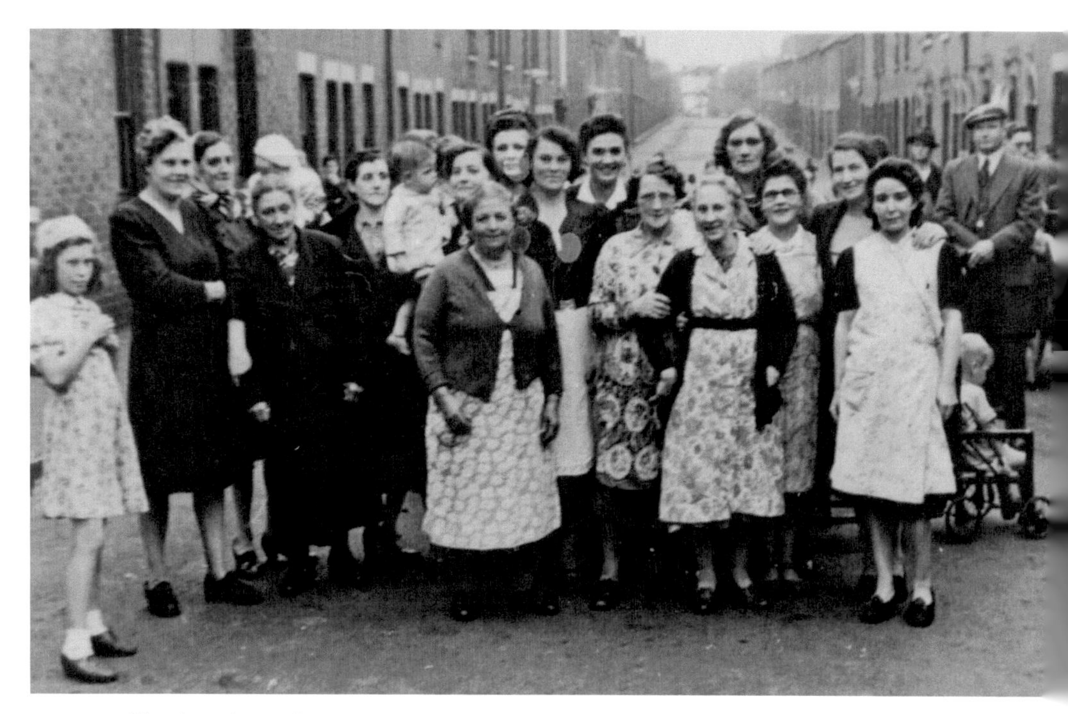

A group of local residents all gathered on Beacon Street, Springfield, for a VE Day street party. Beacon Street does not exist anymore, as it was cleared away for newer housing.

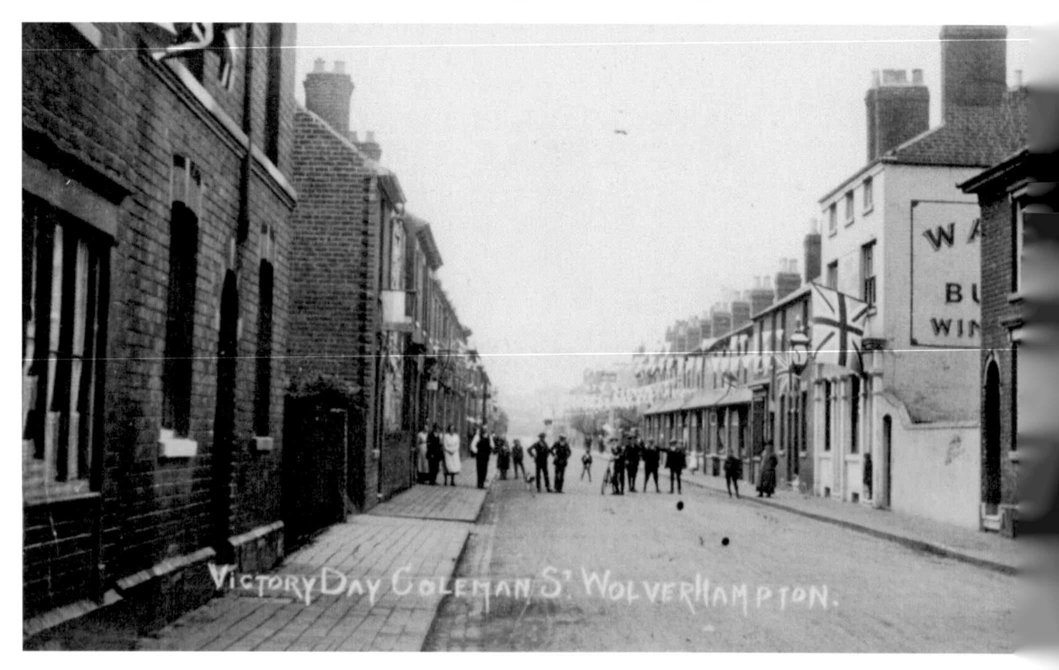

Another street of terraced houses: Coleman Street on the other side of Wolverhampton in Whitmore Reans. And the end of a different war: Victory Day after the First World War is celebrated outside the Three Crowns pub. The pub and much of the terraced housing has gone and Coleman Street is now a cul-de-sac.

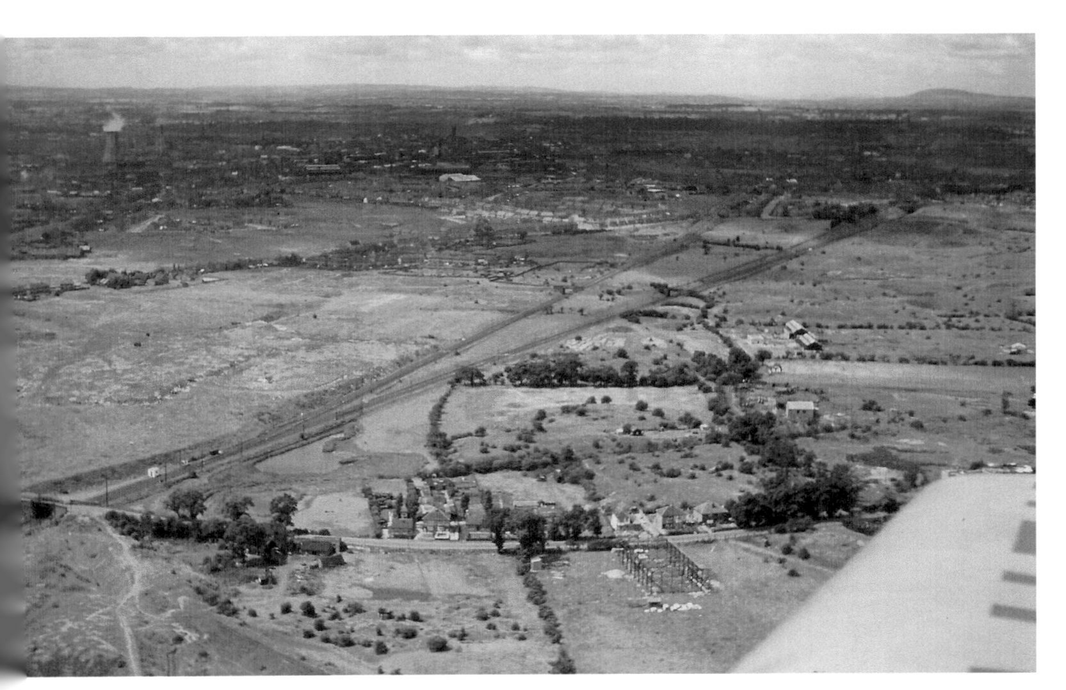

An aerial view of the Deansfield area of Wolverhampton looking towards the town centre, with Deans Road in the foreground, and the Willenhall Road to the left. At the time, just after the war, the whole area was empty, home only to derelict old mine workings. Later, the huge Deansfield Estate was built here.

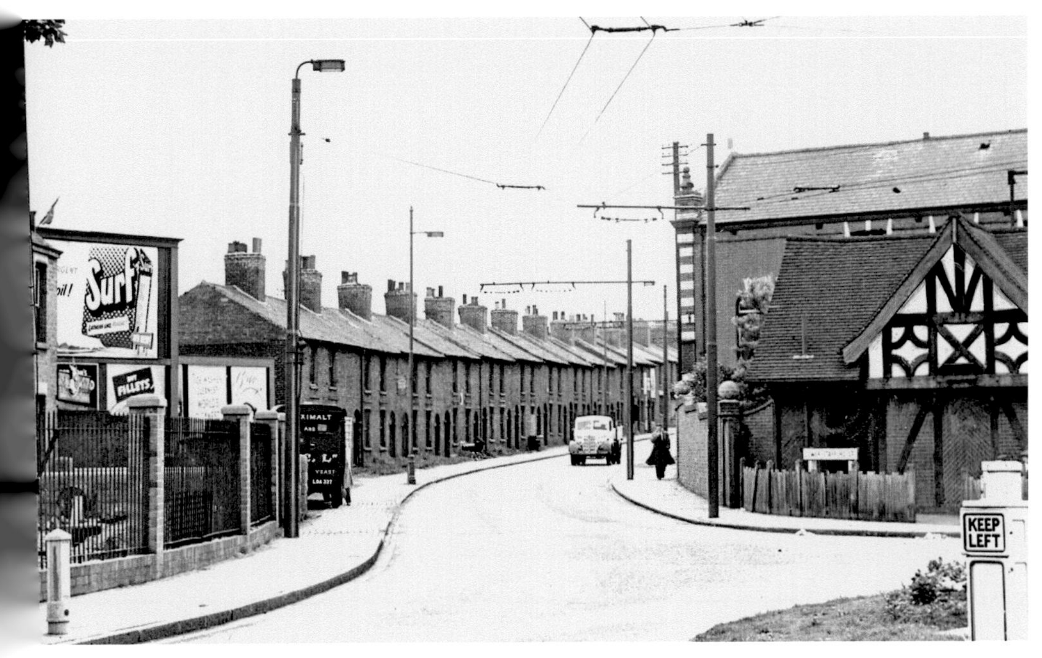

A view of Five Ways island looking up Stafford Street towards the town centre. As Stafford Road/Street was widened into a dual carriageway, all of this was cleared away. Halfords now sits on this corner to the left.

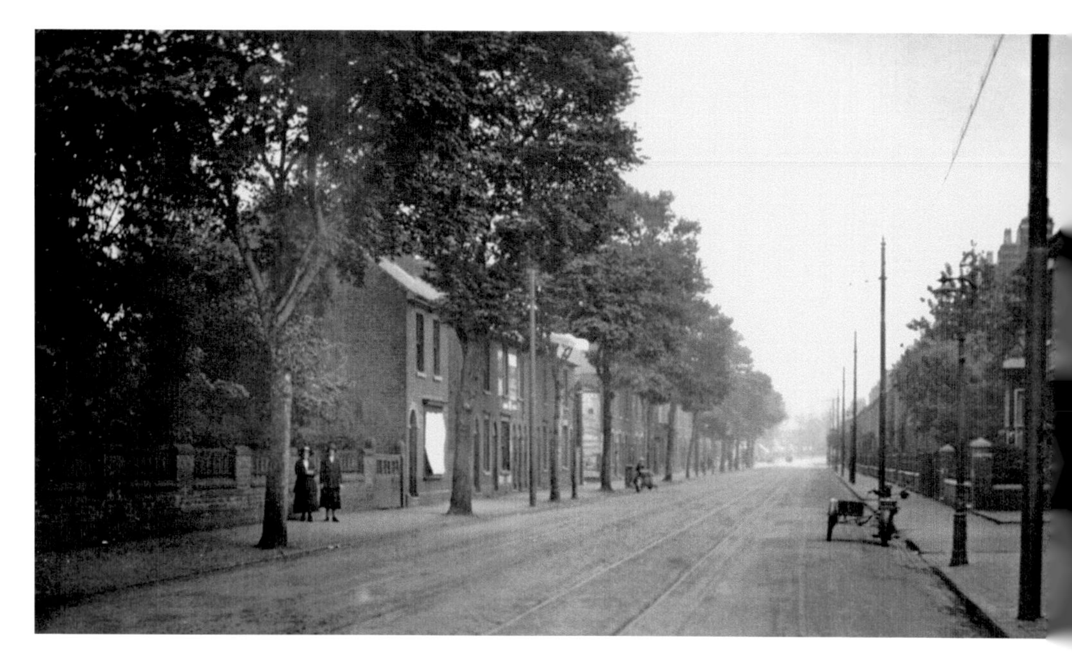

Newhampton Road, Whitmore Reans, a suburb of endless terraced houses. The tram tracks run through with the wall of St Andrew's Vicarage to the left, but the only traffic is a parked motorbike and side car. It has been a long time since this road looked so empty.

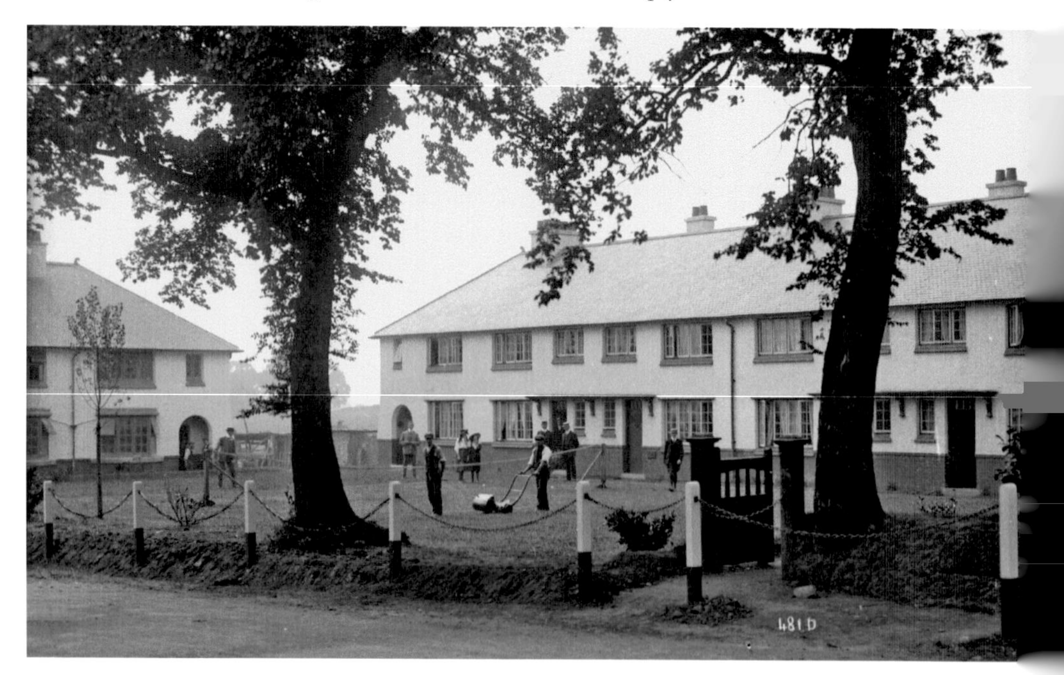

In the early days of the twentieth century, the garden city movement swept the country and efforts were made to build new towns and suburbs with green spaces and gardens instead of back-to-back terraced houses. The result of this in Wolverhampton was Park Village, which opened in 1908. The houses seen here are some of those that were built. They are still there today too, though they no longer have hand mowers on their front gardens, which have been paved over for parking.

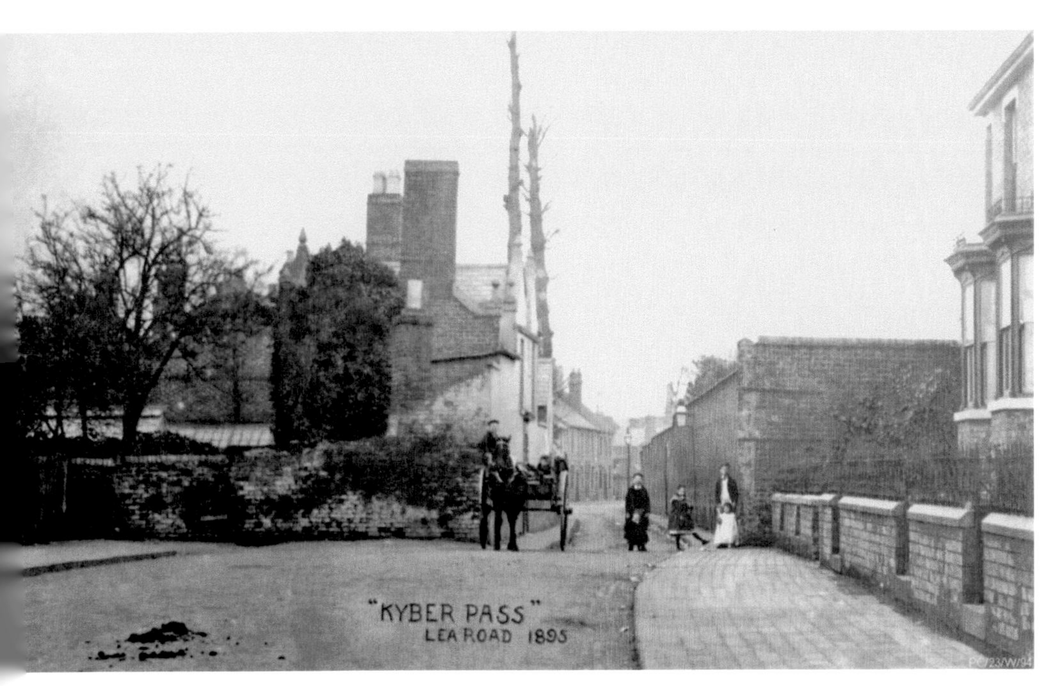

In the nineteenth century, Lea Road was just a lane leading to Lea Farm. As housing expanded out of the town westwards this constriction was left, known locally as 'the Khyber Pass' (the mountain pass connecting Afghanistan and India). The housing on the left was removed to allow the road to be widened.

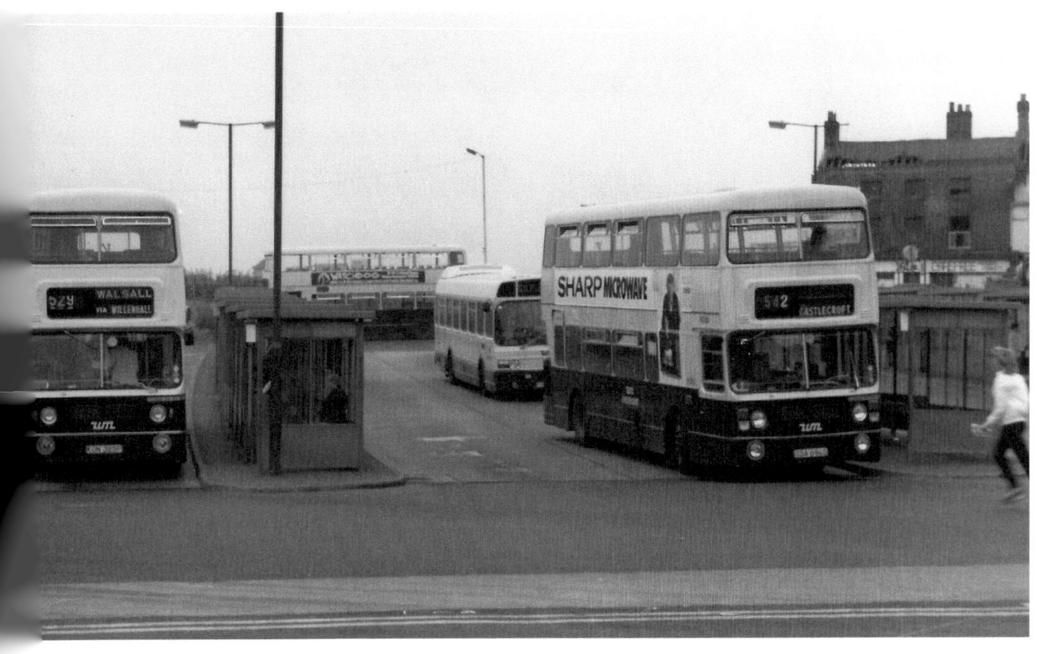

The old 'toast rack' style bus station in 1988, full of buses in WMPTE colours. As always, someone is running to catch a bus – probably the Walsall service to the left. The building in the background is at the top of Horseley Fields.

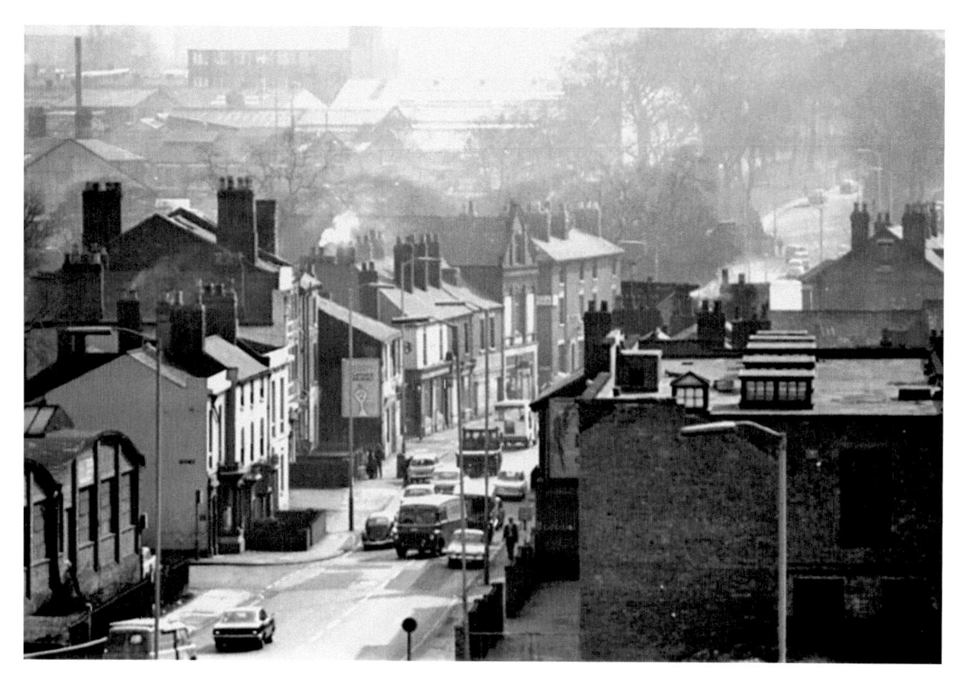

Before Penn Road was widened into a dual carriageway, and before the ring road sliced through, the area looked like this, with the factories of Blakenhall in the background.

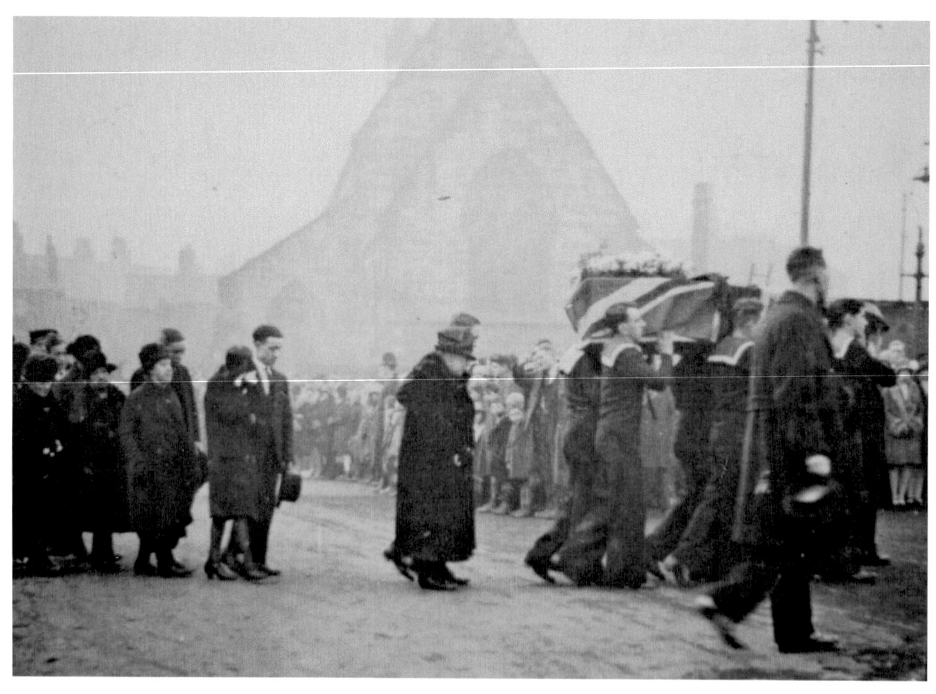

In the 1920s Harry Parks Temple, a sailor on leave, jumped into the pool on Stowheath Lane to try and save two boys from drowning. He lost his own life and the local community came out in droves to honour him at his funeral at St James' Church, Horseley Fields. The old church looming in the mist was replaced with a new one further out of town as housing moved out of the area.

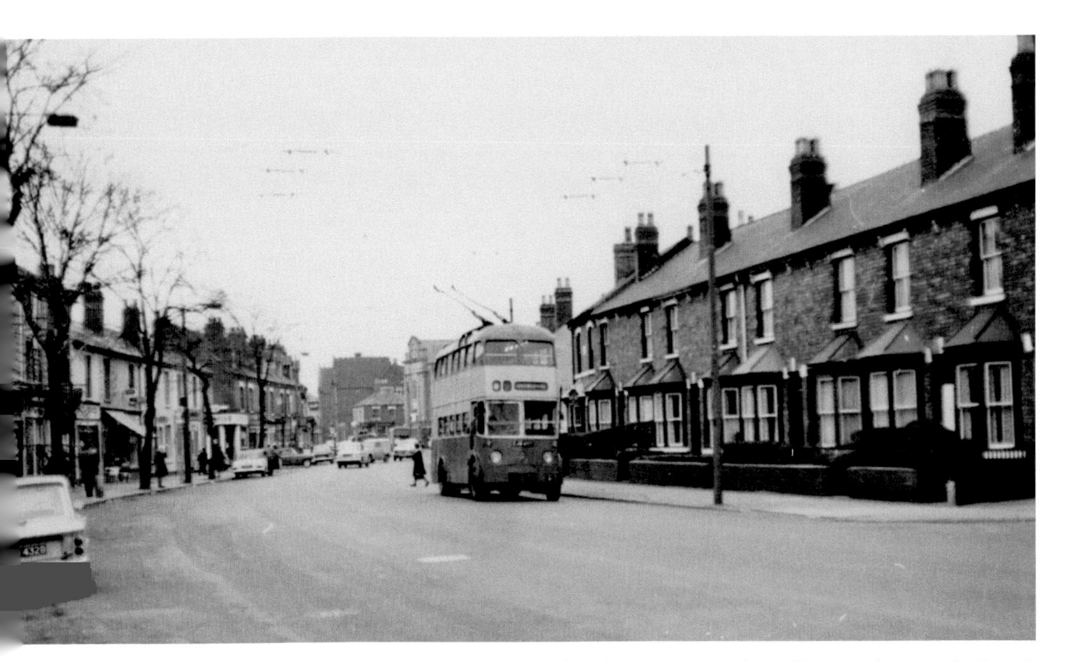

One area of the inner town that has retained much of its heart is around Dudley Road. Here the No. 8 trolleybus has just passed Johnson Street with Dudley Road School in the background. A little of the housing on the right has been replaced, but much is just the same.

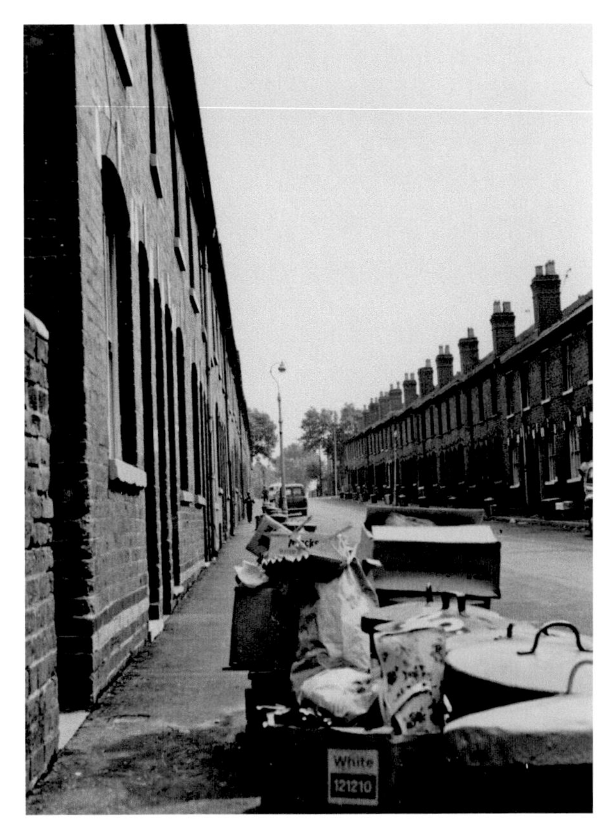

A scene typical of the terraced housing of All Saints on 'bin day'. Johnson Street in 1963 points to the distant cooling tower of the power station. The terraces have now all gone, replaced by new housing.

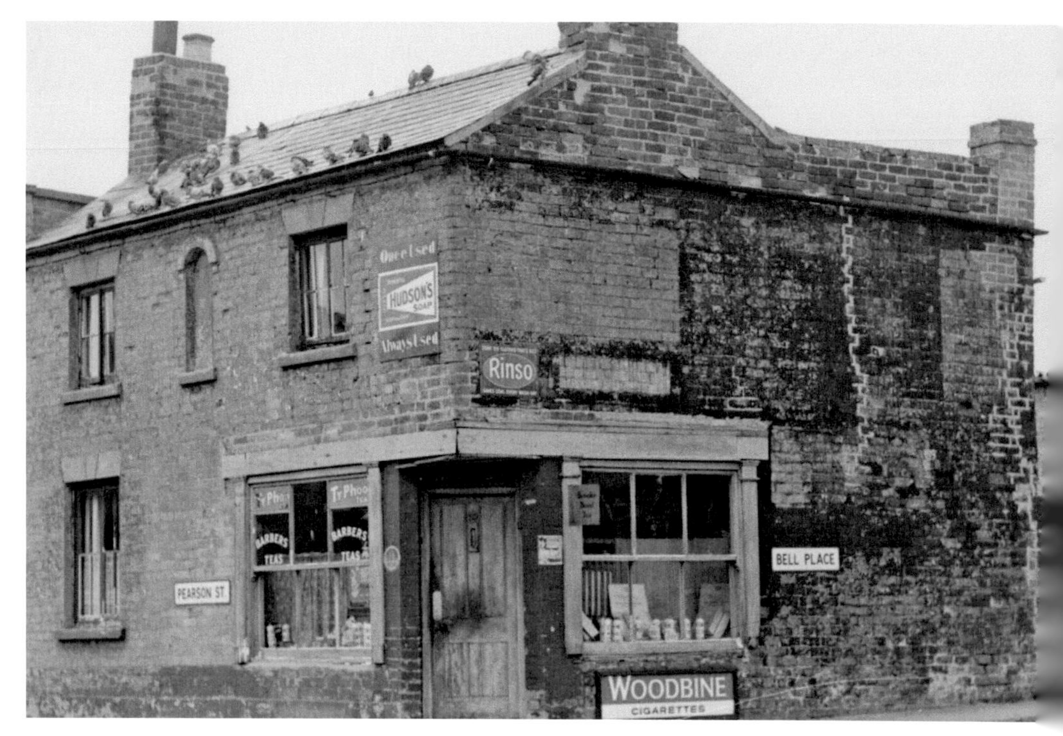

The corner shop on the corner of Bell Place and Pearson Street, which runs parallel to Dudley Road to the west. Corner shops are a thing of the past as industry has claimed this area.

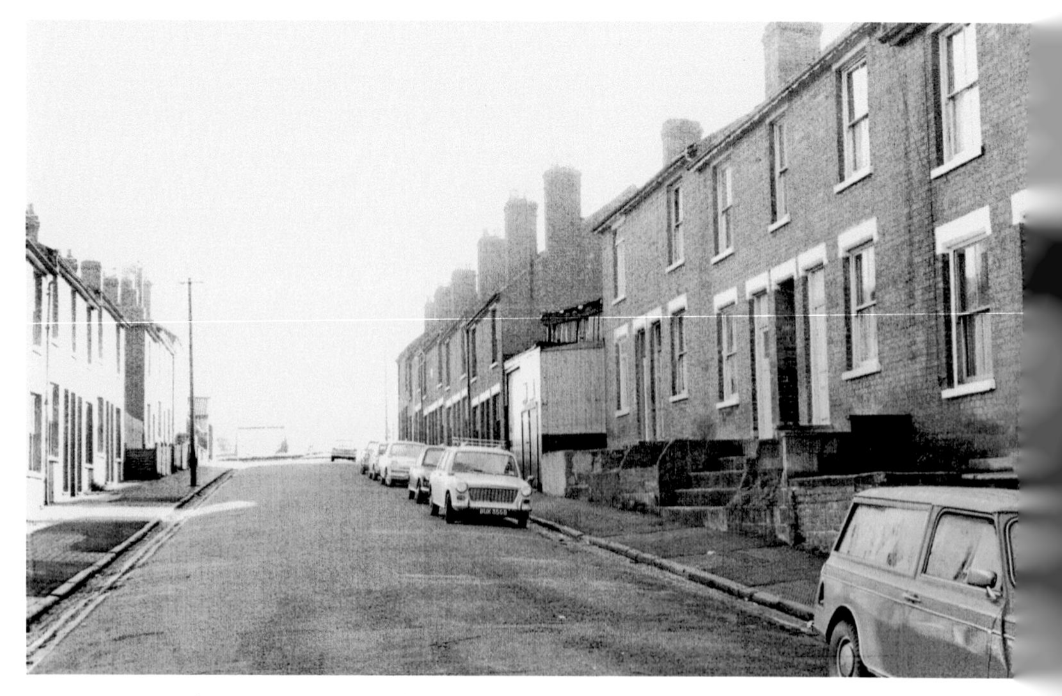

Nursery Street in the 1960s, running up from North Street to Stafford Street. It was paralleled by Camp Street, Crescent Row and Red Hill Street, which have all been built over with university buildings.

4

Lost Leisure

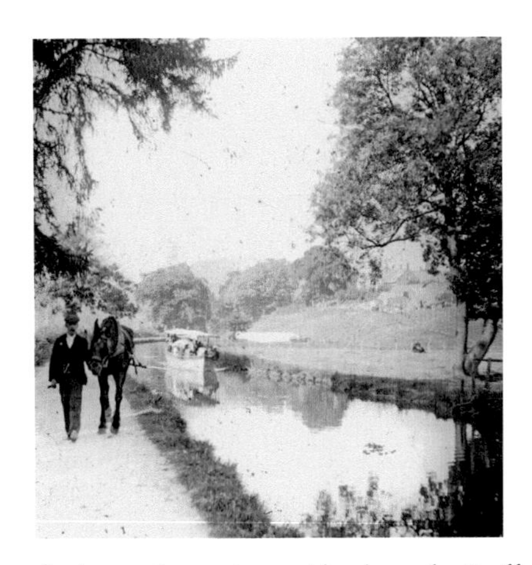

The simple, quiet pleasure of a horse-drawn boat ride along the Staffs & Worcs Canal, heading from Compton and out into the countryside beyond Wightwick. Such boat trips were offered from several places in the town, but no more.

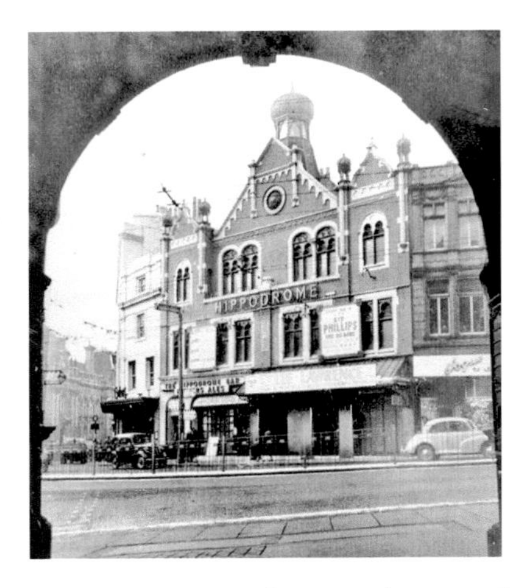

One of the two major theatres in the town was the Hippodrome at the bottom of Queen Square, famous for variety shows. Here, Sid Phillips and his band are playing. Formerly the Empire Palace, the building was knocked down when variety died and replaced by a Times furniture store, and now the Slug and Lettuce pub.

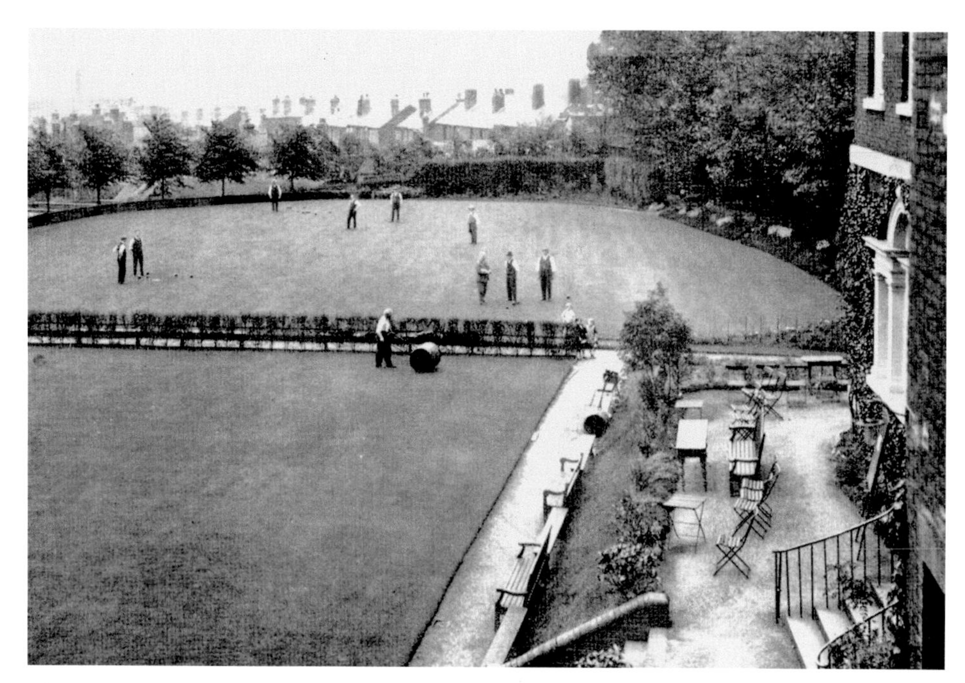

The two bowling greens at the rear of the Molineux Hotel, with the houses of Molineux Street stretching down the hill behind. When this photograph was taken the local football team had not yet eyed Molineux Pleasure Gardens as a possible new home.

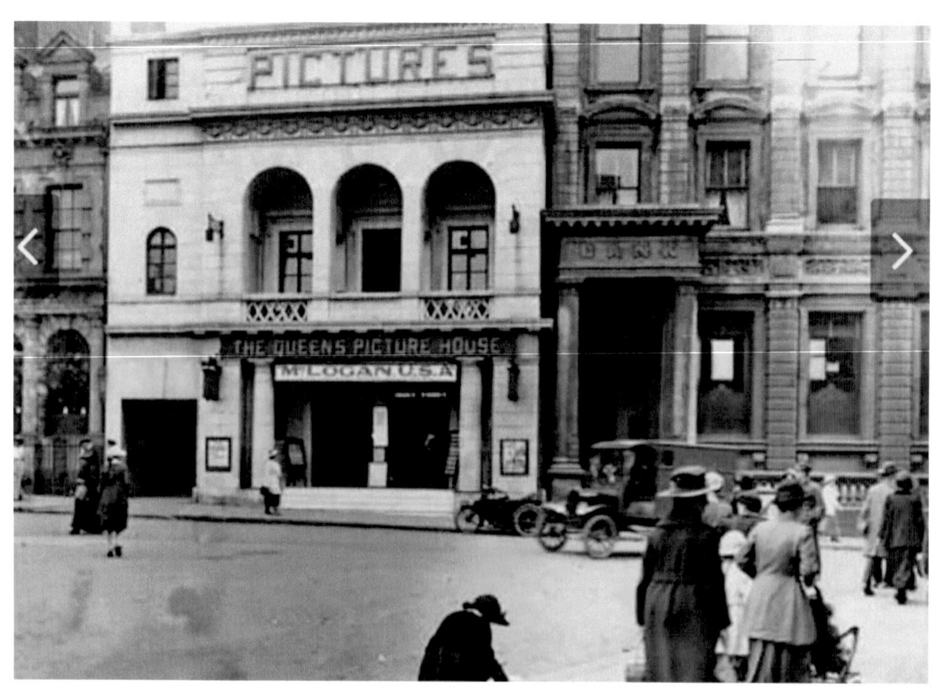

The Queens Picture House at the top of Queen Square, one of the earliest cinemas in the town. It is more widely remembered, however, for its later incarnation as a dance hall. It has now been taken over by its neighbour, Lloyds Bank.

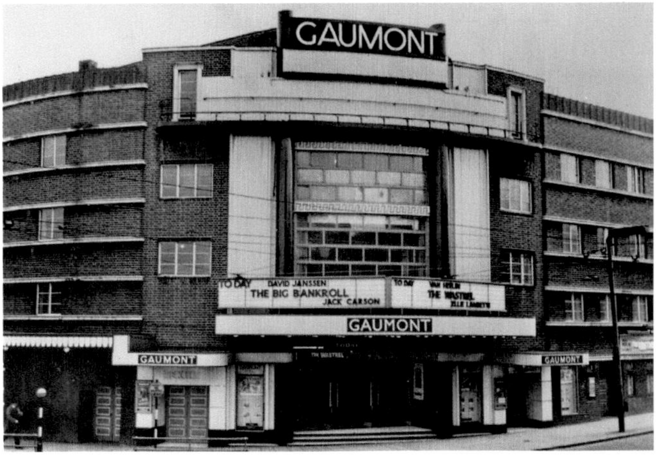

The Gaumont Cinema on Snow Hill was just as famous for its pop concerts, with the likes of the Beatles, as its films. It was built in 1937 on the site of the old Agricultural Hall, but was replaced by a Wilkinson's and is currently occupied by Retail Plus.

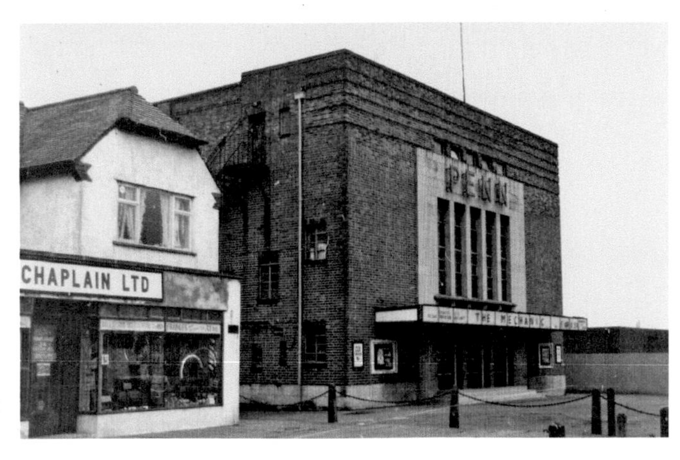

Many of the town's suburbs had their own cinema. On Warstones Road, Penn Cinema was one of a chain of forty-six owned by B. T. Davies. It's shown in 1972, the year before it closed. It was replaced by a Gateway supermarket, now a Co-op, but the shop next door survives.

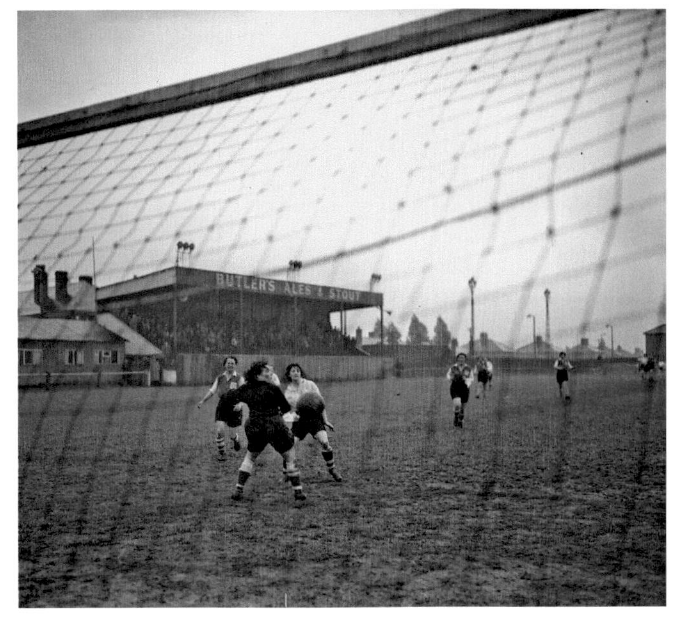

The relatively recent burst of interest in women's football might make us think it's a new phenomenon, but it's not. The ban on it was lifted in 1968, which should date this match, though it looks older than that. The game is being played at Bilston Town FC's Queen Street ground, which opened in 1919, and there seems a healthy crowd in the stand.

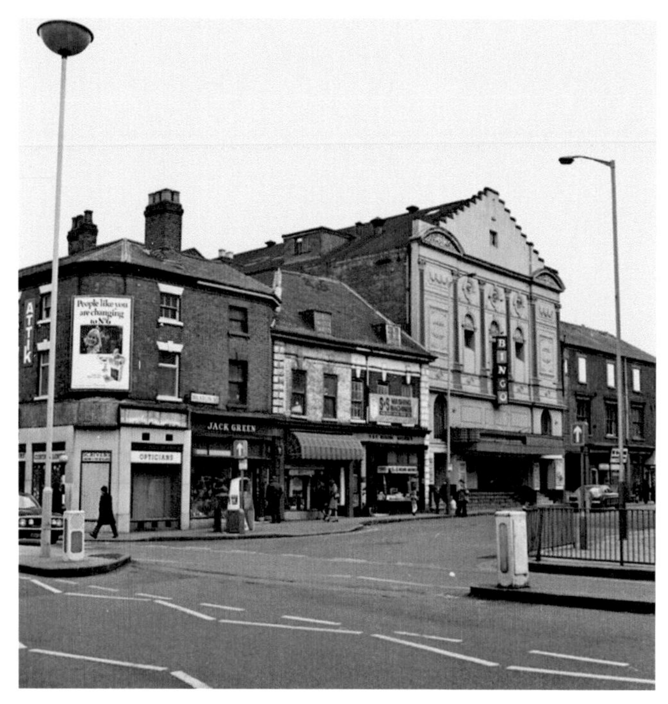

There was another Clifton Cinema in the town centre, opposite the Savoy on Bilston Street, and here already converted to Bingo. It had a longer history than most, having been the Prince of Wales Theatre from 1863 and then renamed the Hippodrome. It became a cinema in 1931, but it has now gone, along with the buildings each side, and the police station occupies the site.

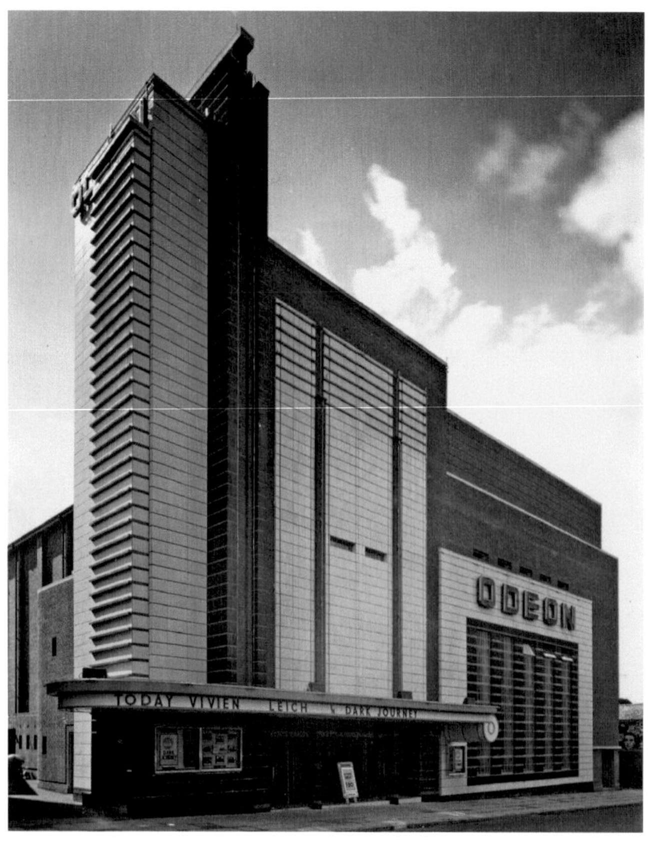

Perhaps the premier cinema in the town was the magnificent Odeon on Skinner Street, seen here showing Vivien Leigh in *Dark Journey*. It was turned into a three-screen venue, but did not survive the cinema downturn and is now the Diamond Banqueting Suite.

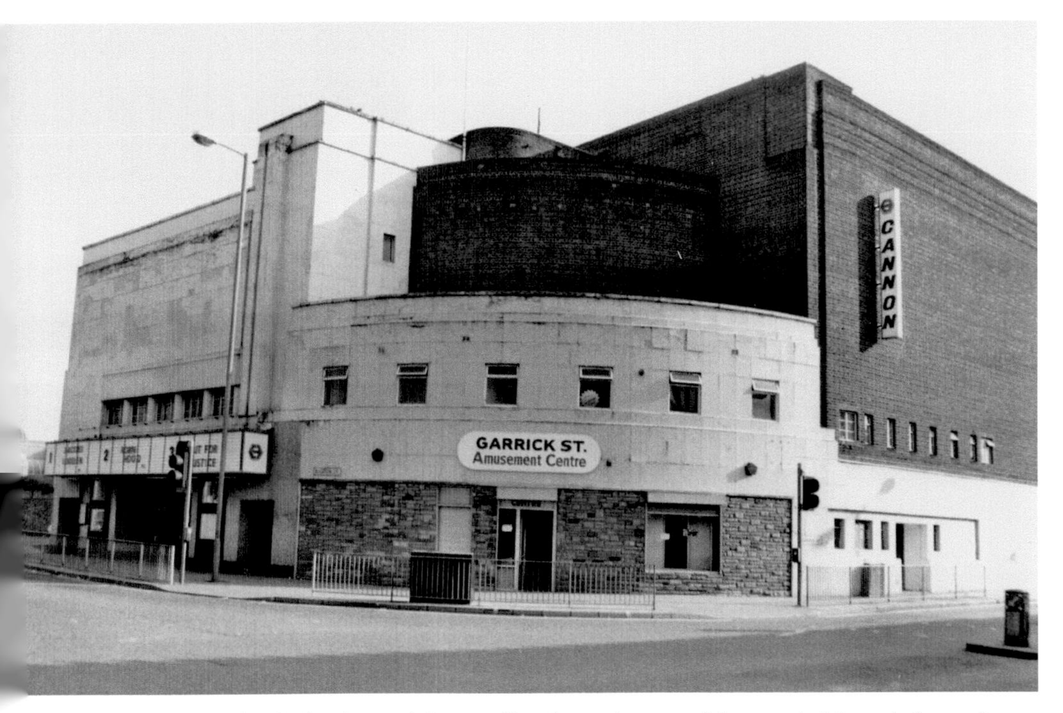

This building has fought hard to redefine itself and remain part of the town's leisure industry. It was the Savoy Cinema when built in 1937, then it became the ABC, and here it has been turned into the three-screen Cannon Cinema with an amusement centre in the former café alongside. Later, it became Atlantis nightclub, then Faces. It has now succumbed and been demolished.

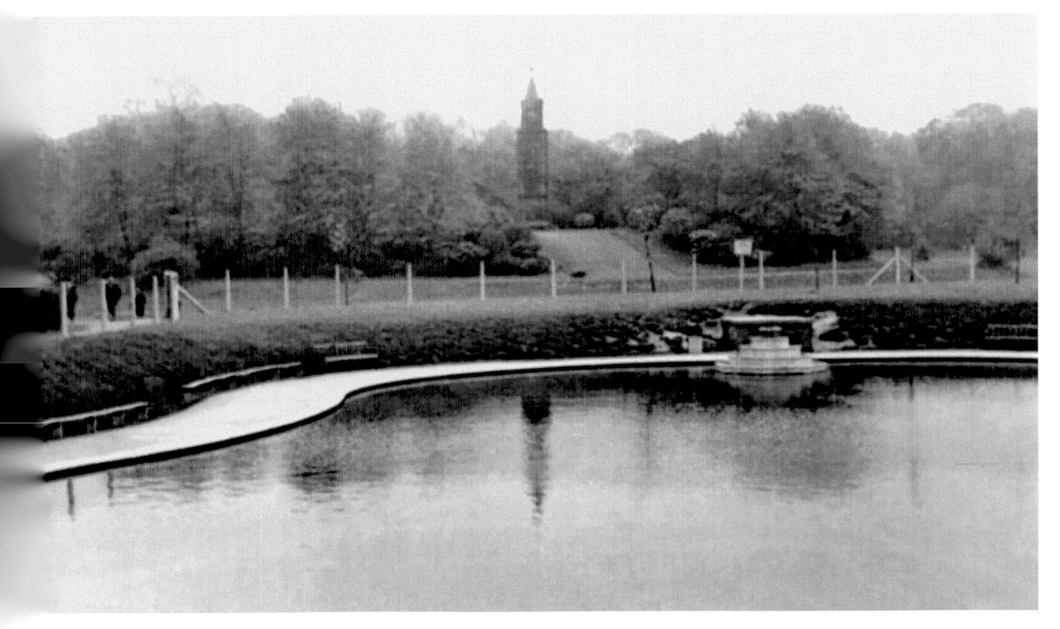

The Victorians blessed the town with two large municipal parks – East and West. They both survive, but East Park has always seemed the orphan, perhaps because the lake (shown here) has gone, leaking into the mine workings that lay beneath.

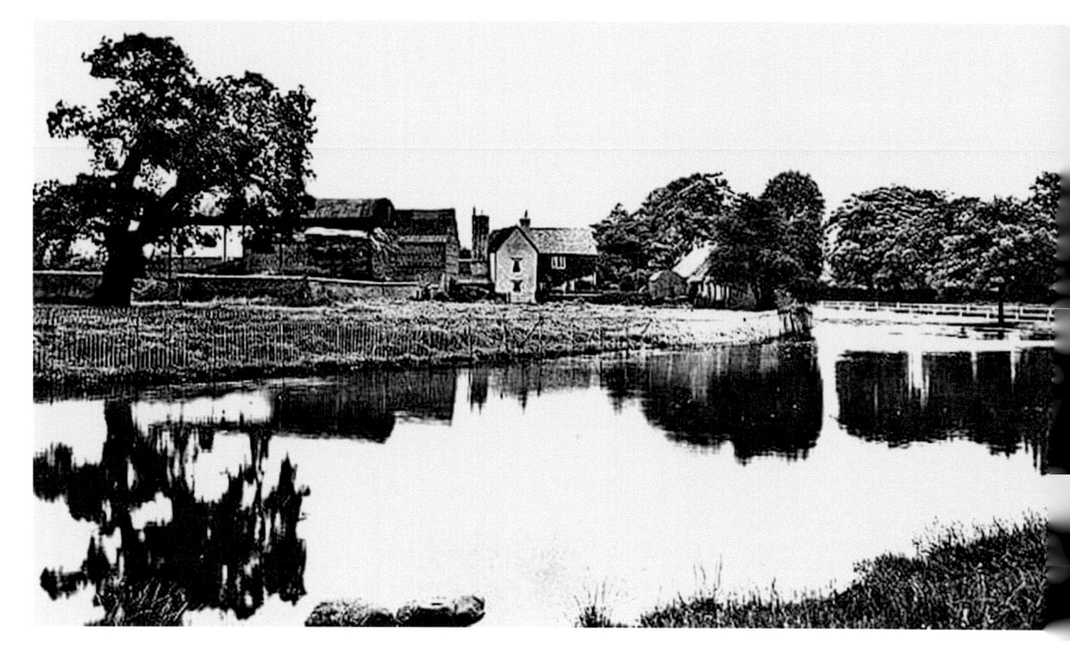

In hot weather Tettenhall Paddling Pool becomes one of the most popular leisure features in the city, but it began life as a pond at Upper Green Farm, shown in the background. After the Swindley family donated the land to the people of the town, the council converted the pond to a paddling pool in 1934 at the expense of Mr Graham, owner of the *Express and Star*.

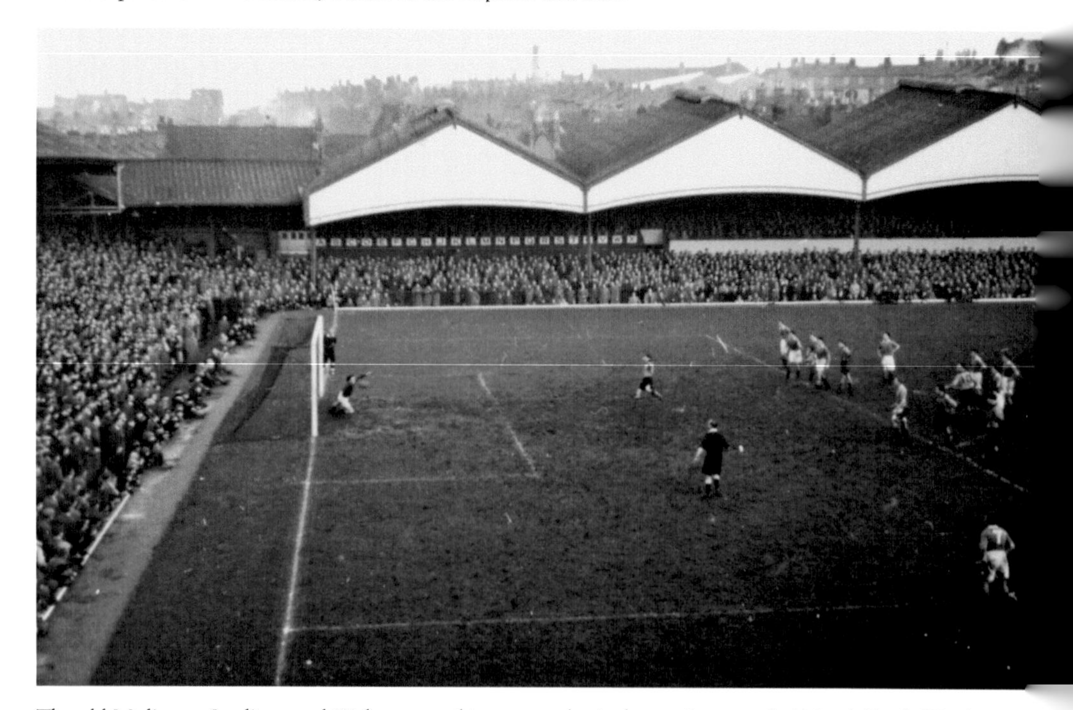

The old Molineux Stadium and Wolves are taking a penalty in front of a crowded North Bank. We don't know if they scored, but the keeper is off his line and is close to saving it. The seven-bay roof of the Molineux Street stand, designed by Archie Leith, was the unique signature of the stadium.

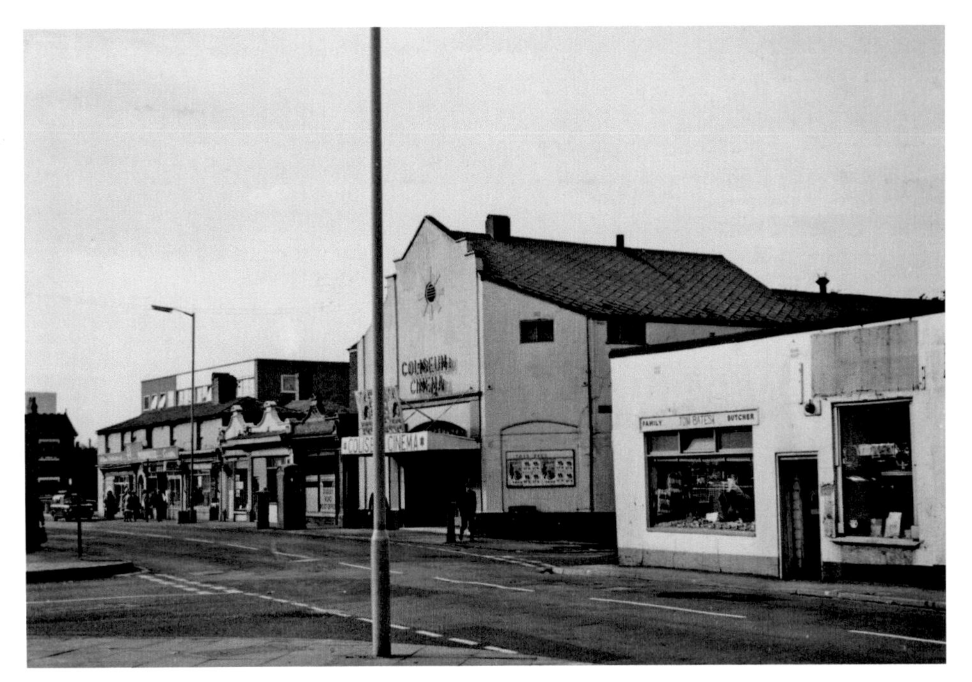

The Coliseum on Dudley Road, near Frederick Street, was built in 1912 and survived a little longer than many of the urban cinemas by switching to showing Asian films. By doing this it catered for the local community, which is what such cinemas were all about. It was demolished in 1980, an indirect victim of the ring road.

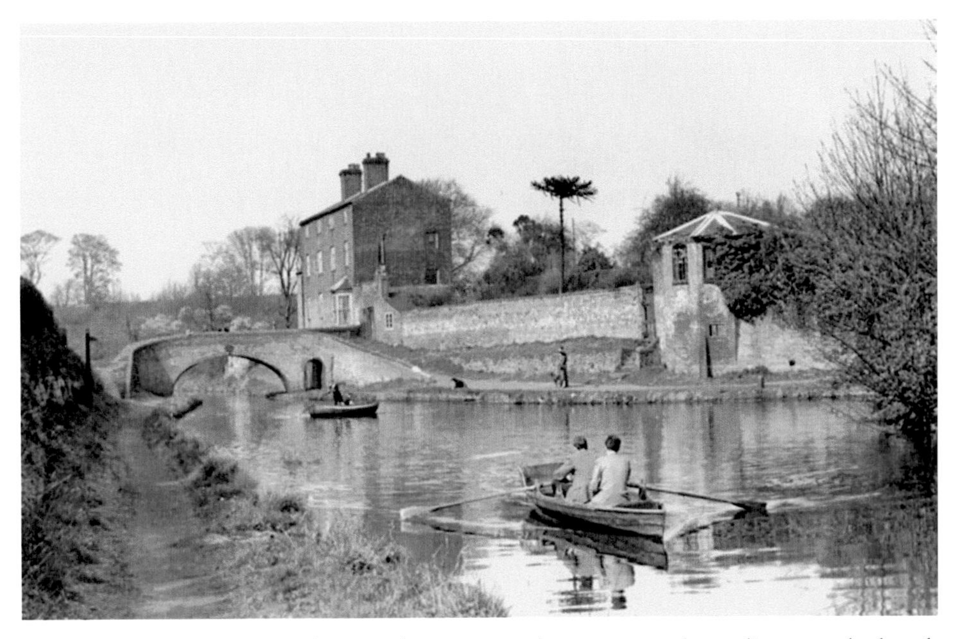

Rowing a boat on the canal is another pastime that seems to have disappeared, though Wolverhampton Canoe Club has used this water for sixty years. The two boats here are by Aldersley Junction, seen when the four cottages of the Staffs & Worcs Canal and the hexagonal tollhouse were all still standing.

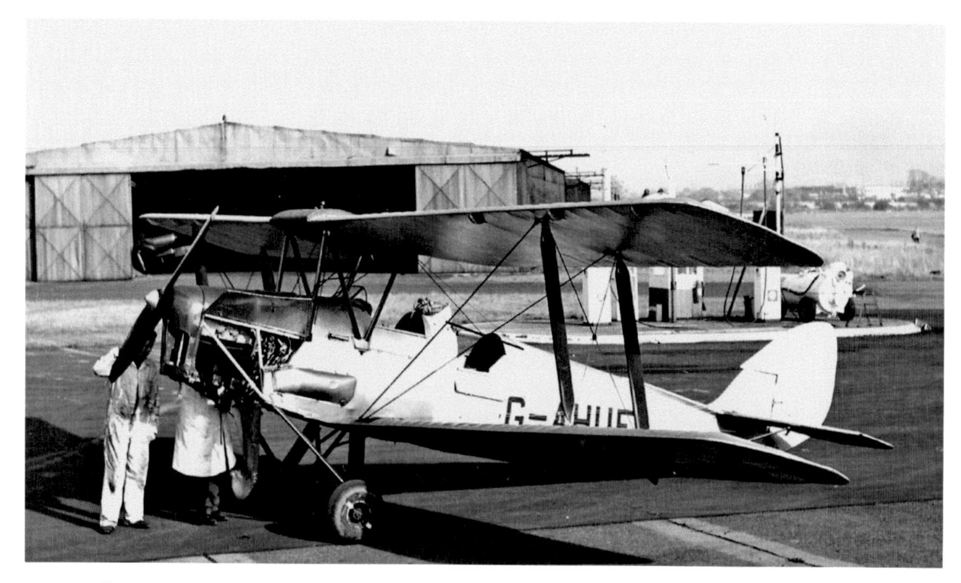

Leisure flying was possible from Wolverhampton Municipal Airport from 1936 to its closure in 1971. Here G-AHUE, a Wolverhampton Aero Club Tiger Moth (the most common type seen at Pendeford in its thirty-six years of existence) is serviced in front of the maintenance hangar with the petrol pumps behind.

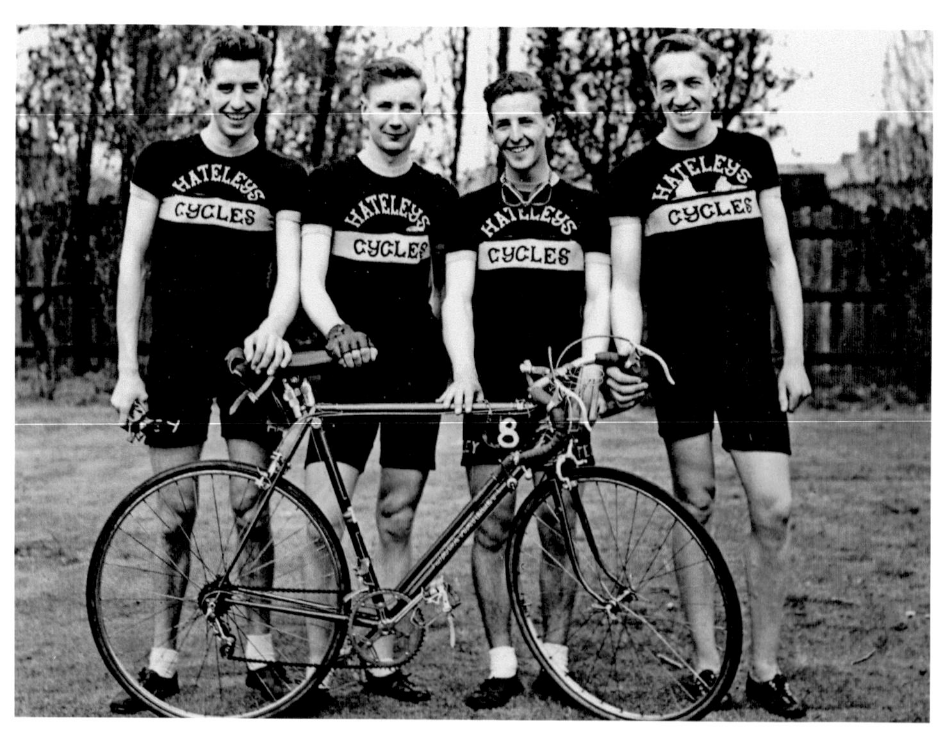

There were a number of cycling clubs in the town, and Wolverhampton Wheelers still operate, but in the 1950s there were also three works cycle racing teams. This is the Hateley Team on Stafford Road, sponsored by Jack Hateley, who also hosted the Wolverhampton Olympic Cycling Club in his shop.

5

Lost Transport

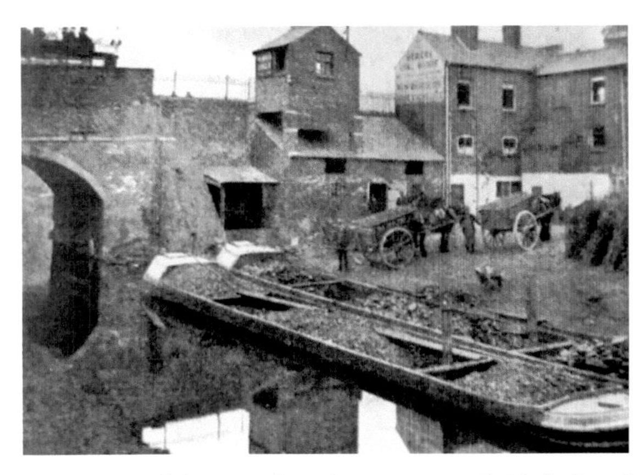

A blurred but interesting view of three modes of transport available before the First World War. Weaver's Coal Wharf lay by the canal at Newbridge. Most canal/road junctions had coal wharfs because narrowboats hauled coal from the coalfields, which was then delivered by horse and cart. Over the bridge, a Lorain system tram is travelling to Tettenhall. The bridge and everything else in this photograph, including the Newbridge Inn on the road to the right, was cleared away in the 1930s and a new bridge built.

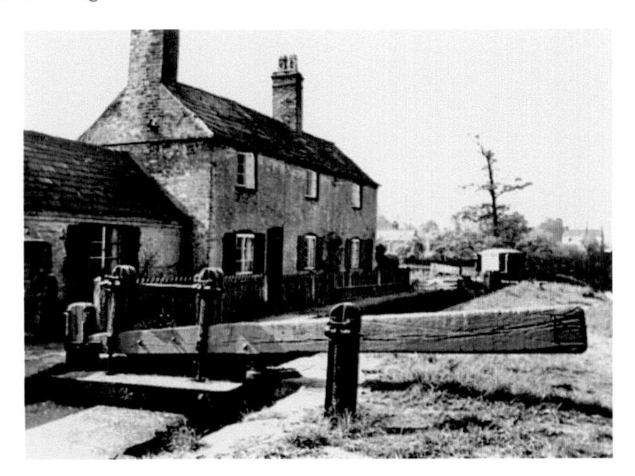

The lock-keeper's cottage at Compton Lock, where the construction of the Staffs & Worcs Canal was started in 1772, revolutionising bulk transport in Great Britain and allowing Wolverhampton and Black Country coal and iron products to reach the world. The cottage no longer exists.

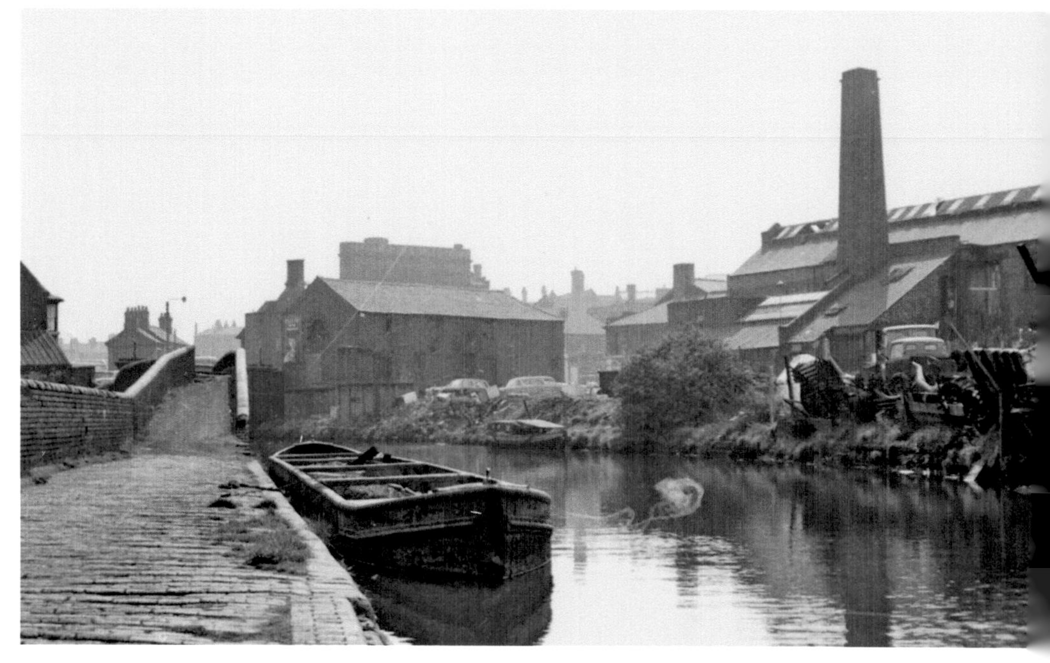

From the Staffs & Worcs Canal, the Birmingham Canal Navigations (BCN) climbed twenty-one locks to here, just before the Wednesfield Road. Carvers building merchants is to the right and the Chubbs factory can just be seen in the background.

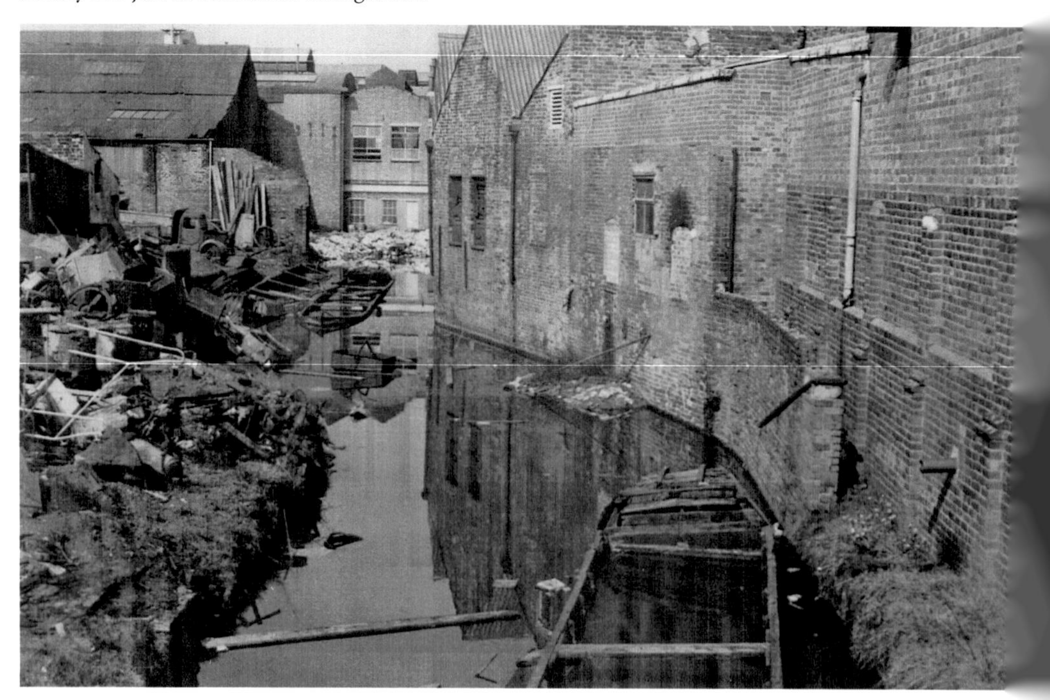

The derelict Minerva Wharf in Horseley Fields, built to serve the Minerva Iron and Steel Company. There were at least twenty wharves and basins through the Horseley Fields area, serving the companies that sited themselves alongside the canal because of its vital transport links.

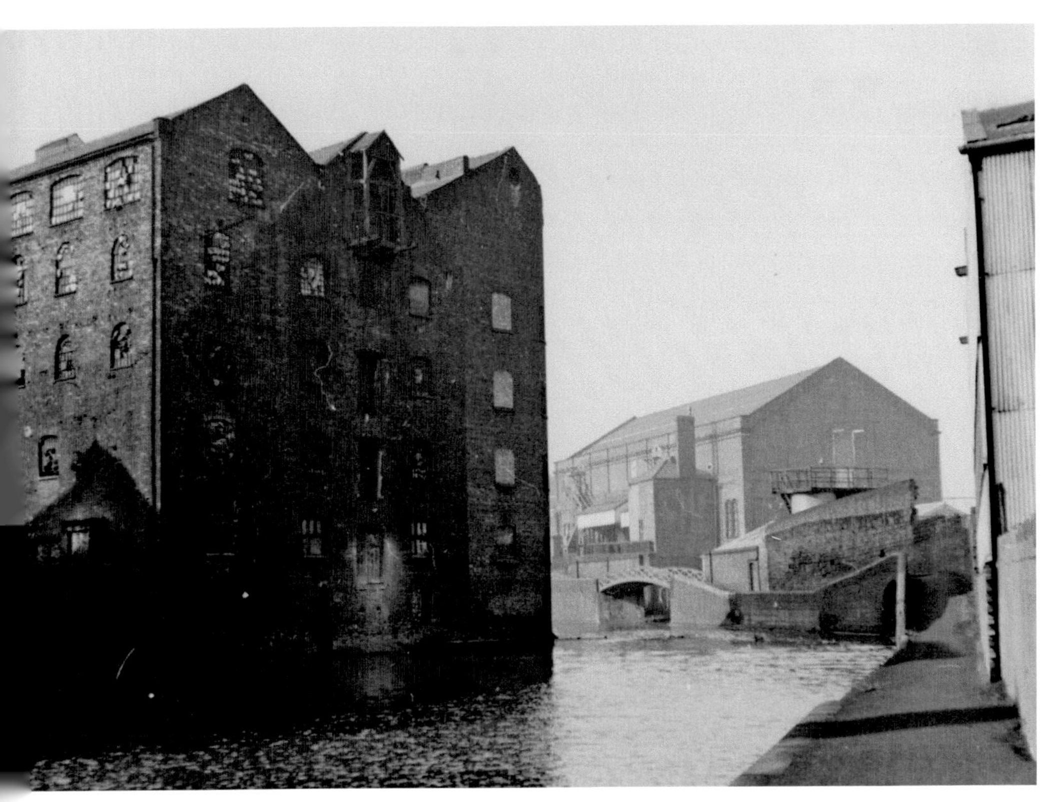

The corn warehouse built alongside the BCN in Horseley Fields. Where nowadays companies build near motorway junctions, 200 years ago they built next to a canal.

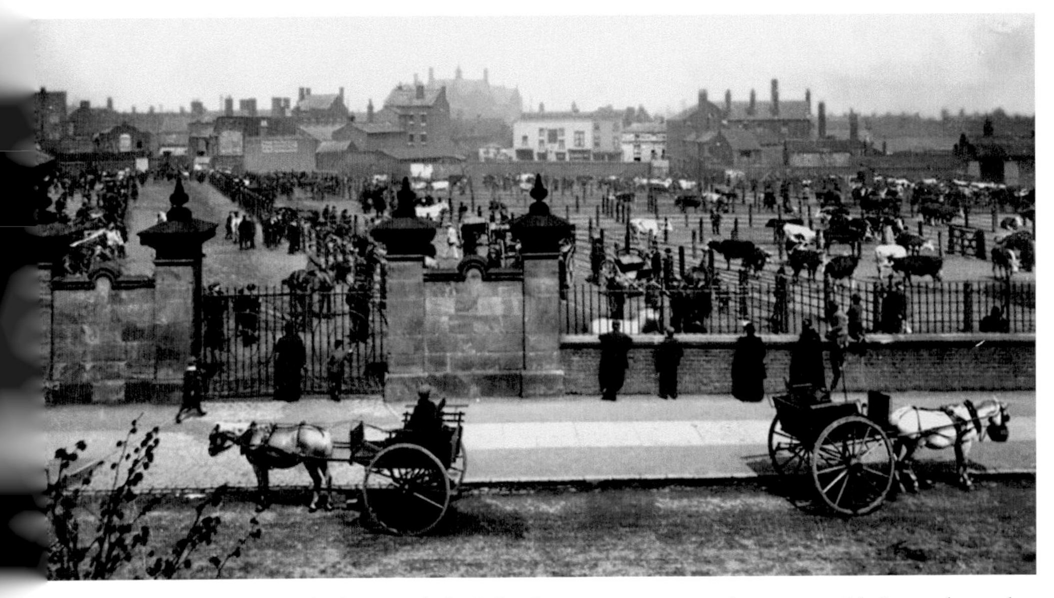

Before canals were dug, the horse ruled. Wolverhampton was a market town with its cattle market in Cleveland Road, where livestock arrived on foot (or hoof). People used pony and traps, like those parked at the kerb, if they could afford them, otherwise they walked.

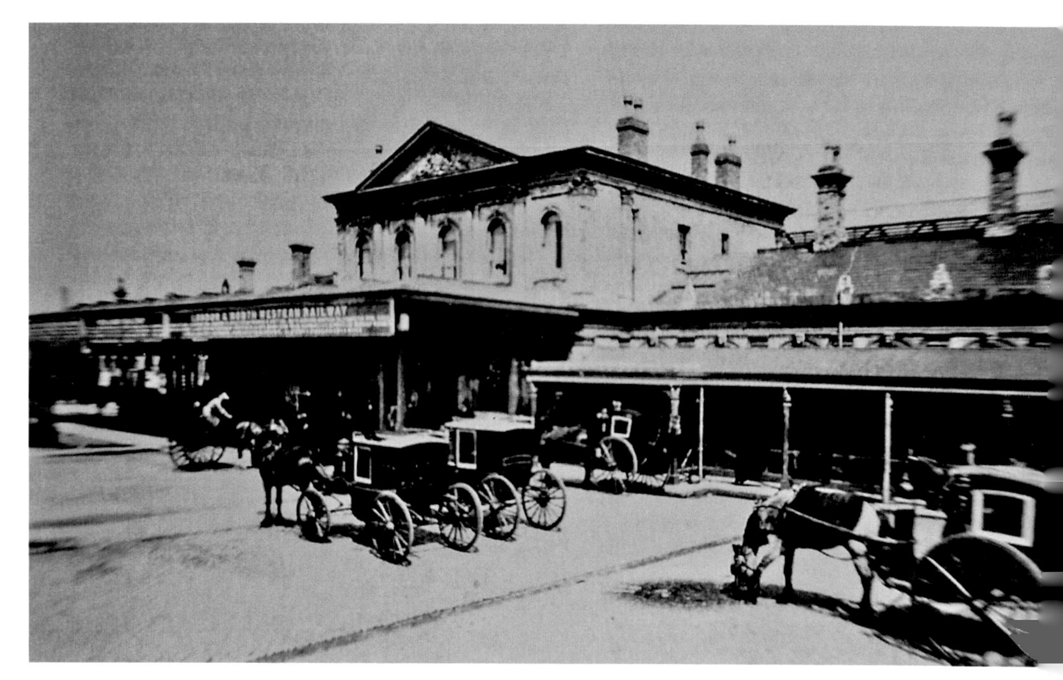

Wolverhampton's Queen Street station, which later became known as High Level, after the adjacent Low Level station was opened. Here, Hansom cabs await passengers from the London Midland & Scottish Railway. This station was replaced by an unloved concrete replacement in the 1960s, and has now been rebuilt once again.

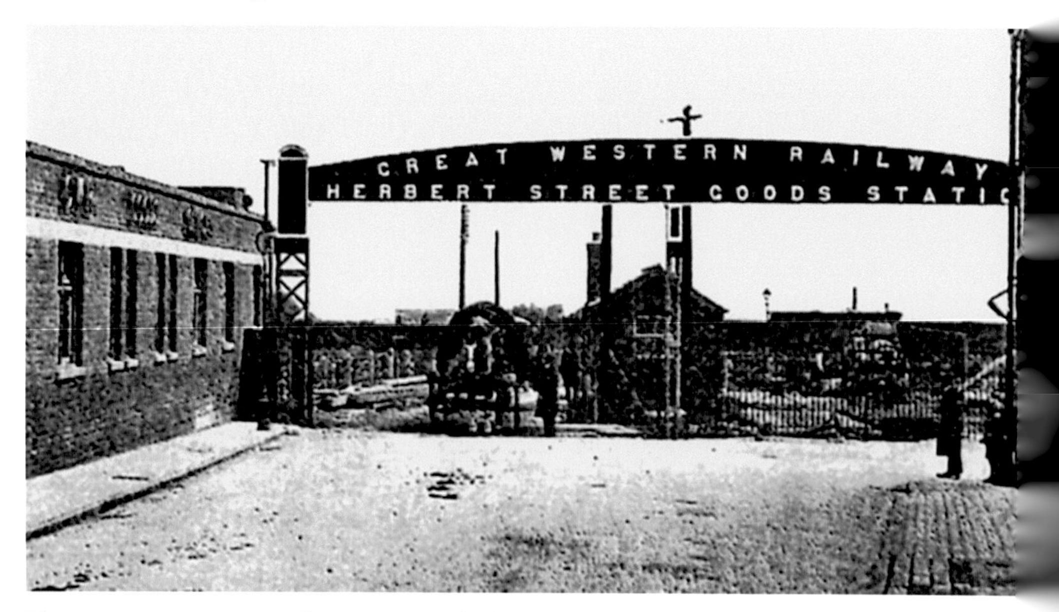

The entrance to GWR's Herbert Street goods depot, which had been built by the Birmingham & Shrewsbury Railway in 1848, with Victoria Basin forming a railway/canal interchange. When GWR took over the company, both GWR's broad-gauge and standard-gauge tracks were laid in the depot for trans-shipment, as the lines north of Wolverhampton remained of standard gauge. The depot closed in 1970.

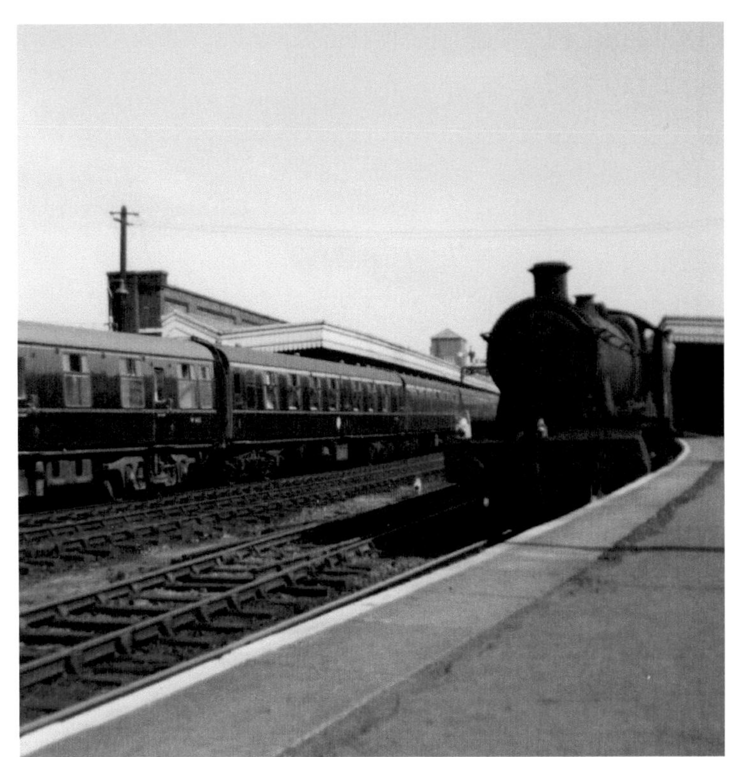

In summer 1969 an ex-GWR Hall Class locomotive waits in Low Level station to take the 5.40 p.m. to Birkenhead, the last regular steam-hauled service from Wolverhampton.

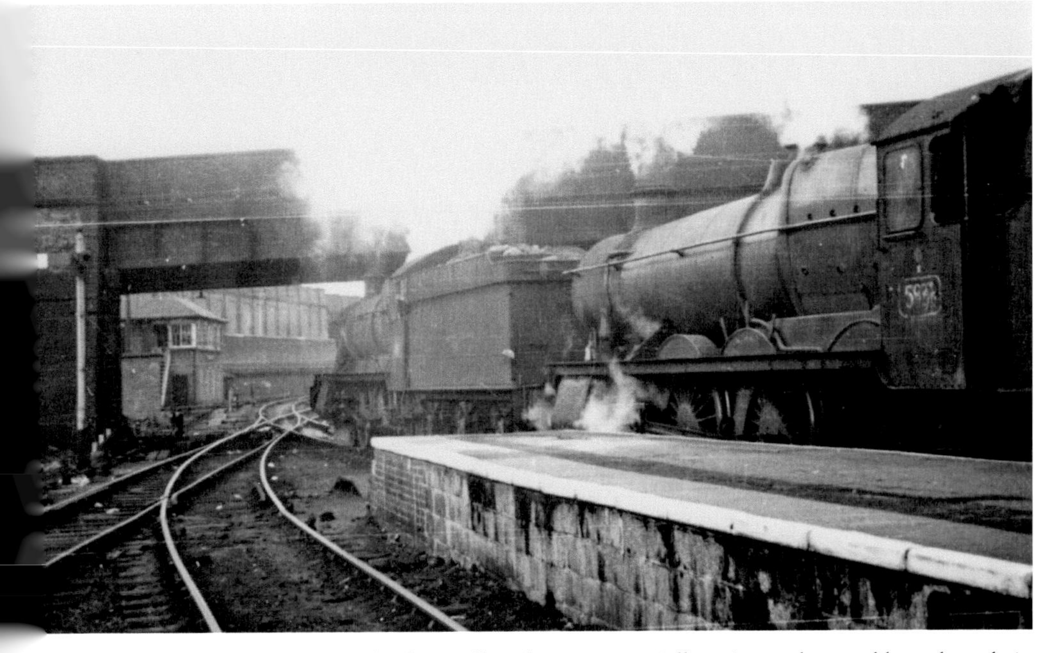

Two Hall Class engines, *Thornbridge Hall* and *Kingsway Hall*, wait on the northbound track in April 1965 with the Wednesfield Road bridge just in front of them. Low Level opened in 1854 as the northernmost broad-gauge station, converted to standard gauge in 1869. It closed to passenger traffic in 1972, becoming a parcels depot, and then closed completely in 1981.

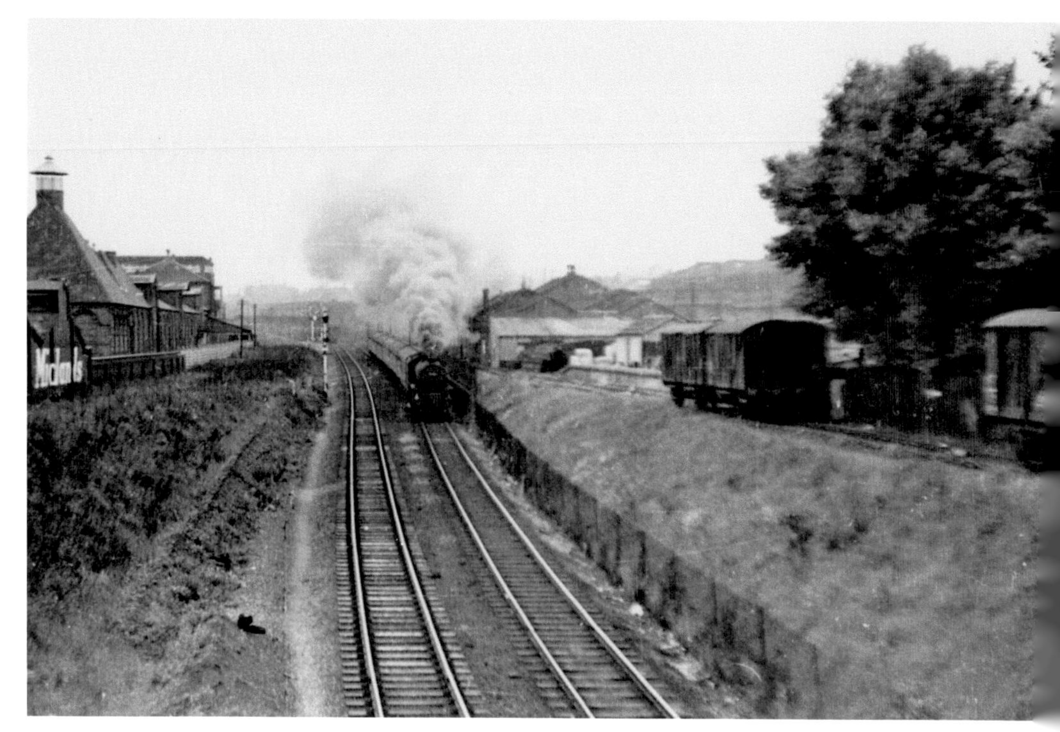

An ex-LMS Class 5 loco leaves Low Level hauling the Birkenhead train in 1966. It is passing Williams Butler's Springfield Brewery on the left as it approaches Cannock Road Bridge.

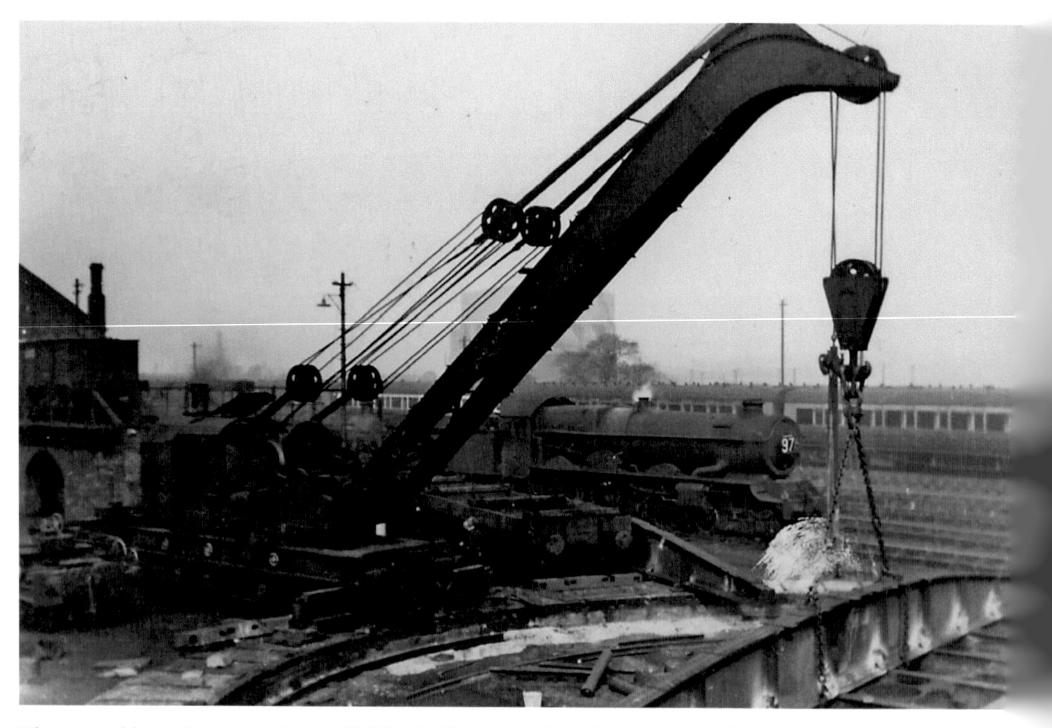

The turntable and crane at Dunstall. The Stafford Road works were one of the largest in the country.

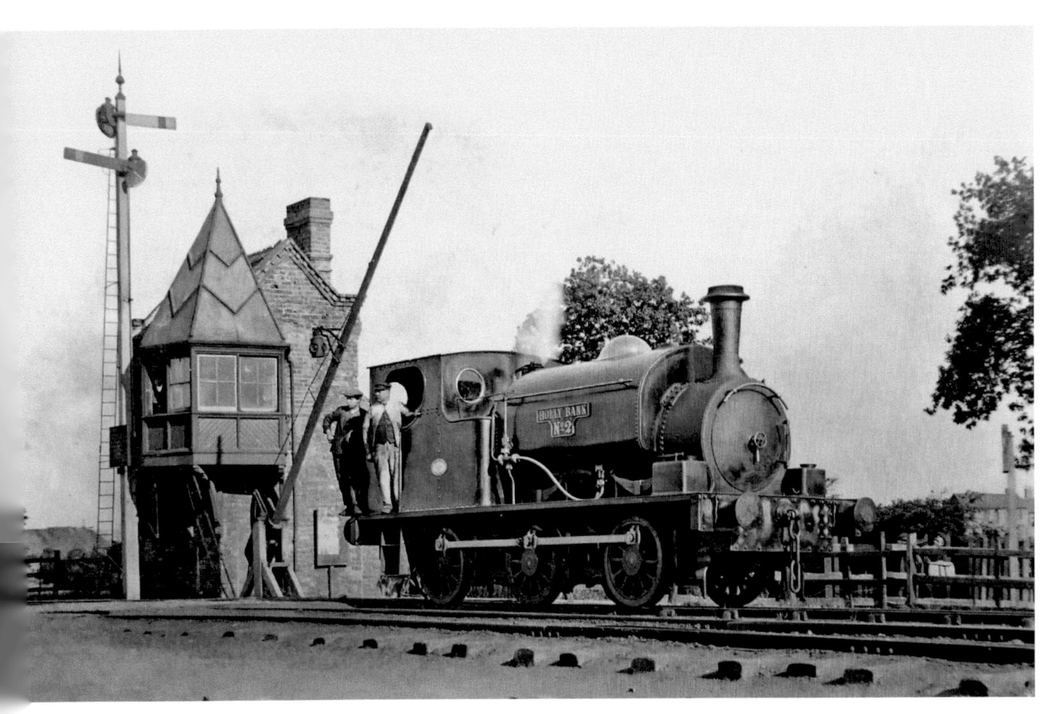

This distinctive signal box operated the road crossing on Bursnips Road, Essington, letting *Holly Bank No. 2* cross over. Where companies had previously had their own canal basin, now many operated their own private railway system.

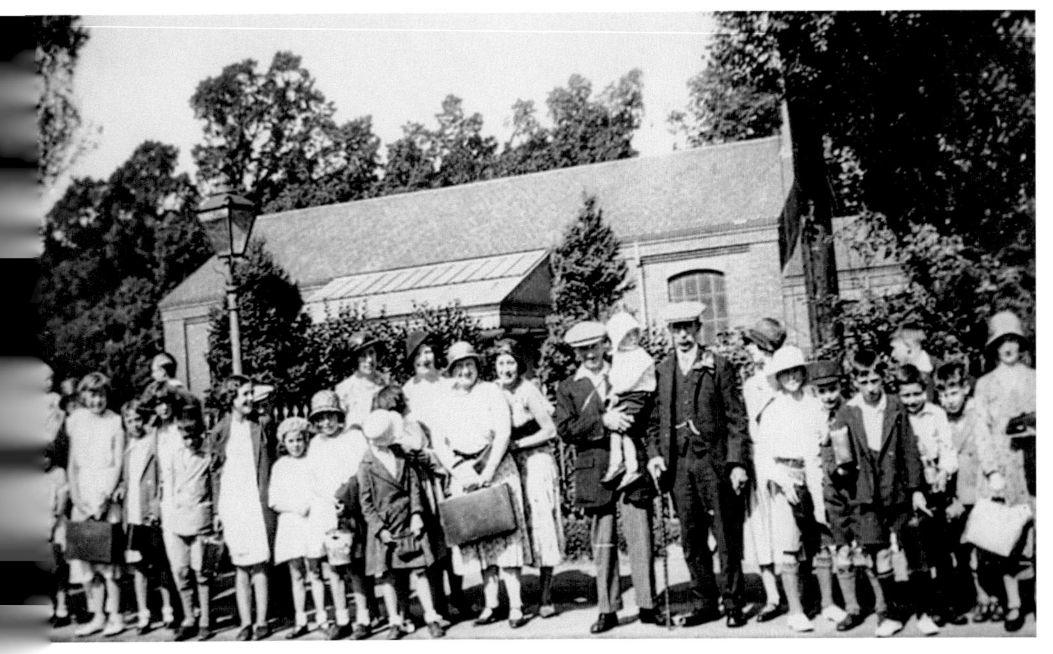

The railway line through Tettenhall only operated for forty years. Here, in 1932, people wait on the platform for a special train to take them on a day trip to Rhyl. It is notable there is no exhortation to stand back a metre from the platform edge.

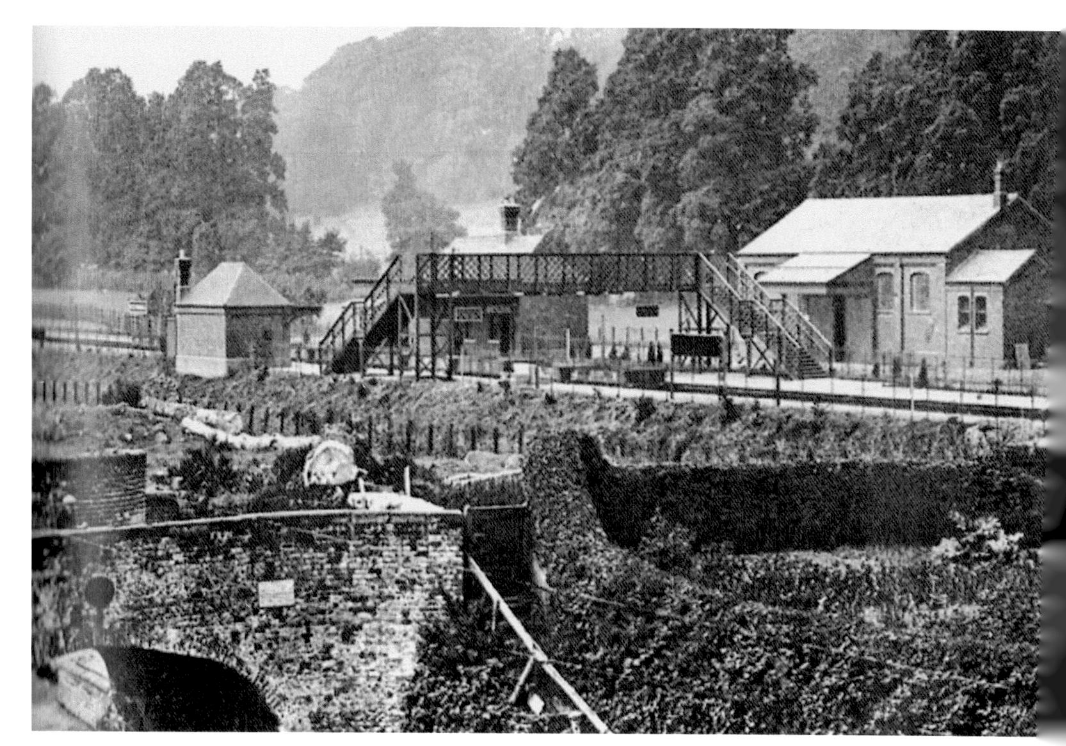

Great Western Railway's Tettenhall station opened in 1925 after a protracted development, halted by the First World War. This photograph, taken from the Tettenhall Road, shows how rural the location was then, with the old canal bridge in the foreground. The station footbridge was removed when it was decided that the second set of rails were not going to be laid through the station, with the cessation of regular passenger services in 1932.

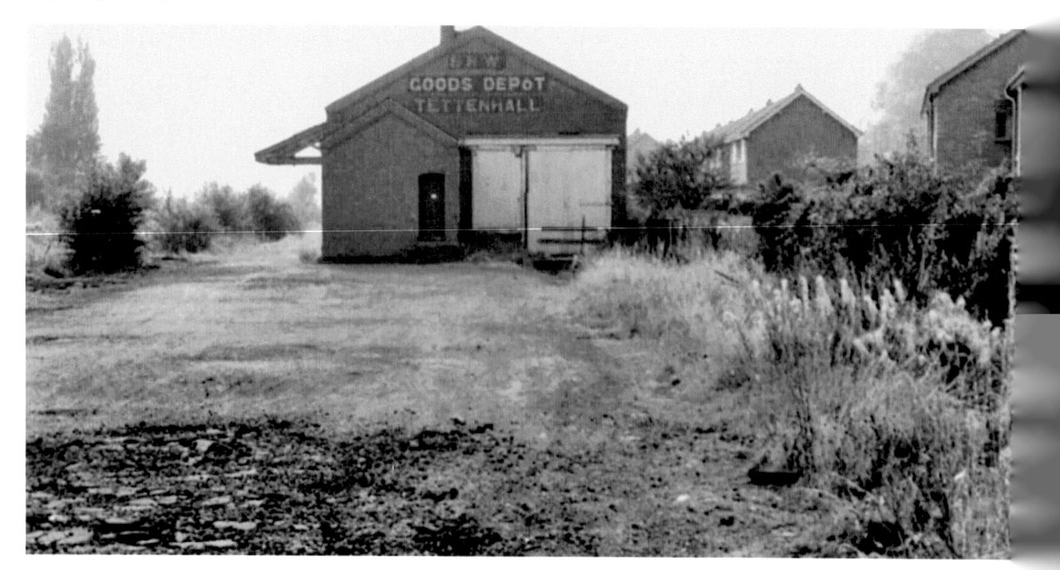

After closure in 1965 the station at Tettenhall fell into dereliction, and here the goods depot awaits a new purpose. Used as a warehouse for a little while, it has now finally been rejuvenated as the Tettenhall Transport Heritage Centre, the city's first transport museum.

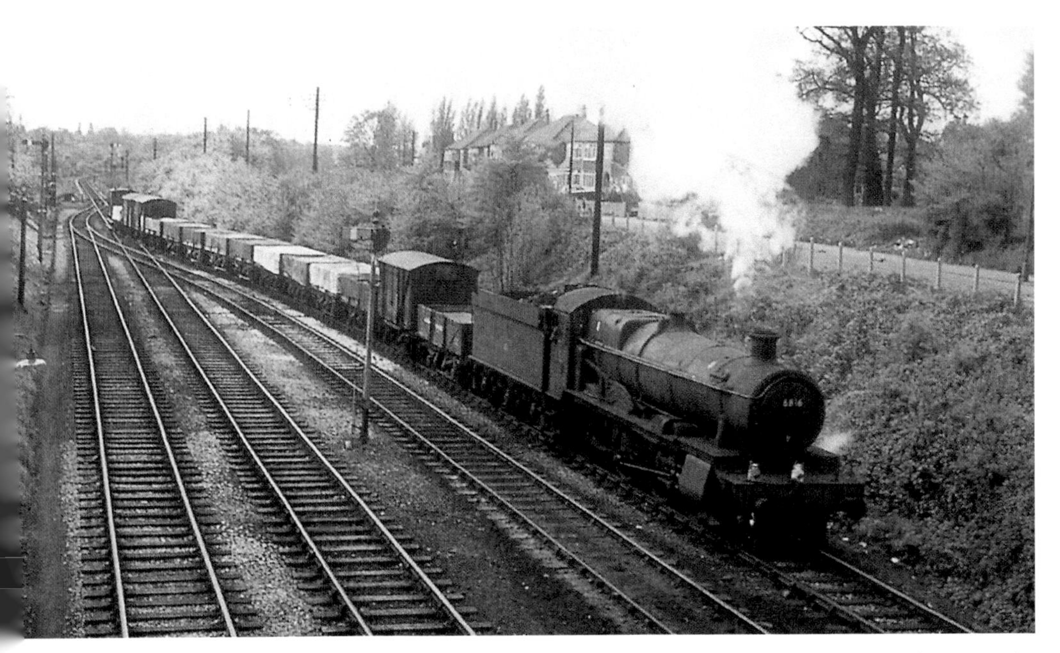

The end of the line through Tettenhall at Oxley Junction shows unfulfilled ambition. Twin lines join the Wolverhampton to Shrewsbury line going north and south, but then they are reduced to one, because the second set of rails was never laid on what set out to be the Wolverhampton to Bridgnorth Railway. The branch from Wombourne through Halfpenny Green to Bridgnorth was never built.

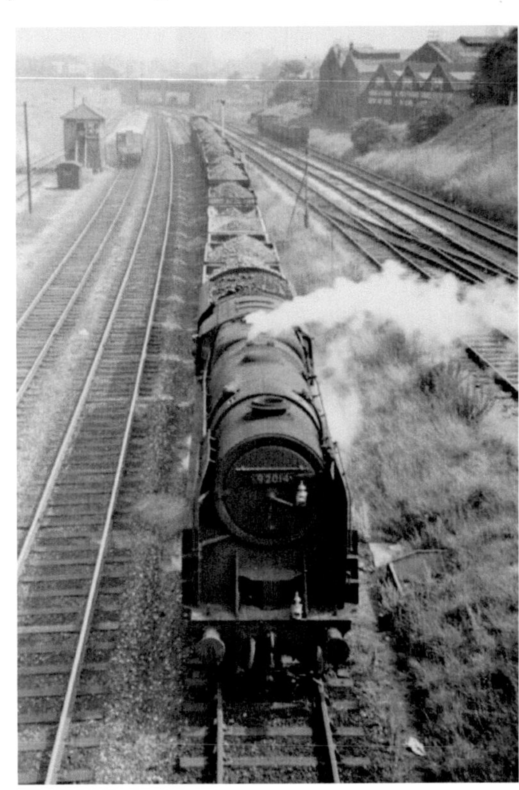

From the Monmore Green bridge a train leaves Low Level station, passing a parcels diesel motor unit (DMU) standing by the signal box.

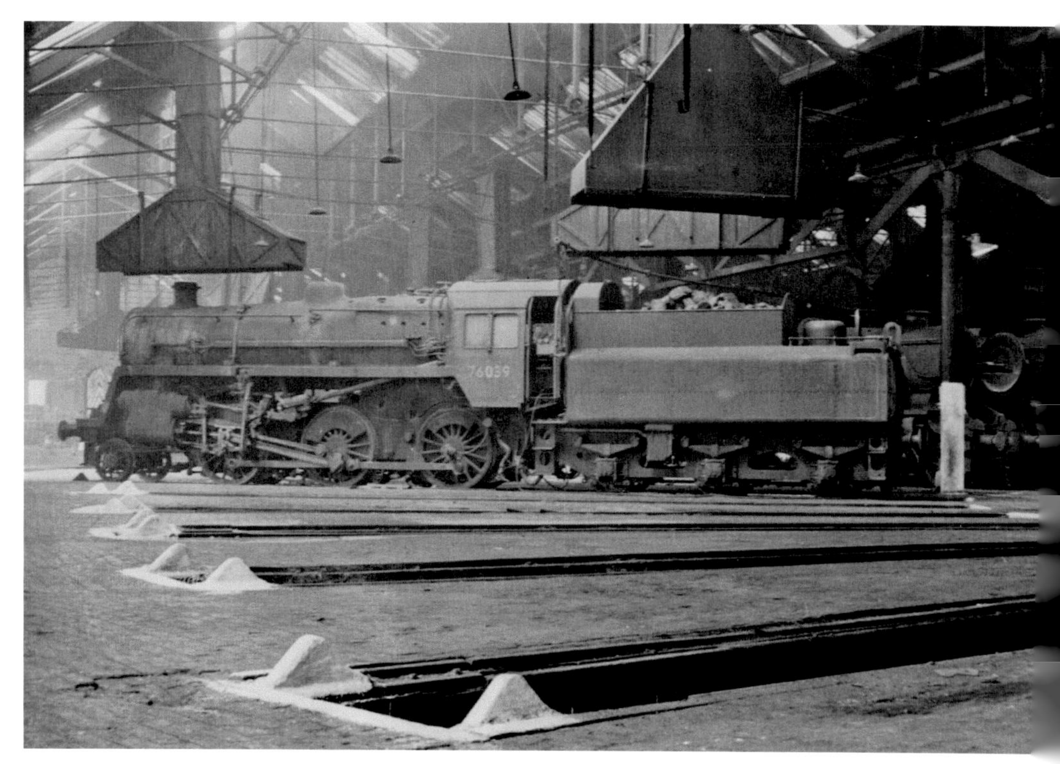

Inside Oxley engine sheds just before closure in 1966, locomotive No. 76039 awaits disposal.

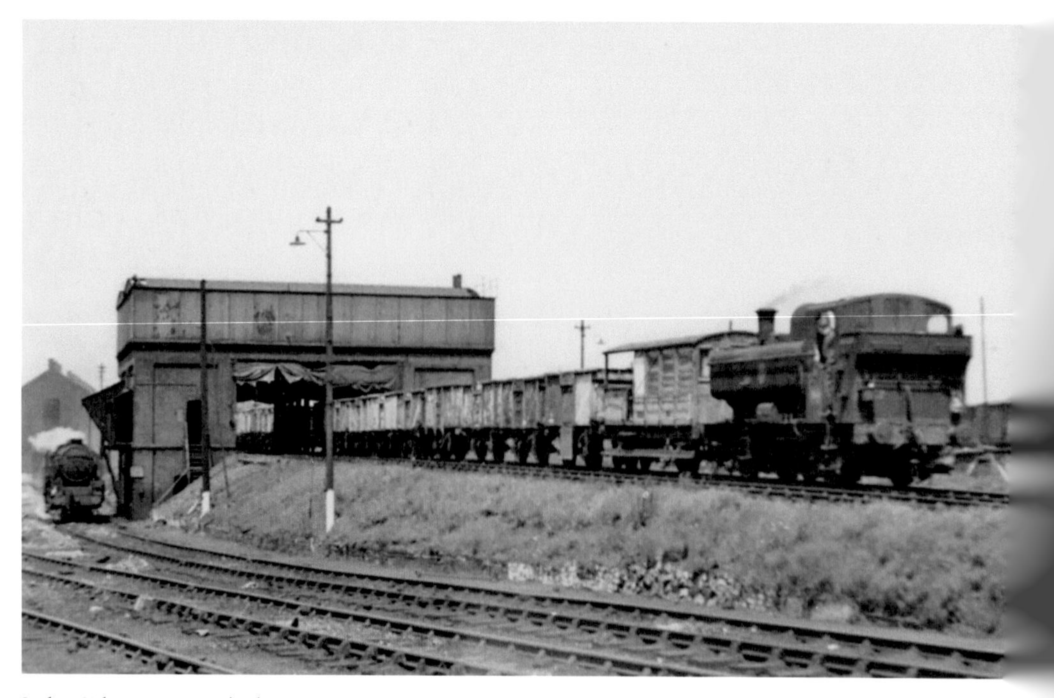

Oxley Sidings occupied a huge site, with a train shed, engine shed and goods sidings on two levels. Here a tank engine stands at the coaling stage in 1966.

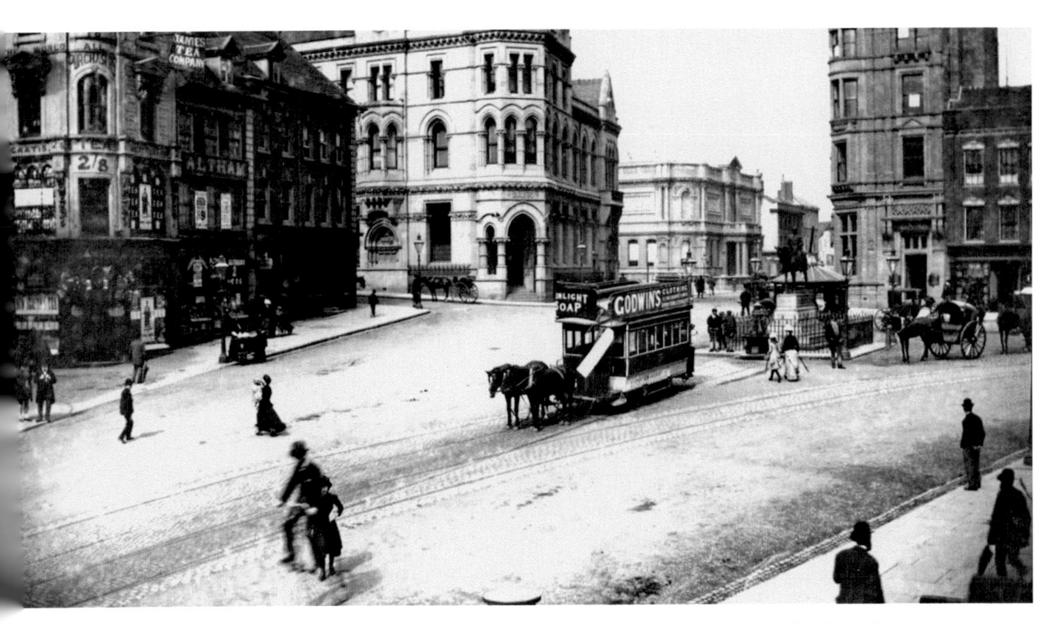

The first horse-drawn tram lines to Tettenhall, Willenhall and Bilston were laid ready for opening in 1878. Here two horses wait patiently in Queen Square to take a tram to Tettenhall as Prince Albert's statue watches on. A steam-hauled tram was trialled for six months, but the good people along the Tettenhall Road objected and the horses operated until electricity arrived in 1902.

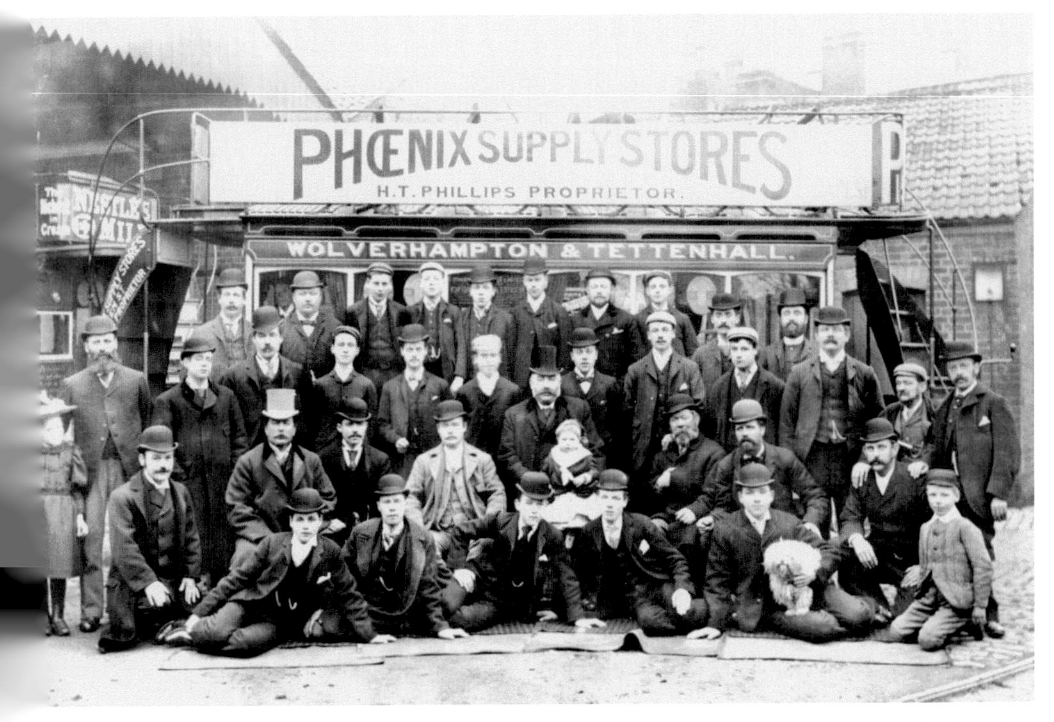

The main tram depot for the private Wolverhampton Tramways Company was at Newbridge Here the staff pose for the photograph, with three children and a dog. The corporation later bought out the company and prepared for electrification.

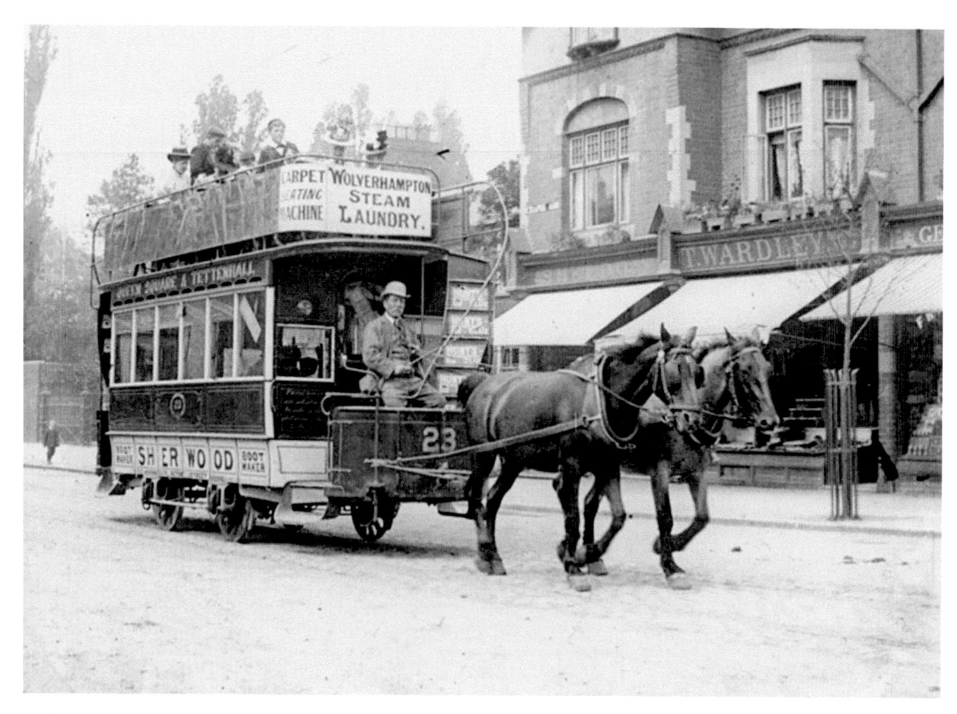

A horse-drawn tram passes into Chapel Ash on the route from Newbridge to Queen Square. As the driver is not in uniform, this is before the tramways were bought by the corporation in 1899. The buildings behind are still there, though of course with new tenants.

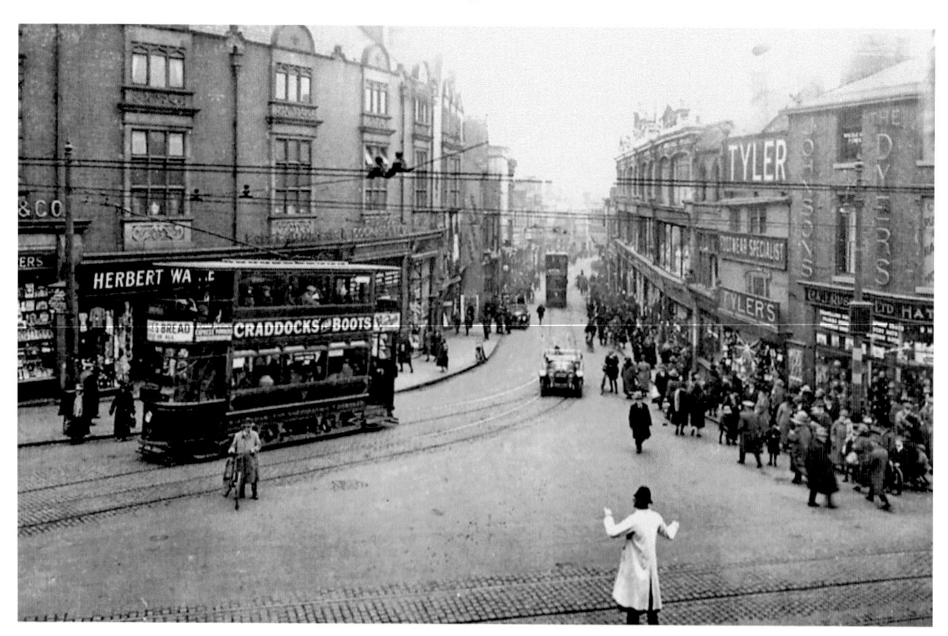

After the First World War, the much-enlarged tram system was converted to overhead collection. Here a tram turns down Victoria Street, much narrower then, as the buildings on the right were not yet demolished to make way for Beatties department store. The traffic policeman directs just two trams and a car.

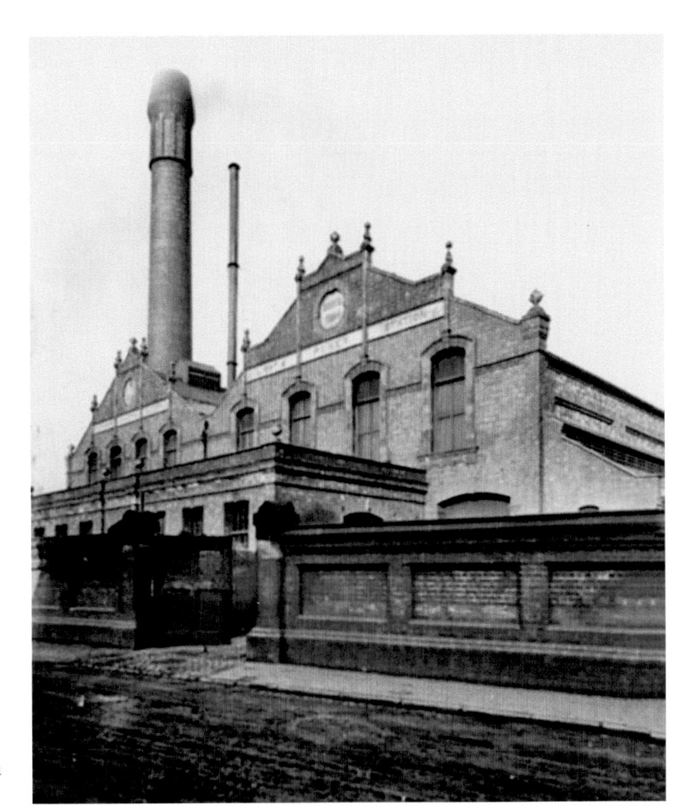

Power for the tramways system and the later trolleybuses was supplied by Wolverhampton's own Municipal Power Station in Commercial Road, originally equipped with two wooden cooling towers and later by one in concrete. Coal was brought in by canal at the rear.

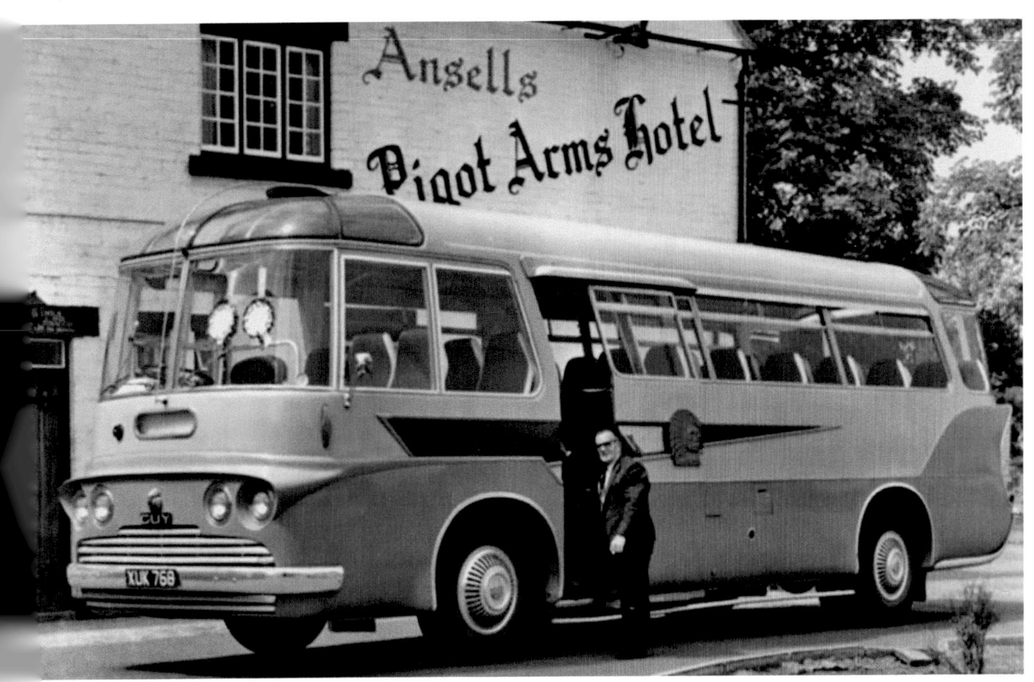

A new Guy Motors forty-one-seat Warrior coach with Burlingham bodywork in a posed shot outside the Pigot Arms in Pattingham. This was one of only two such coaches built.

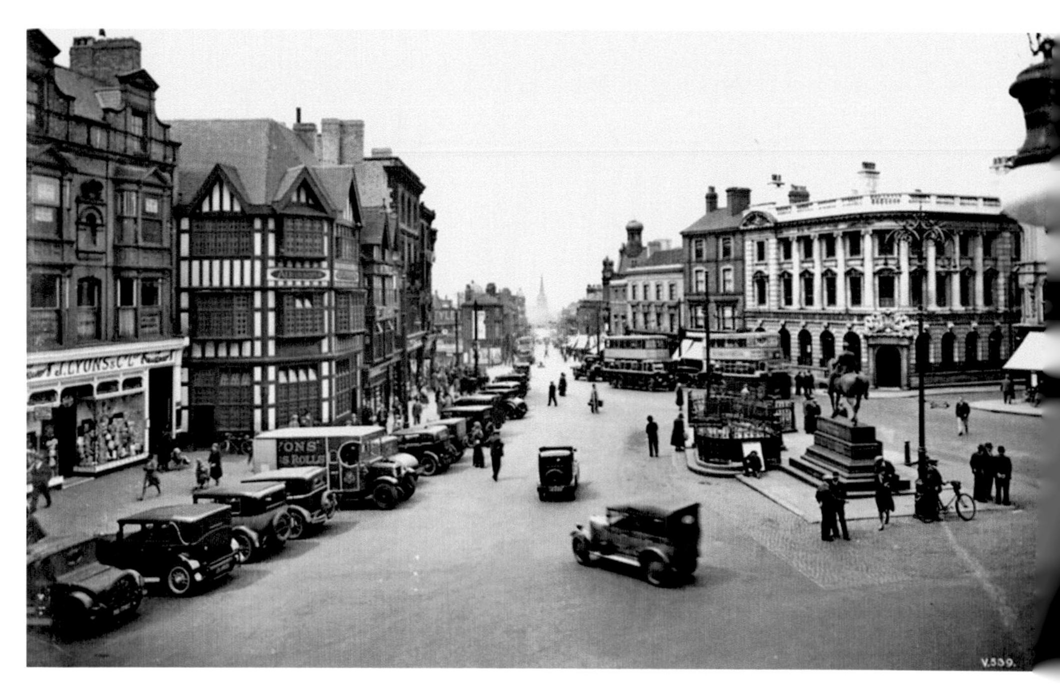

Queen Square from the top of Lloyds Bank with two Guy BTX trolleybuses ascending. It seems the overhead trolleybus wires have been removed from the image. It was a time when people could stand in the middle of the road happily chatting, perhaps having met one another going to the central underground toilets.

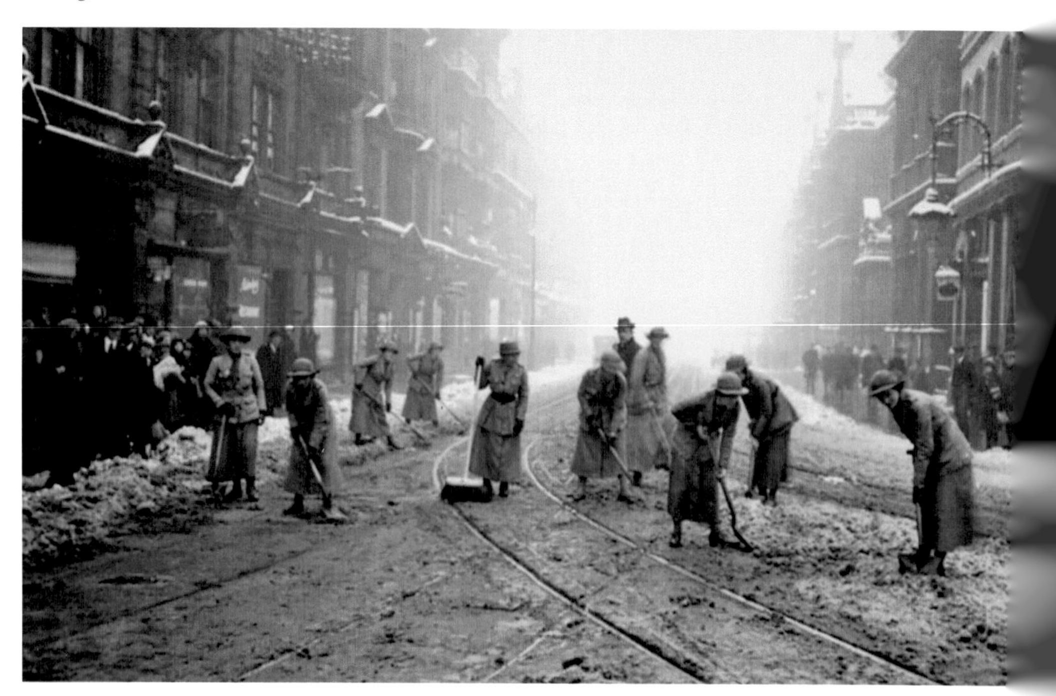

Lichfield Street during the First World War. An army of women keep the tram tracks clear of snow. It's interesting that the trams were clearly still running in such weather, even with a surface contact system.

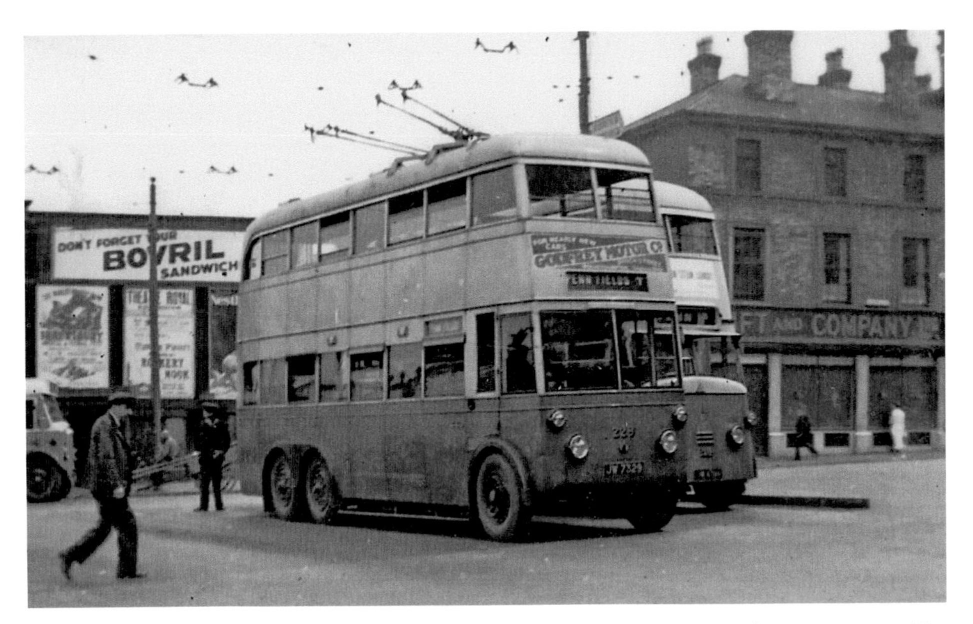

Two trolleybuses stand in the centre of Victoria Square in December 1935, the nearest Guy BTX waiting to go to Penn Fields. Victoria Square was used as a central hub for the trolleybus system, though loading was in the middle of the road.

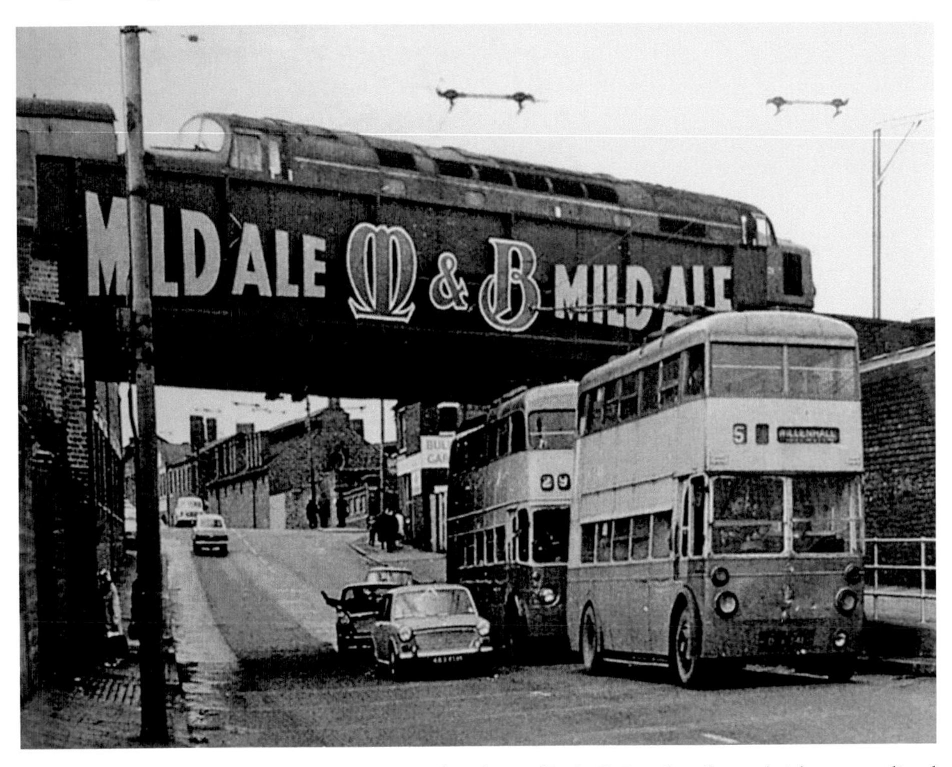

Two trolleybuses, Nos 5 and 29, pass under the Willenhall Road railway bridge as a diesel locomotive passes over in the mid-1960s. This was one of the bridges where the road had to be lowered to allow double-deckers to pass beneath.

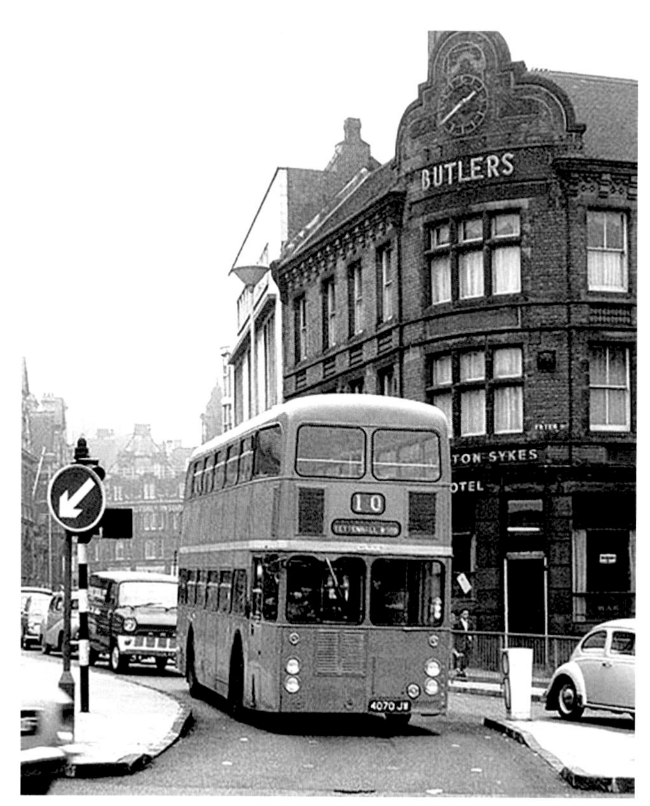

A Guy Wulfrunian motor bus on trial with Wolverhampton Transport passes the Sir Tatton Sykes pub. The advanced nature of the Wulfrunian and the expense of developing it sent Guy Motors into financial difficulty after their Arab model had been in production for many years.

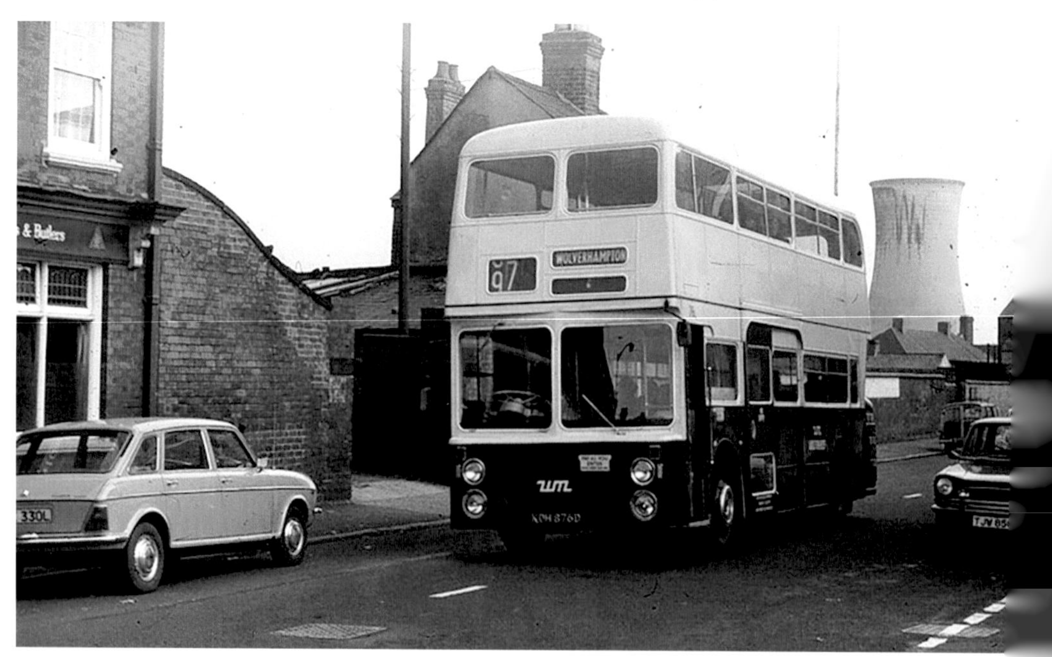

The green and yellow of Wolverhampton Transport buses disappeared from the streets with amalgamation of all West Midlands passenger services in 1973. The blue and grey of WMPTE buses then appeared, like on this Daimler Fleetline passing the Red Cow on the Bilston Road.

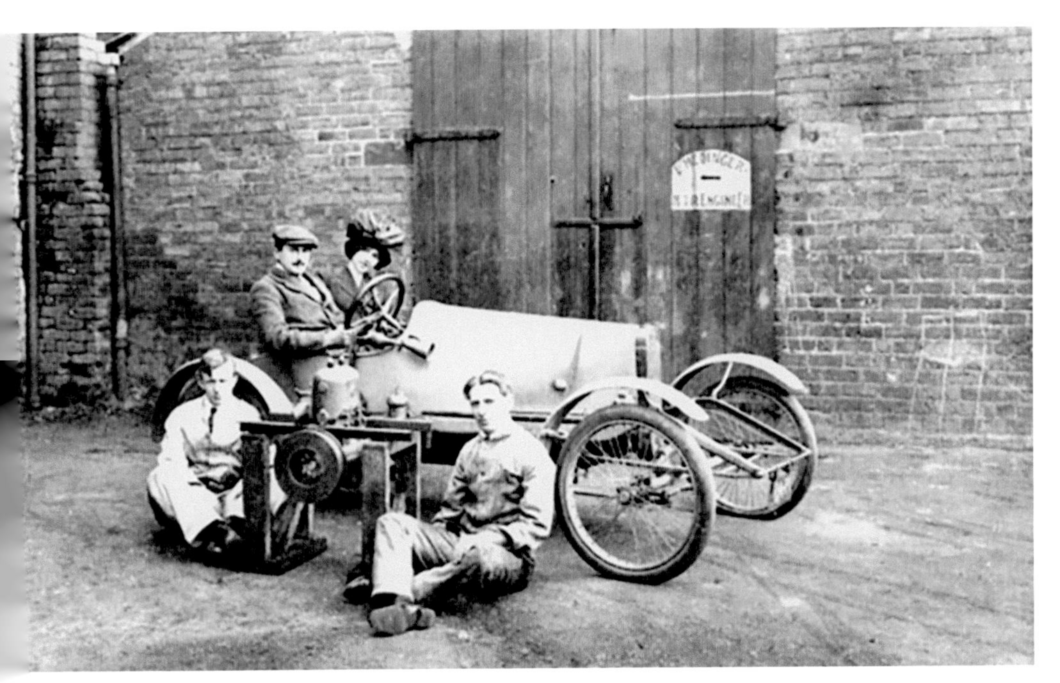

Wolverhampton has had many car manufacturers, but the most obscure was Emil Medinger. He was an Austrian employed by Sunbeam as a racing driver, but in 1912 he set up the Medinger Motor Car Co. in Worcester Street and built this two-stroke cycle car and engine, apparently capable of 60 mph. He was interned during the war as an enemy alien and never built a second car.

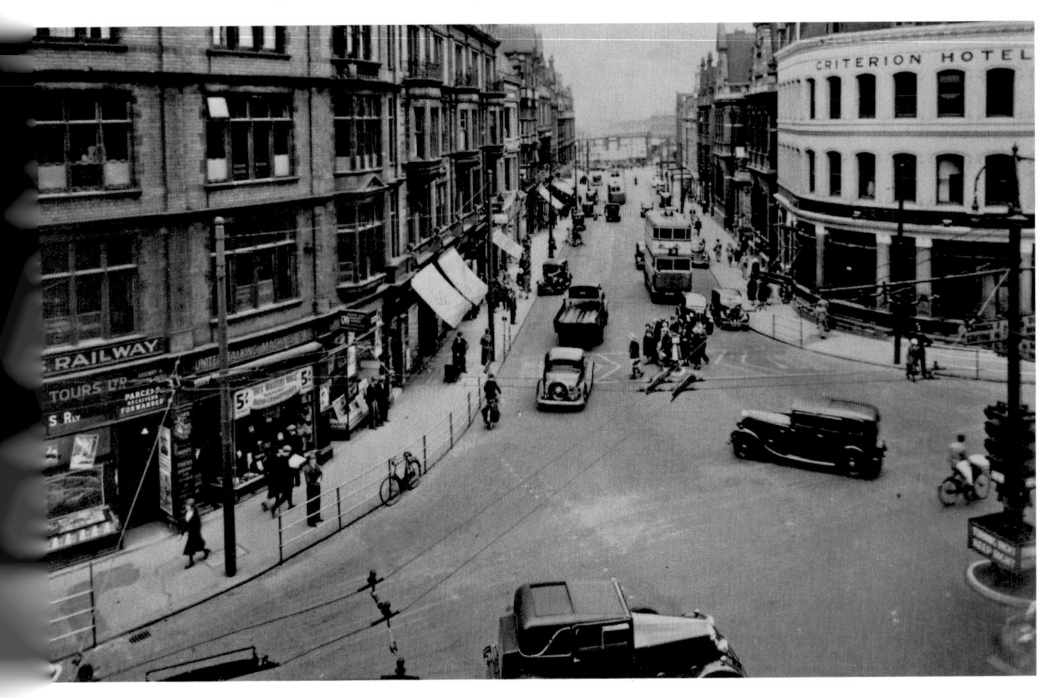

Princess Square with a trolleybus about to pass the Criterion Hotel. The significant thing in the scene is the traffic lights; this location saw the first use of automatic traffic lights in Europe.

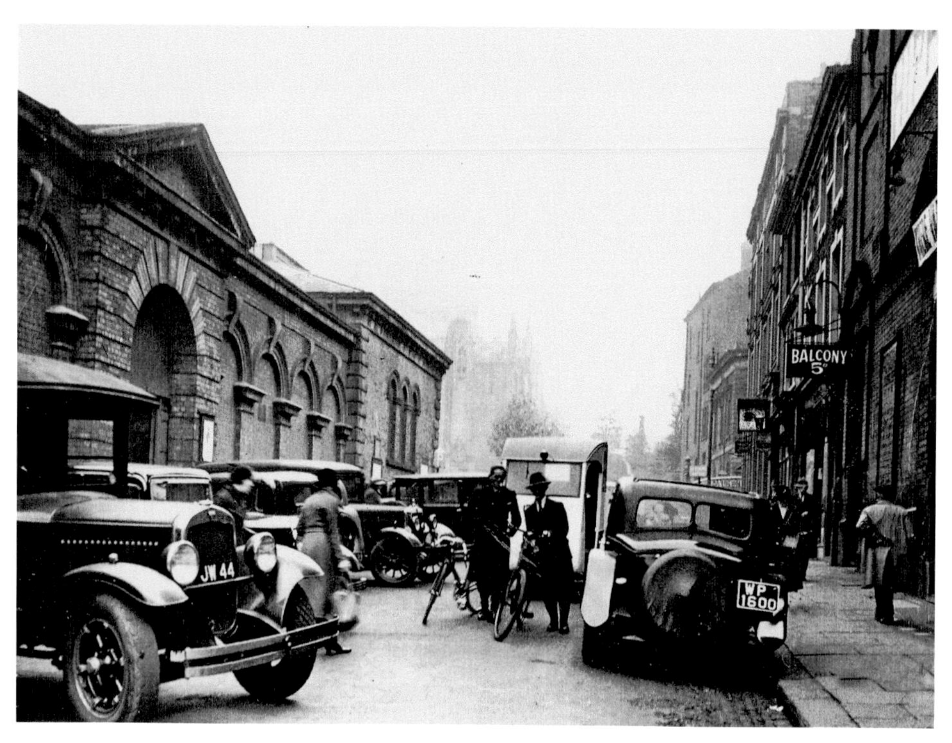

Even in the 1920s car parking was a problem. Here in Cheapside, between the Retail Market and the rear of the Hippodrome, chaos seems to be happening.

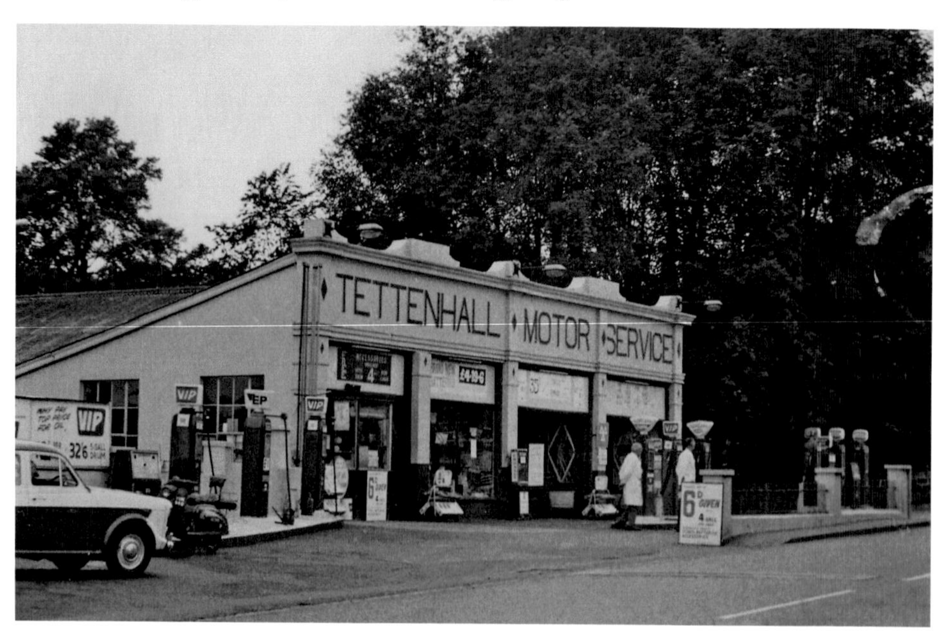

In the 1930s Tettenhall & Newbridge Motor Services opened a garage on the corner of Henwood Road at the bottom of the Rock. The front was later doubled in size, and during the war the rear workshops were added. Later the front range of buildings seen here were cleared away and a large canopy was erected over modern pumps. The building is now a Majestic Wine warehouse.

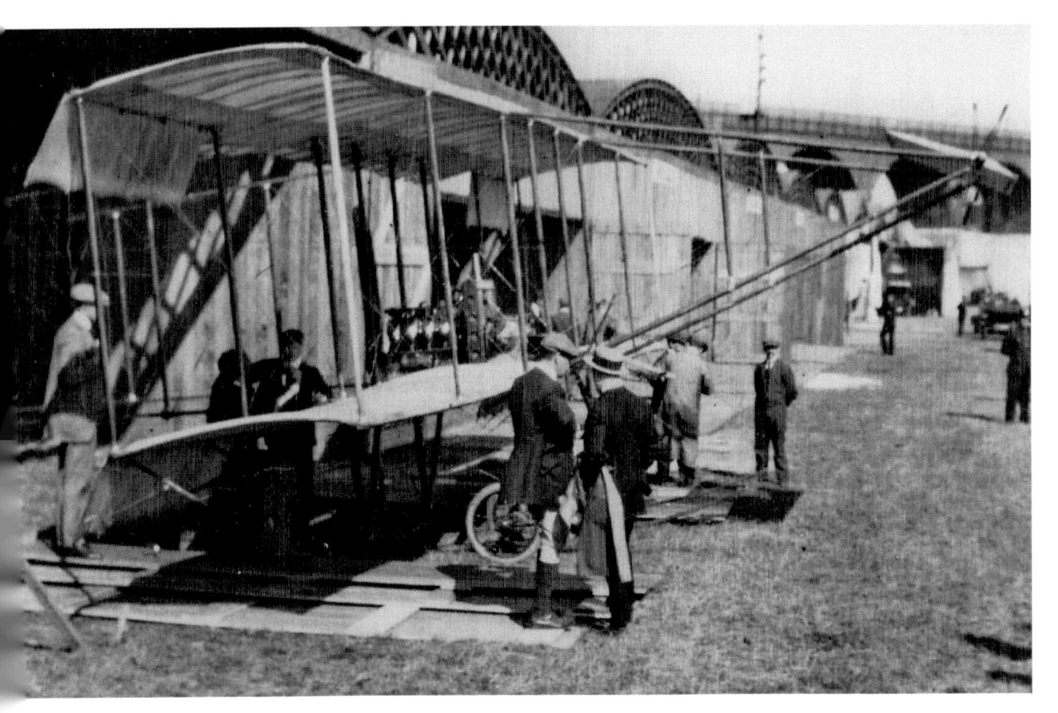

In 1910, aviation came to Wolverhampton. In June, Dunstall Park Racecourse became the town's first airfield, and these hangars were built for the first All-British Flying Meeting. Claude-Grahame White's Farman biplane stands outside of one.

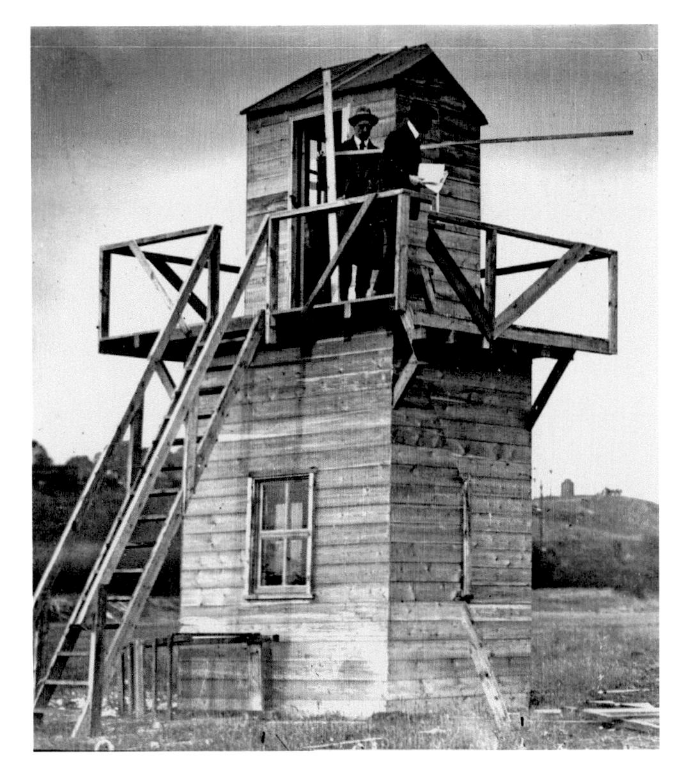

In the middle of the racecourse the town's first 'control tower' was built, with signalling to the aviators by flags. The town is one of the few to have had an airfield for over 100 years. After Dunstall Park there was Perton, then the Municipal Airport at Pendeford, and, since 1971, Halfpenny Green.

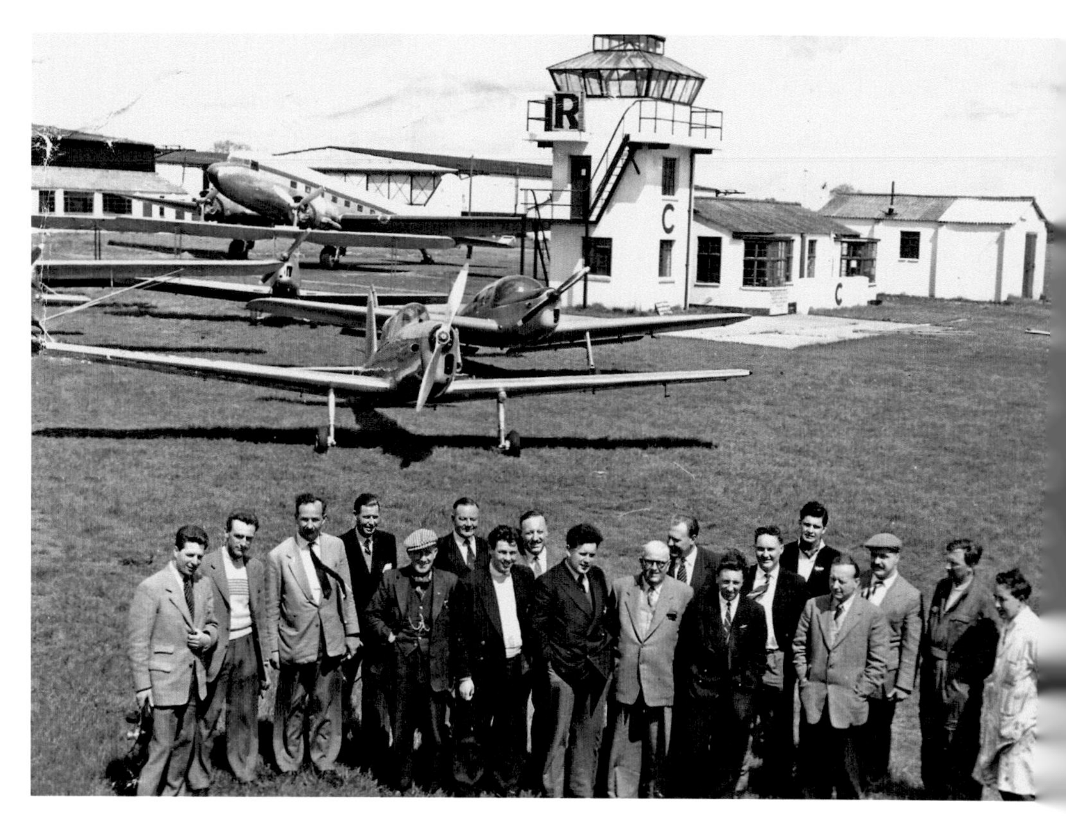

Don Everall ran the airfield for many years and serviced its own airliners there. Here the staff, with Don and Peter Everall in the centre, stand in front of the Aero Club's Chipmunk, Messenger, Tiger Moths and a DC-3, with the control tower to the right.

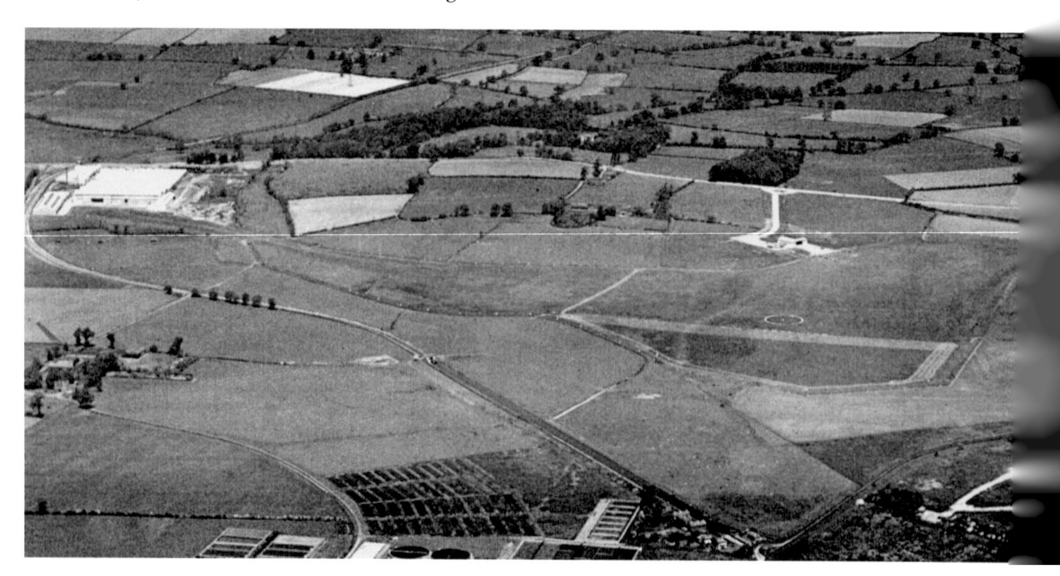

The Municipal Airport just after being built at Pendeford in 1936, with the white shape of Boulton Paul's brand-new factory to the left and the sole hangar and clubhouse to the right. The Barnhurst sewage beds lie in the foreground.

6

Lost Street Scenes

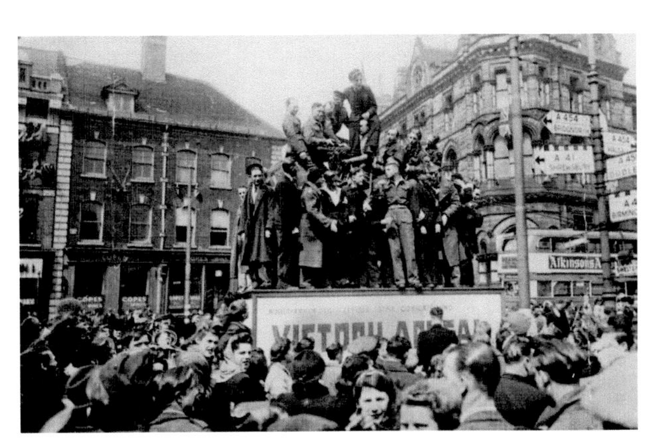

VE Day celebrations in Queen Square. Revellers cling to 'the man on the 'oss', as Prince Albert is invariably known. One cause to celebrate was that Wolverhampton had escaped much of the destruction inflicted elsewhere by the Luftwaffe. A planned air raid on the same scale as the Coventry one had been cancelled.

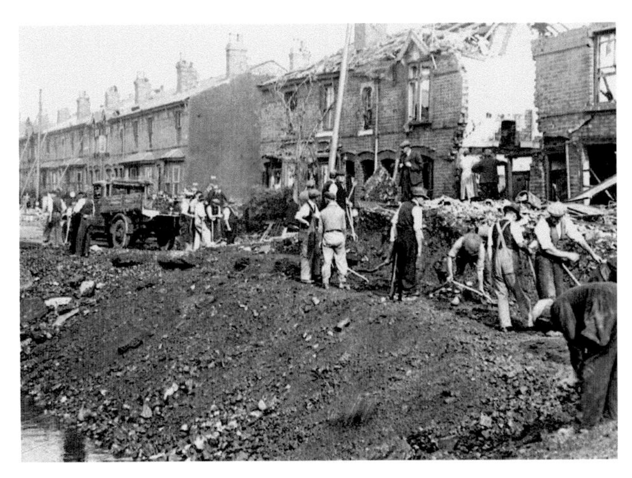

Bombs had fallen, however, including a large one that left this crater in the Willenhall Road, just east of Coventry Street. Destruction to buildings was minimal. The terrace of houses in the background is still there and the damaged ones alongside the crater have since been demolished for the start of Brooklands Parade.

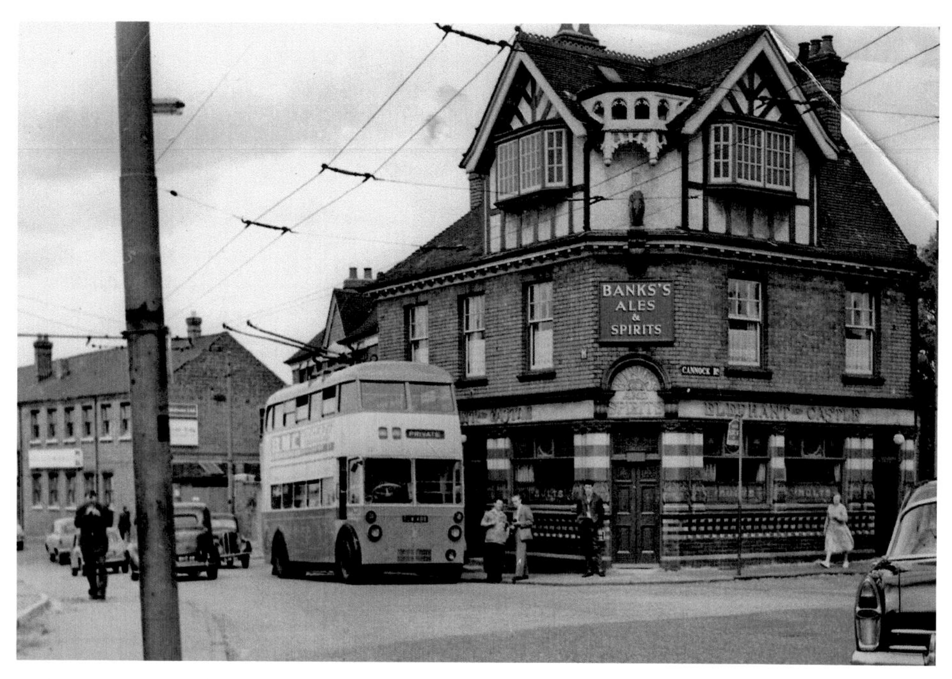

Redevelopment in the 1960s and 1970s caused far more to be lost, including the most lamented pub in Wolverhampton, the Elephant & Castle, on the corner of Cannock Road and Stafford Street. Everything within this scene is now gone, including trolleybuses of course. A replica of the Elephant & Castle has been built in the Black Country Living Museum.

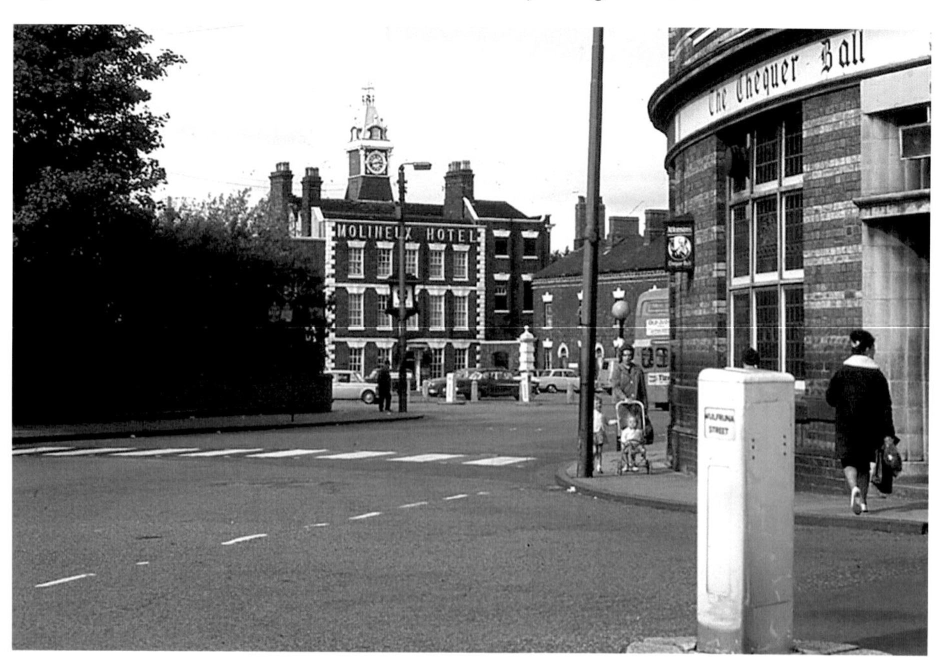

Another much missed pub is the Chequer Ball, with its ornate brickwork, seen on the right on the corner of North Street and Wulfruna Street. In the background the Molineux Hotel survives as the City Archives, but again everything else has gone.

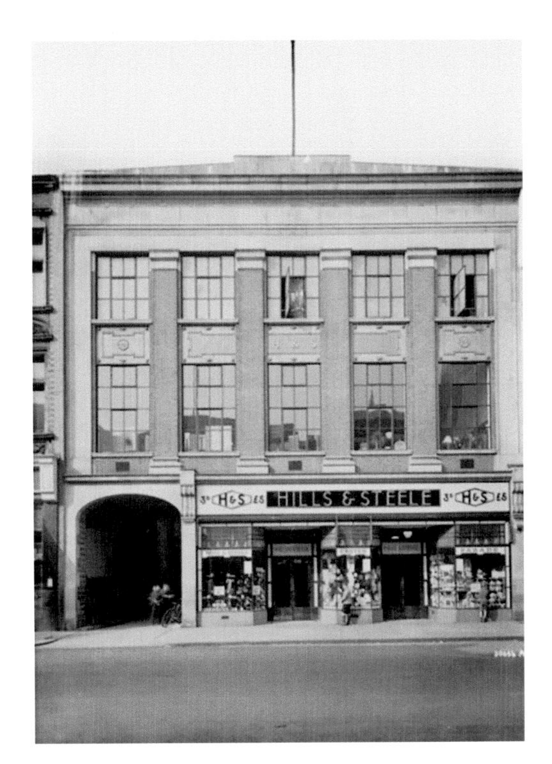

The ghost of some institutions survive longer than most. Hills and Steele was a store in Dudley Street, closed and replaced by British Home Stores (later BHS). For years afterwards some Wulfrunians, including my mother, still called it 'Hills and Steeles'.

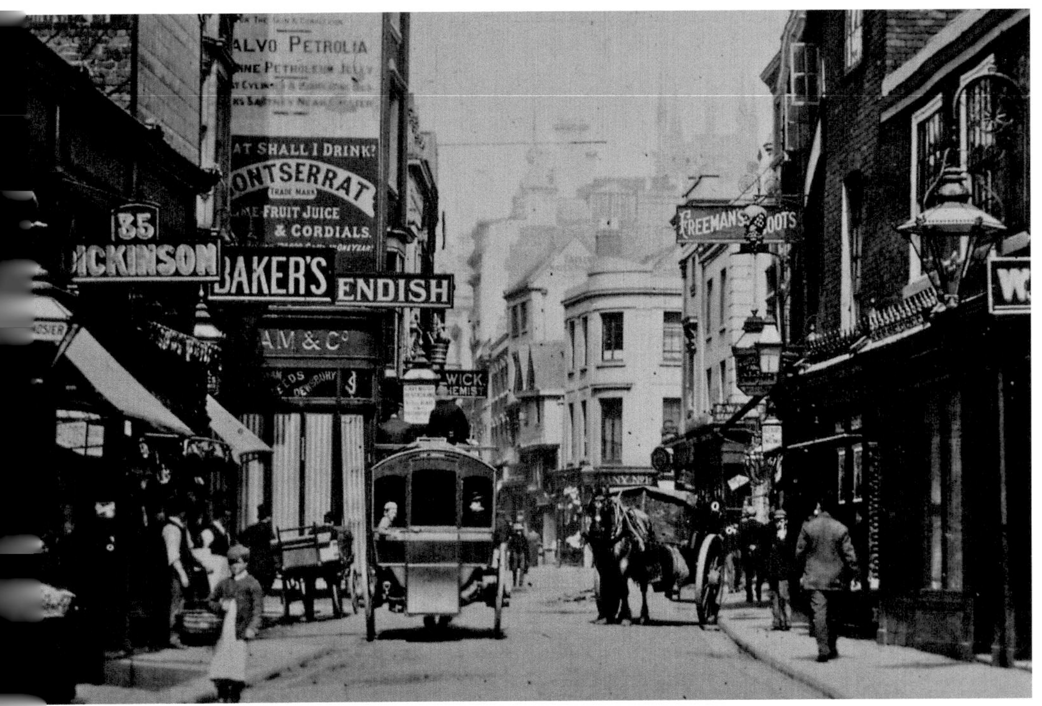

Dudley Street has long been the main shopping street in the town, even when horse-drawn buses passed along it and deliveries were by horse and cart. The buildings on the right of this picture were later replaced, however.

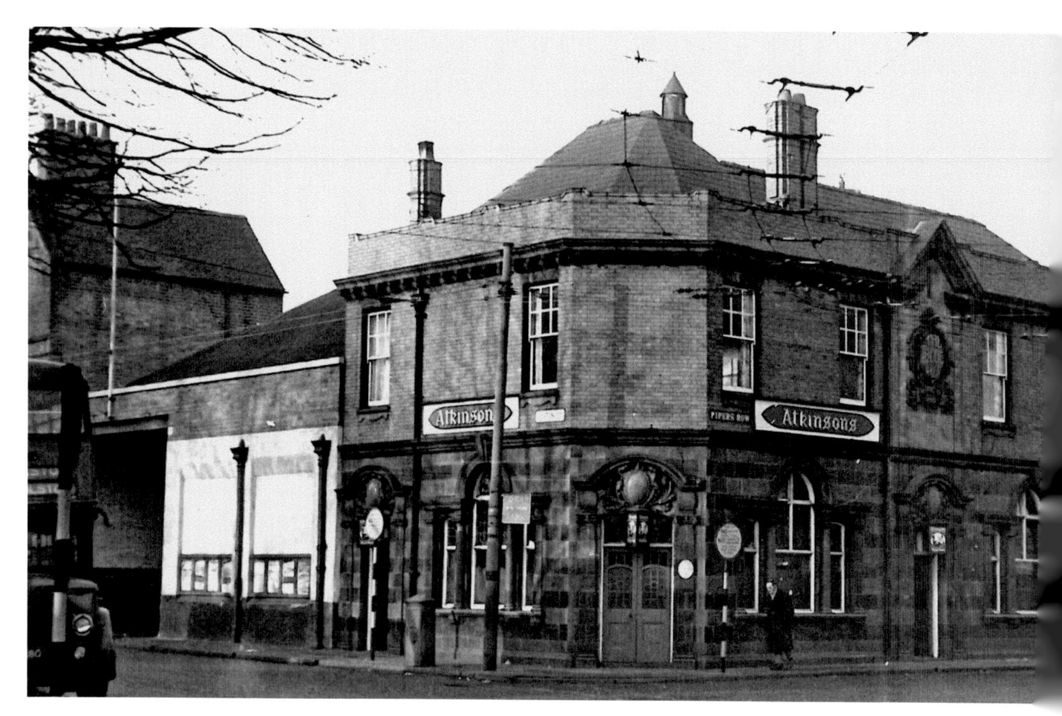

Wolverhampton has lost many pubs over the years – hundreds, in fact. This one, the Blue Ball, sat on the corner of Piper's Row (to the right) and Bilston Street. The police station has since taken over this corner.

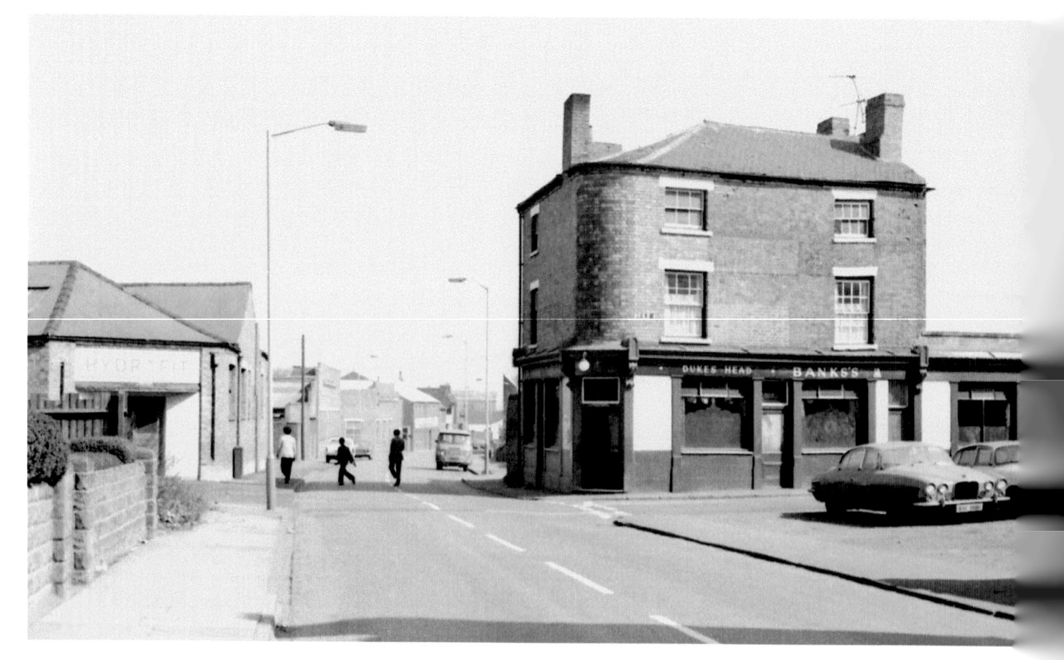

Other pubs, like the Dukes Head on the corner of Duke Street and Walsall Street, have closed but found a new use. In this case, as flats above a fish and chip shop. The rest of this part of Walsall Street is much the same.

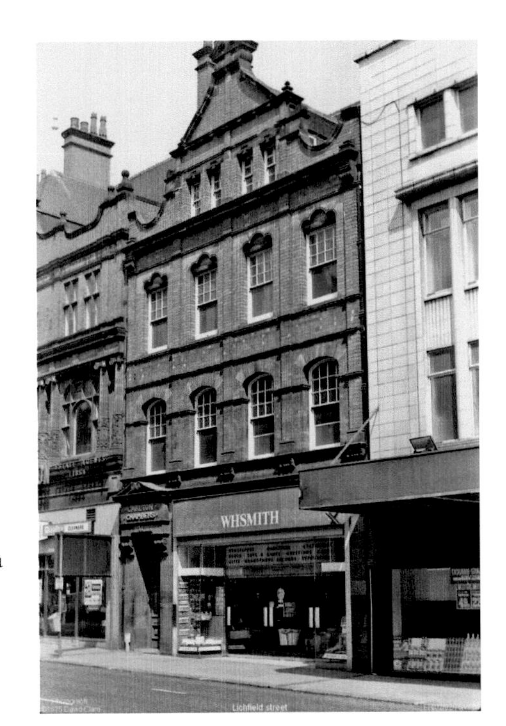

At the time of writing the city does not have a WHSmith shop, which seems incredible. This much-loved shop once occupied a site next to the art deco Co-operative store in Lichfield Street for many years, until relocating to the Mander Centre.

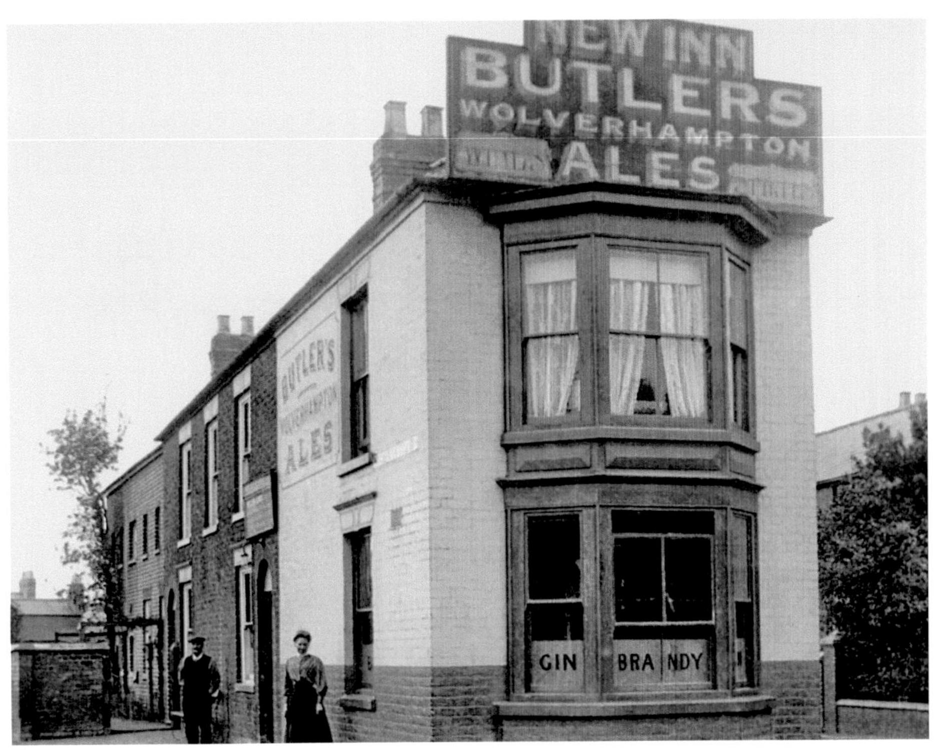

The New Inn, squeezed in the fork between Castlecroft Road and Finchfield Road West, has gone but was replaced by another pub, named the Chestnut Tree, set much further back from the corner.

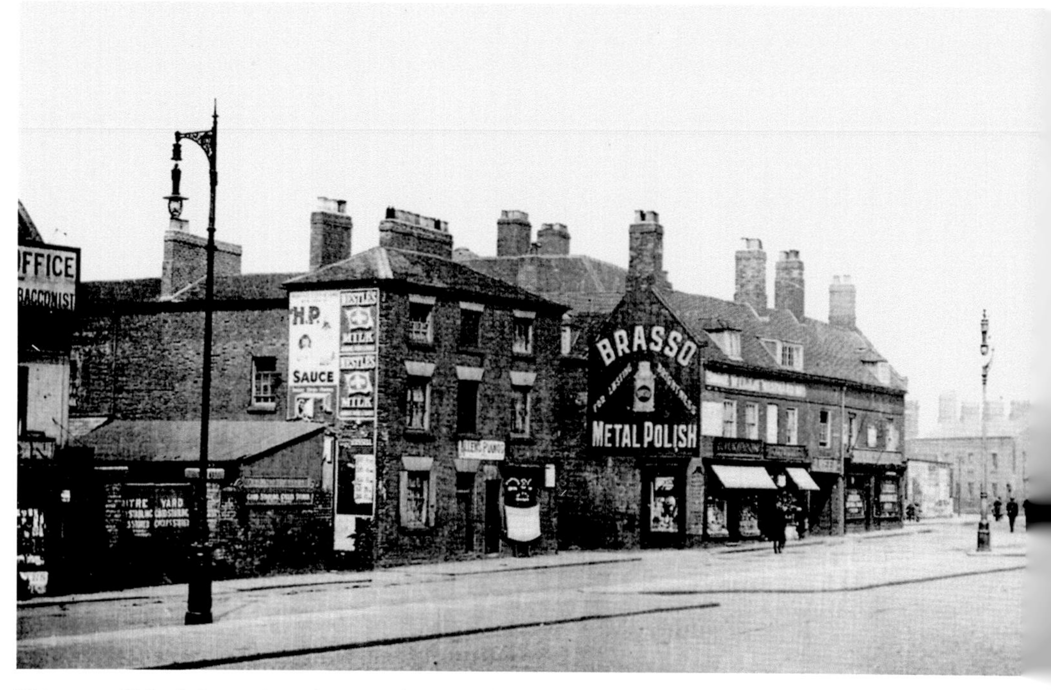

This part of North Street, just above Molineux Fold (seen in the background) and leading to Molineux House would now be up in the air. The ring road cuts right through this area at a much lower level, and below even that is the 'Wolves' subway leading to the stadium.

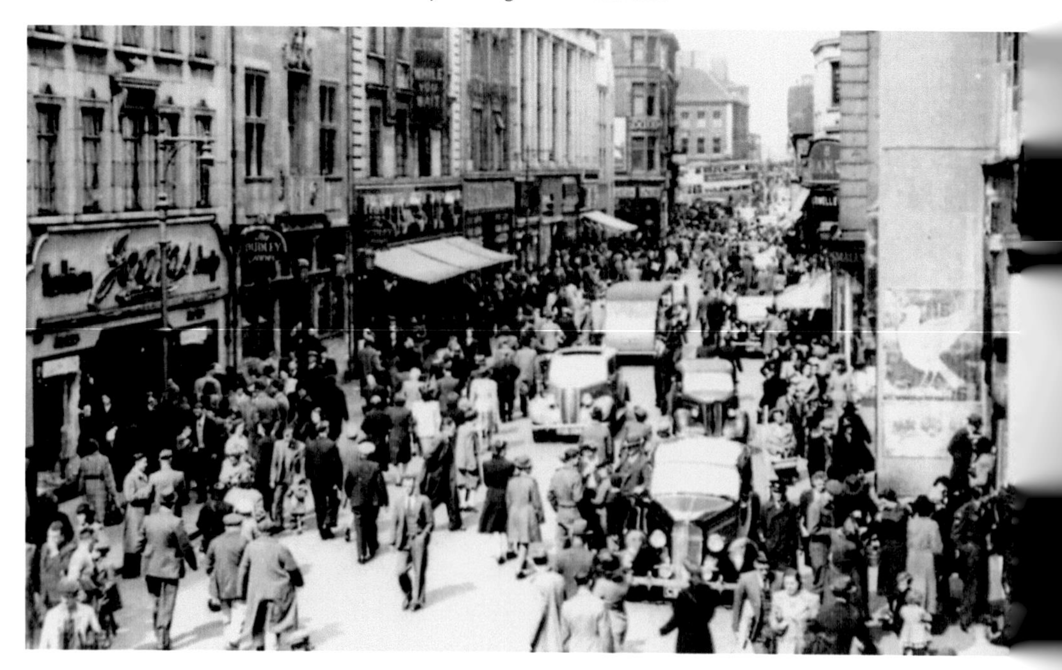

Proof that even in the 1950s the people of Wolverhampton treated Dudley Street as if it was pedestrianised, as it actually is today. Drivers negotiated it at walking pace as people wandered across it without looking both ways.

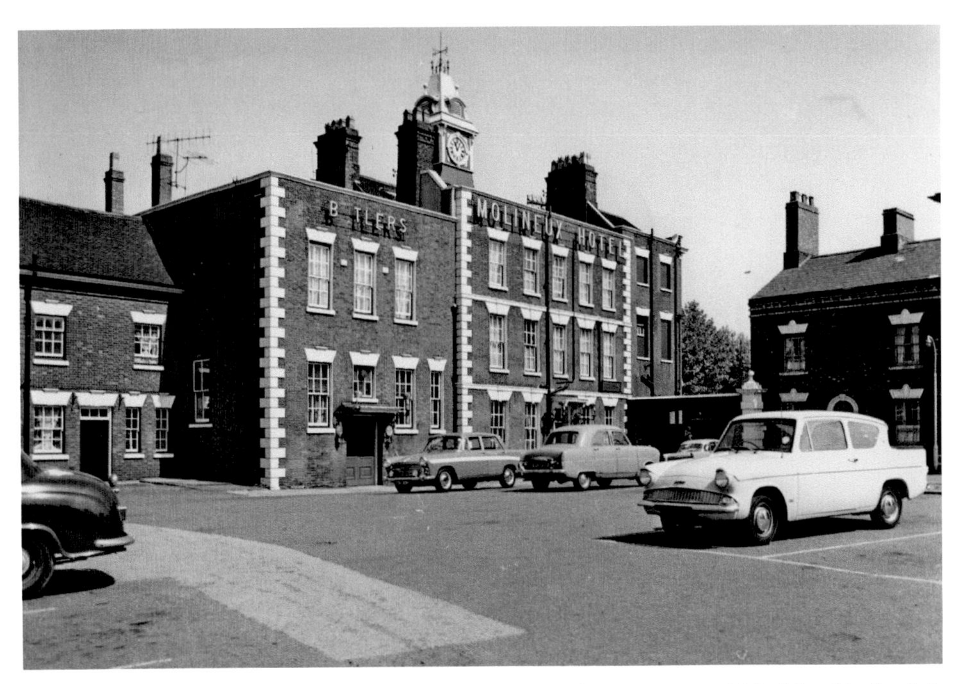

This is the 300-year-old Molineux Hotel, built by one John Rotton in 1720. After his death it became the home of Benjamin Molineux. When housing had encroached on all sides it was turned into a hotel. Shown in the 1960s just before the ring road cut it off from the town centre, it was nearing the end of its heyday.

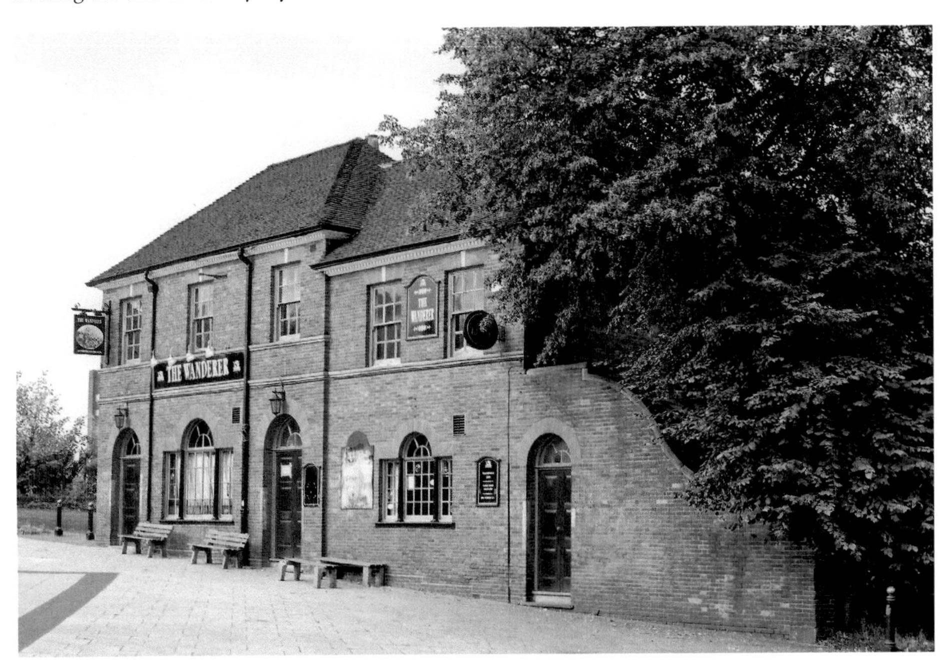

Just down the hill from the Molineux Hotel was the 'top' Fox, later renamed the Wanderer. The other Fox in the town was by Penn Road island. The Wanderer has now been demolished to be replaced by extra car parking space.

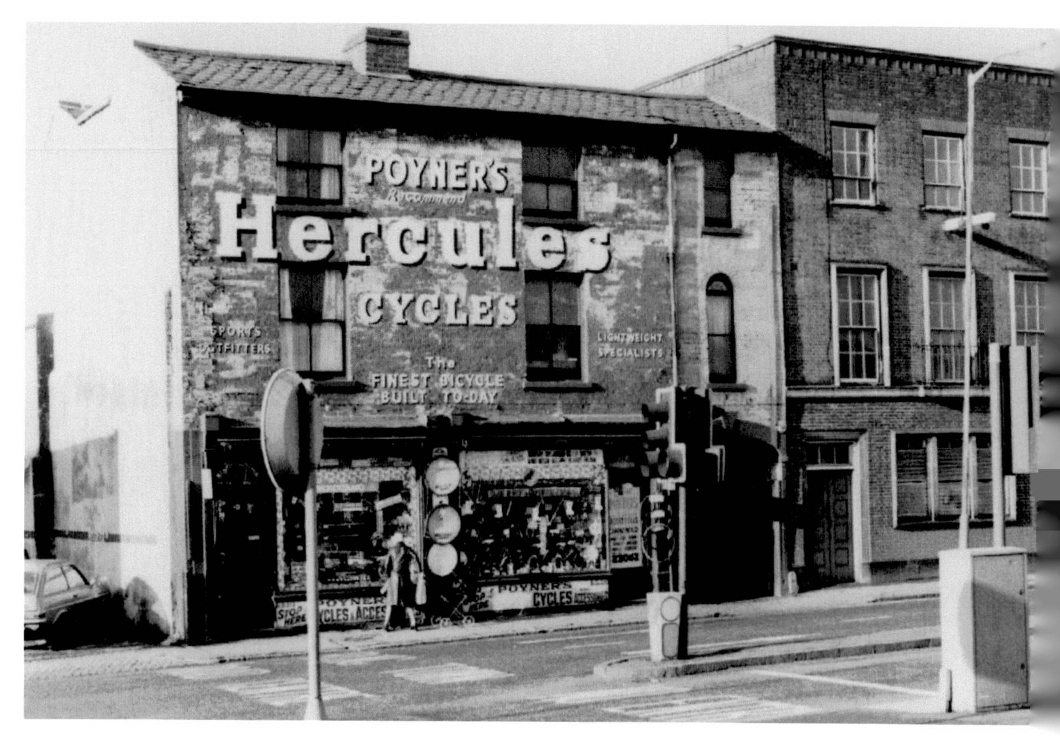

Every quarter of the town used to have its local cycle shop. Poyner's on Dudley Street heavily advertises Hercules Cycles, not a Wolverhampton-made brand. This was yet another casualty of the ring road.

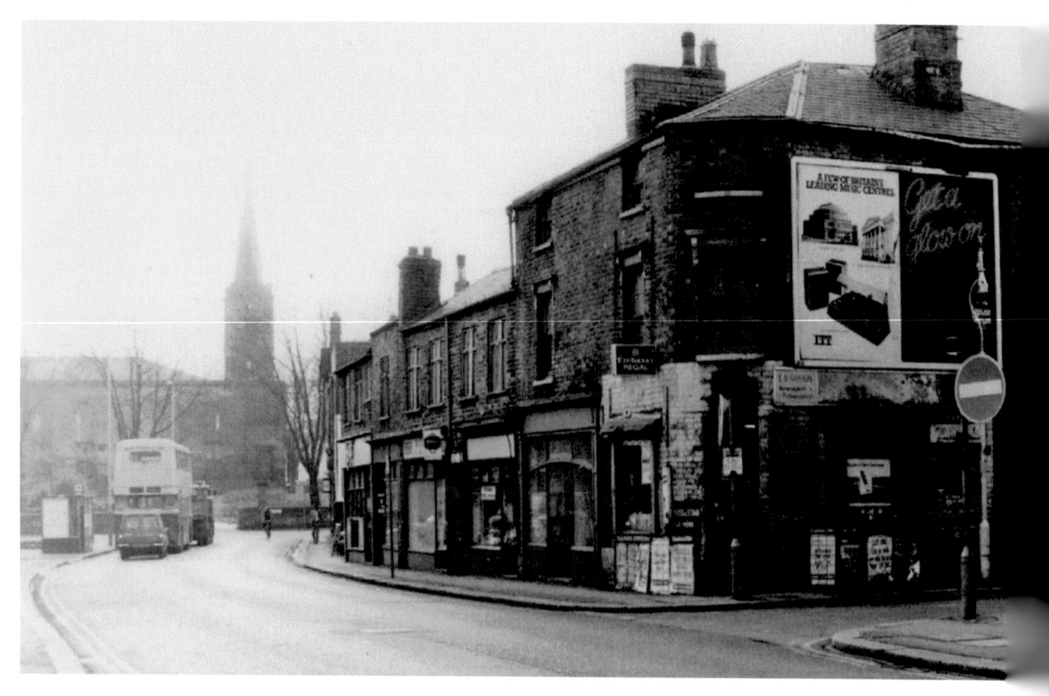

One end of Piper's Row in the 1970s, with St George's Church in the background and Tower Street to the right. The church became a Sainsbury's and the buildings to the right have all been cleared away.

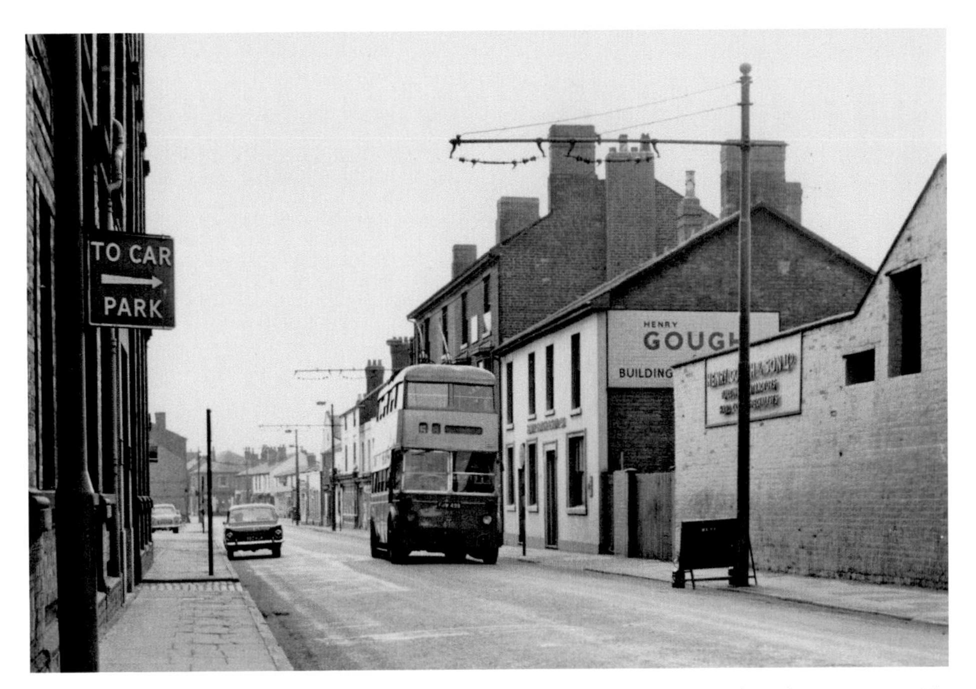

A Mk 1 Cortina and a trolleybus travelling away from the town centre date this scene outside Henry Gough's, the builders, to the early 1960s. This section of Dudley Road is next to what is now the St John's Retail Park, which would be to the left, though none of the buildings in the photograph remain.

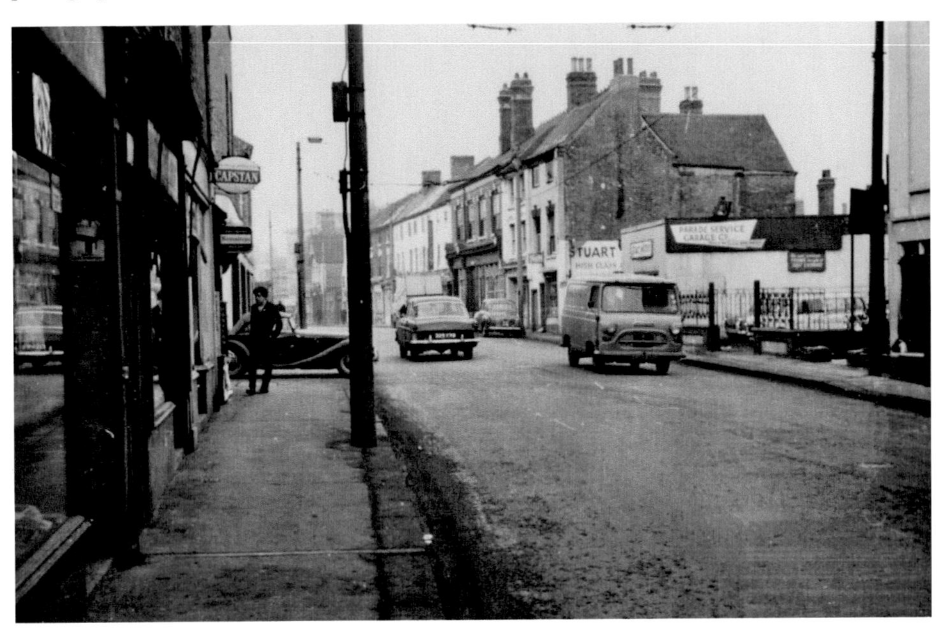

The central section of Piper's Row looking towards Victoria Square, with the Parade Service Garage to the right, where the new bus station now lies. Nothing in this photograph remains – a phrase I have used many times through this book. Tram tracks now run down Piper's Row, though at the time of writing a tram has still not yet passed along them.

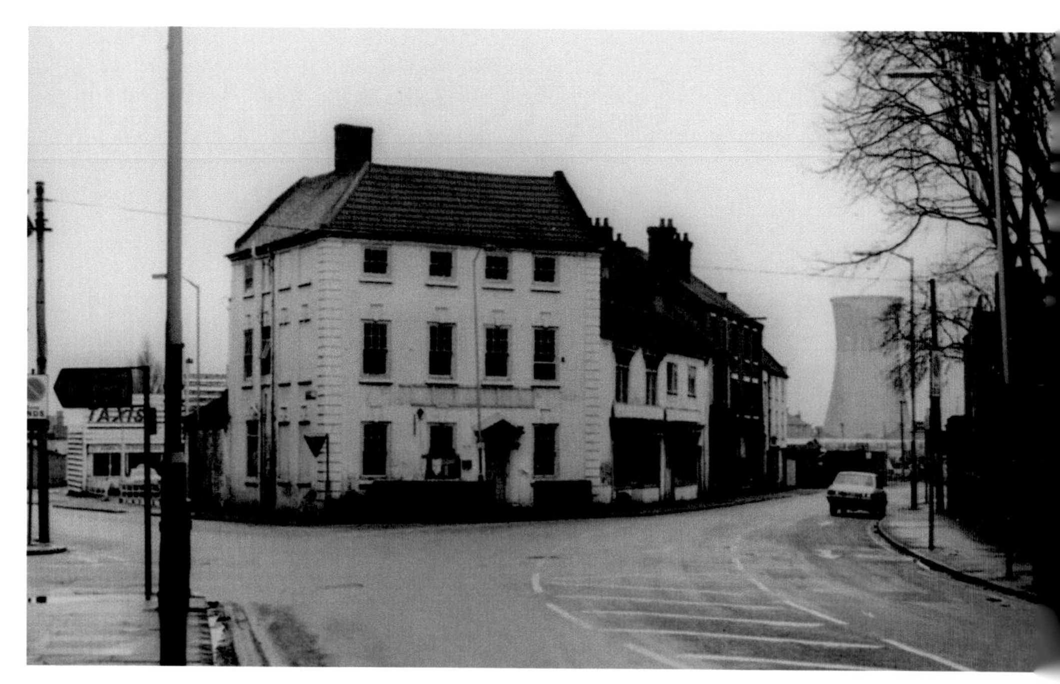

The fork in the road by the end of Piper's Row, with Walsall Street to the left and Bilston Street to the right. The trees in St George's churchyard are on the right. Like so many street scenes in the inner part of the city, this bears almost no relationship to what exists today. The Metro tracks now run through here to the Wishbone Bridge over the ring road.

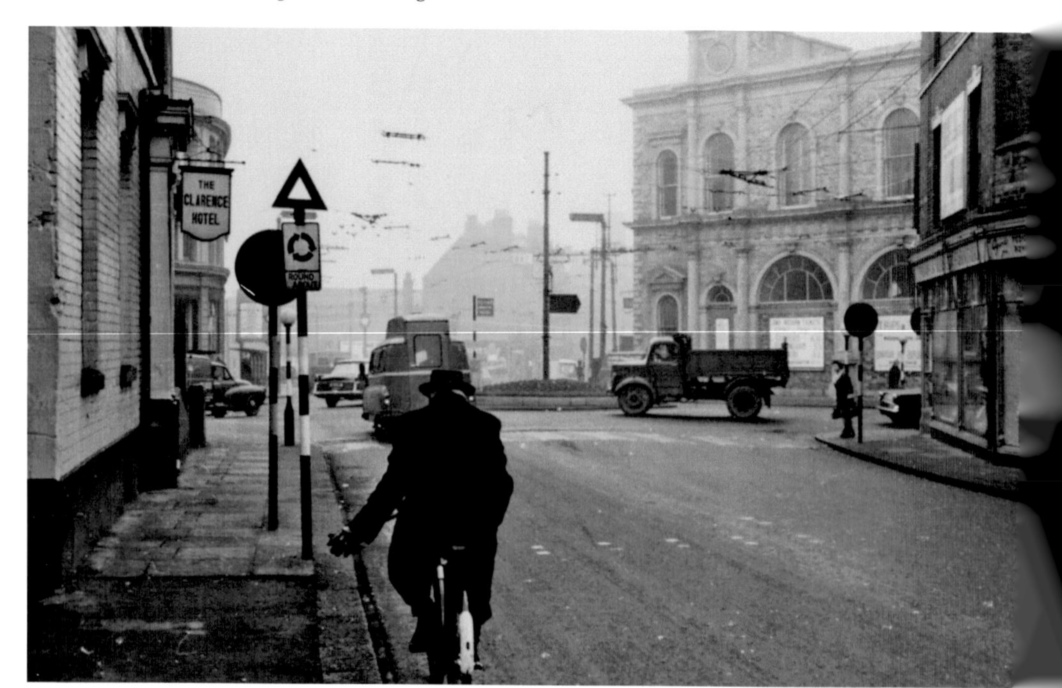

The other end of Piper's Row, with the Queen's Building ahead. The road to the right of the roundabout is the top of Horseley Fields, and to the left, where the cyclist is indicating he might go, is Queen Street.

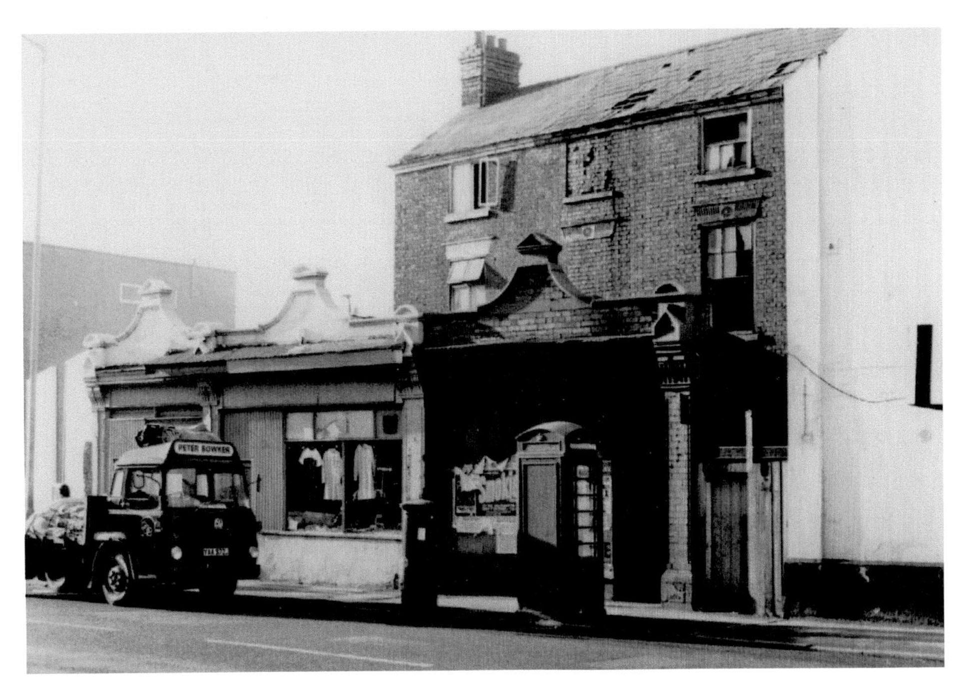

H. M. Grazier (post office and tobacconist) on Dudley Road next to the Coliseum cinema, with the postbox and telephone box seen outside. This and the dress shop next door are built in the front garden of the Georgian house behind, which looks rather rundown and does not have long to survive as the ring road threatens.

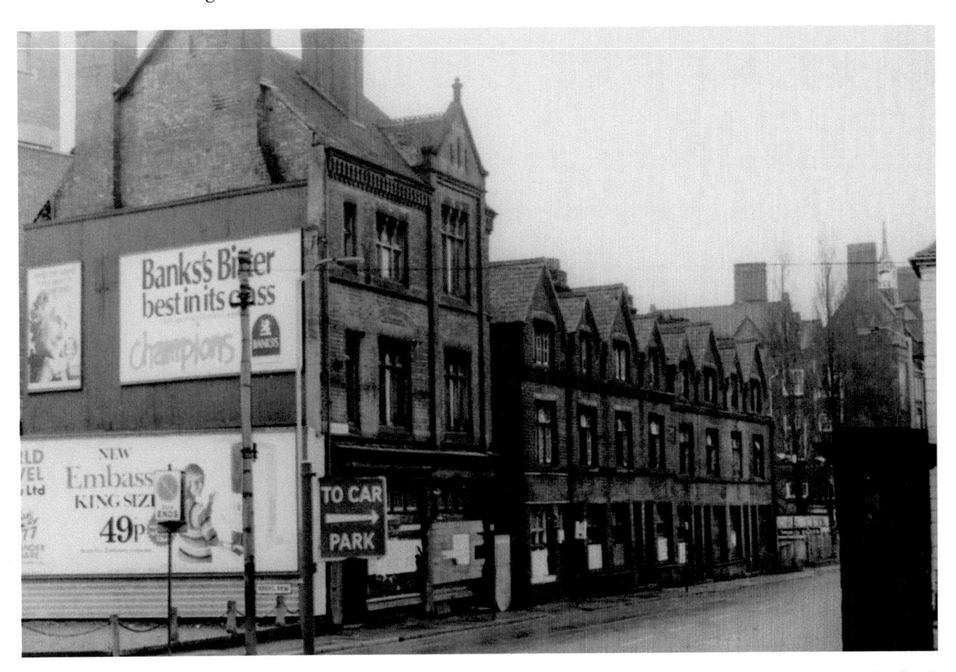

The start of Walsall Street with two shops, one of them a barbers, then houses, and the Walsall Street schools beyond, primary and secondary. Walsall Street now starts on the other side of the ring road.

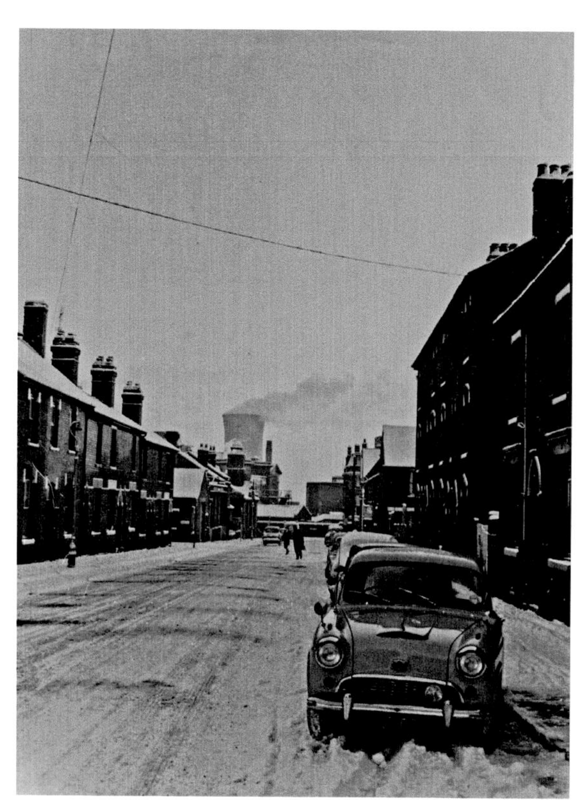

A snowy day in Powlett Street in the 1960s with the cooling tower seen in the distance. Powlett Street ran from Snow Hill, opposite George Street, to Vicarage Road with largely terraced houses, though the White Rose pub was lower down on the right. The ring road sliced through it and the BMW dealership is near the end of the abbreviated remainder.

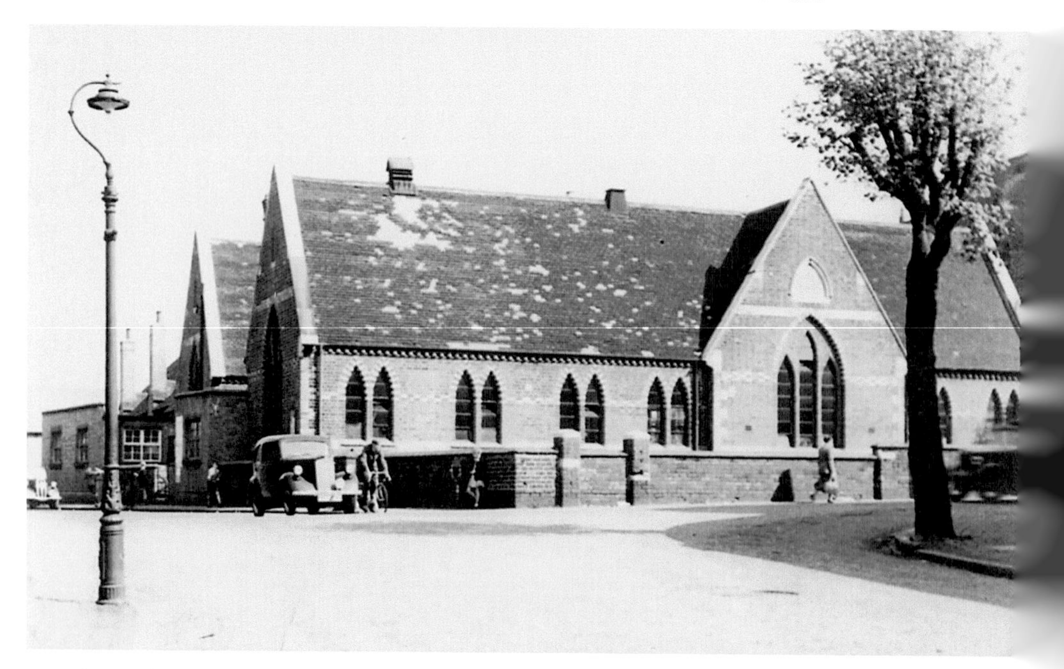

St Luke's School on Upper Villiers Street, famously the birthplace of Wolverhampton Wanderers Football Club. The ornate brickwork of the school matched that of St Luke's Church alongside. The school was demolished and replaced by a new building.

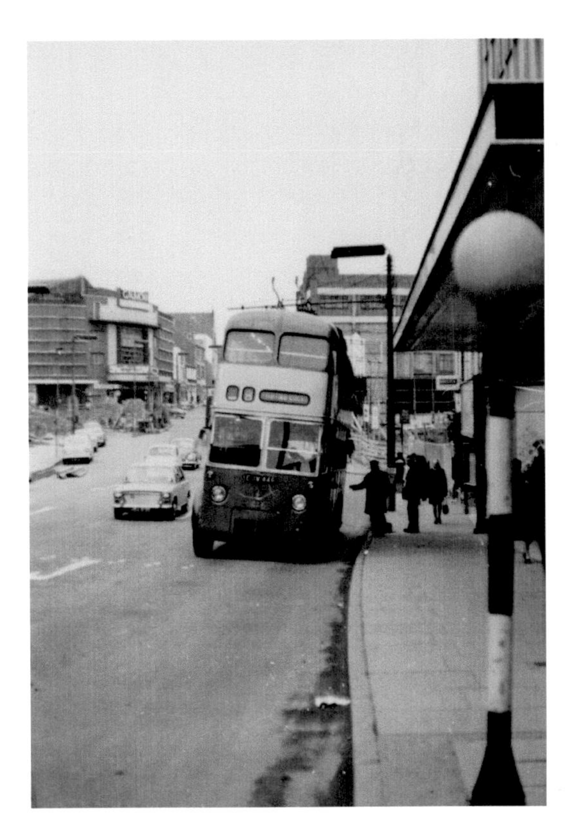

A No. 8 trolleybus drops passengers outside C&A at the bottom of Snow Hill, with the Gaumont Cinema in the background. C&A was later incorporated into the Wulfrun Shopping Centre, which blocked off this whole road.

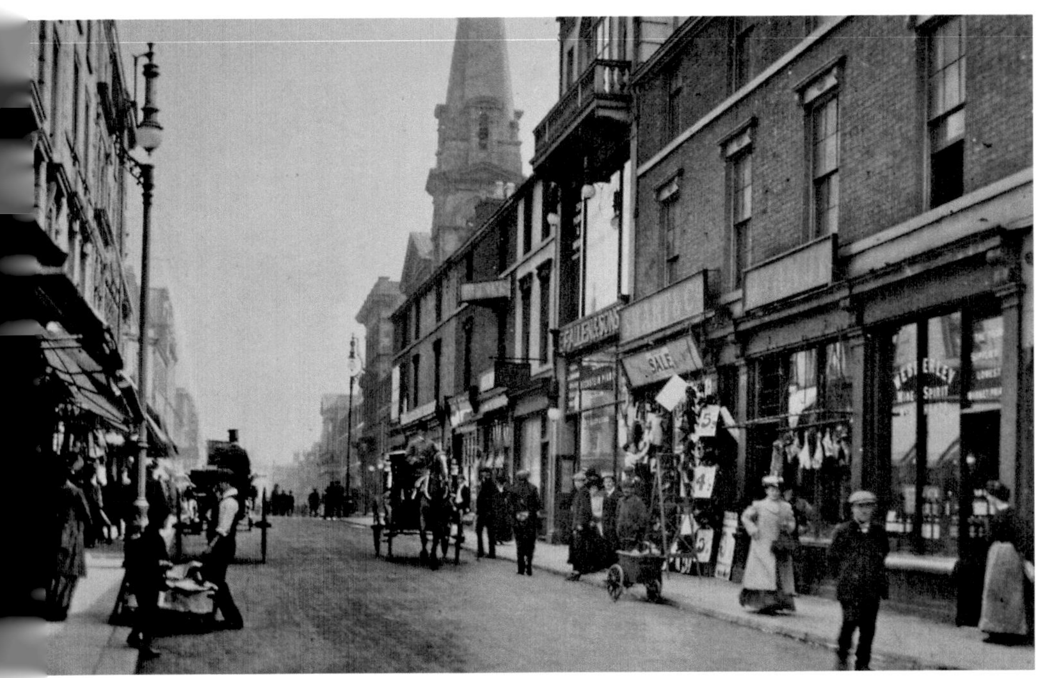

Queen Street over 100 years ago, looking from Dudley Street, with the Congregational Church in the background. Everything in this photograph has now gone, including the church.

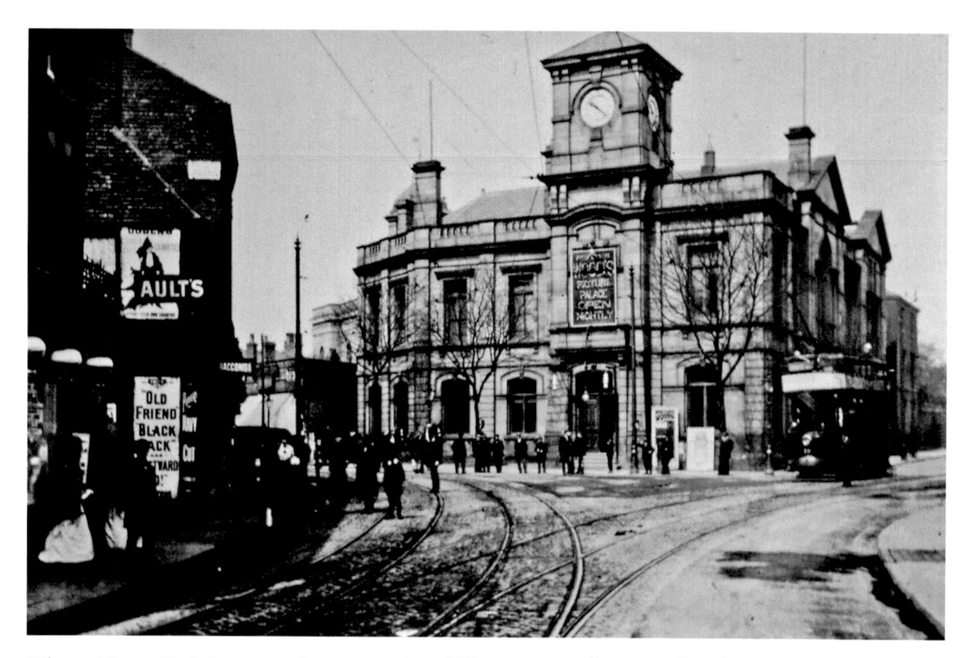

Bilston Town Hall between the wars, when Bilston was still a proud and independent borough. The tram tracks go to the left and right, and a tram with overhead connection is heading to Wolverhampton. The men standing in the road have clearly been told to stand still for the photograph. The Town Hall still exists.

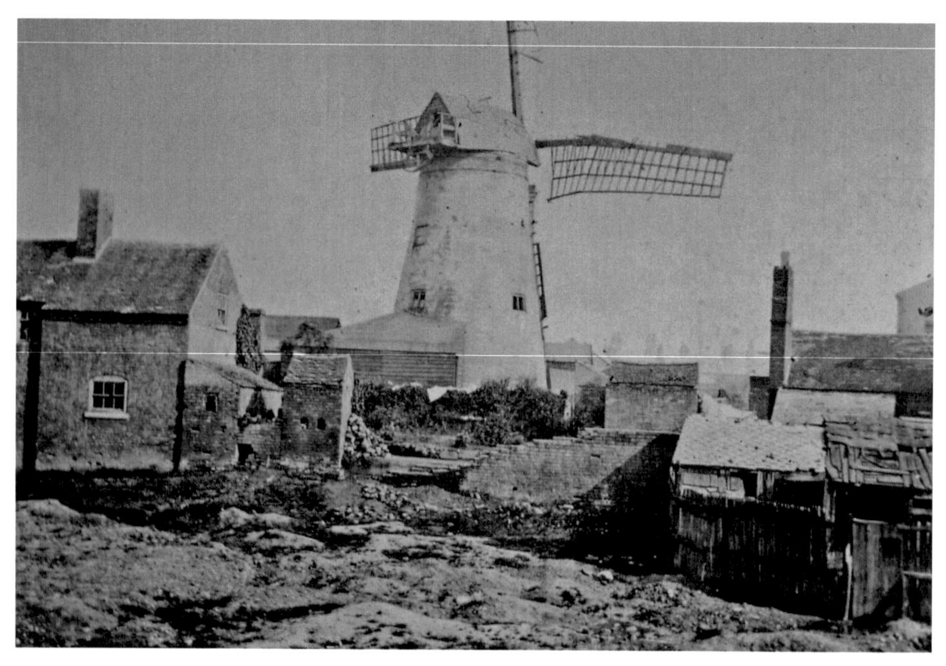

A reminder, like the first photograph in this book, that buildings for which we bemoan the loss were built on the site of even earlier buildings. This is one of two windmills that existed in the town in Victorian times, this one near Stafford Street. A time before Wolverhampton's fossil fuel-burning power station, when wind energy ruled.